Seeking a Theology for Urban Mission

God So
Loves
the City

Edited by

Charles Van Engen
and Jude Tiersma

WIPF & STOCK · Eugene, Oregon

Wipf and Stock Publishers
199 W 8th Ave, Suite 3
Eugene, OR 97401

God So Loves the City
Seeking a Theology for Urban Mission
By Van Engen, Charles and Tiersma, Jude
Copyright©1994 by Van Engen, Charles and Tiersma, Jude
ISBN 13: 978-1-60608-946-0
Publication date 7/8/2009
Previously published by MARC, 1994

Contributing Authors

Christine Accornero has been on the staff of PUMA (Presbyterians United for Missions Advance), and for the past several years has served as Fuller Theological Seminary's director of human resources. Her doctoral research is in the area of stewardship as a biblical and missiological perspective that may create an institutional dynamic that helps Christian managers effectively use the gifts and talents of people in their organizations. She serves the mission community and other non-profit organizations as a management consultant, specializing in personnel and community development, and program evaluation. She hopes to teach mission management at the graduate level.

Atul Y. Aghamkar ministered in two cities in central India with the Christian and Missionary Alliance, primarily as a church planter and pastor. Having earned a B. A. in English literature from Poona University and a B. D. in pastoralia from Union Biblical Seminary, Yavatmal, he completed the M. Th. in missiology at the South Asia Institute of Advanced Christian Studies in Bangalore. His doctoral studies focus on a Christian response to urbanization in India. He hopes to develop strategies for effective urban ministry as part of a training program for urban ministers in South Asia.

Jayakumar Christian was born and raised in India, and has been with World Vision of India since 1978, where he served as associate director for ministry enhancement. He has also been involved in facilitating regional learning events in Kenya, China, the Philippines, Cambodia, and Thailand. He currently serves on the faculty of the Asian Institute of Christian Communication in Thailand. He has a master's degree in community development from India and master's degrees in missiology and theology from Fuller Theological Seminary. His doctoral research deals with the kingdom of God and the powerlessness of the rural poor.

Harvie M. Conn is professor of missions and director of the Urban Missions Program, Westminster Theological Seminary, Philadelphia, Pennsylvania. He served in Korea as an Orthodox Presbyterian missionary from 1960-1972. He is the editor and author of many books, including *Evangelism: Doing Justice and Preaching Grace* (1982), *Eternal Word and Changing Worlds* (1984), and *A Clarified Vision for Urban Mission* (1987). Dr. Conn also serves as editor of the quarterly journal *Urban Mission*.

Richard Gollings has served since 1982 with the Baptist General Conference in church planting in Mexico City and Tijuana. His Th. M. thesis was an oral history and analysis of an indigenous revival movement in a Mexican urban youth drug subculture. He is married and has two children.

Marsha Haney is an ordained minister of the Presbyterian Church, U.S.A. (Greater Atlanta Presbytery). She has served as a pastor, chaplain, and theological educator in Juba, Sudan; Kumba, Cameroon; and as an adjunct professor in the Presbyterian Seminary of the West (Pasadena, California). Rev. Haney recently served as interim pastor of the Redeemer Presbyterian Church in Los Angeles.

J. Timothy Kauffman was a pastor and urban church planter in Berlin and Frankfurt, Germany for twelve years. He presently teaches pastoral formation, urban studies and leadership as an adjunct professor at a number of undergraduate and graduate institutions. His doctoral study seeks to describe the contours of theological education and ministry formation for contextually appropriate ministry in the city. Mr. Kauffman is co-author with Edgar Elliston of *Developing Leaders for Urban Ministries*, along with numerous articles on related subjects.

Kathryn Mowry has served as an associate pastor in two multi-congregational urban churches in transitional communities. She is presently the associate director of the Bresee Institute for Urban Training in Los Angeles. Ms. Mowry's doctoral work involves research into the nature and mission of the local congregation in the city.

Stanley Mutuku Mutunga has done pastoral work and Bible college teaching with the Africa Inland Church of Kenya. A native of Kenya, Dr. Mutunga holds a B. Th. degree from Scott Theological College in Kenya, and an M. A. in missiology and a Ph. D. in intercultural studies from Fuller Theological Seminary's School of World Mission. His current doctoral studies focus on rural-urban migration into Nairobi and its implications for urban ministry.

Mary Thiessen, a Mennonite from rural Canada, received her education degree from Tabor College in Hillsboro, Kansas before moving to the inner city of Los Angeles as a missionary with World Impact. She served as women's director and assisted in the founding of an elementary and middle school during her eighteen years in Los Angeles before beginning her studies at Fuller Theological Seminary. Ms. Thiessen's doctoral studies in the School of World Mission are in the area of healing and renewal for people who live and work in the city.

Jude Tiersma lives and works in a Hispanic immigrant neighborhood in central Los Angeles as part of the Cambria Community, Innerchange. She coordinates the concentration in urban mission in the School of World Mission, Fuller Theological Seminary, where she is pursuing her Ph. D. studies.

Charles Van Engen was born and raised in Mexico, where from 1973-1985 he served the National Presbyterian Church of Mexico in theological education, evangelism, youth ministries, and refugee relief. In 1981 he completed the Ph. D. in missiology from the Free University of Amsterdam under Johannes Verkuyl. He is presently associate professor of theology of mission, church growth, and Latin American studies at Fuller Theological Seminary's School of World Mission.

Contents

Figures

"O Jerusalem, Jerusalem, you who kill the prophets and stone those sent to you, how often I have longed to gather your children together, as a hen gathers her chicks under her wings, but you were not willing! Look, your house is left to you desolate. I tell you, you will not see me again until you say, 'Blessed is he who comes in the name of the Lord.'"

Luke 13:34-35

Foreword

Harvie M. Conn

DONALD MCGAVRAN saw it in 1970. The rush to the cities is on, he affirmed. "Discipling urban populations is perhaps the most urgent task confronting the Church. Bright hope gleams that now is precisely the time to learn how it may be done and to surge forward actually doing it" (McGavran 1970:295).

When McGavran wrote those words, the world contained 2,400 cities with populations of more than 100,000. Some 161 megacities were home to over one million people. Every day in 1970, 51,500 new non-Christians appeared in those cities (Barrett 1994:25).

Twenty-four years later, as this book goes to press in mid-1994, McGavran's call is even more urgent. The number of cities with over 100,000 people has reached 3,730. The megacities number 370 and the number of new non-Christian urban dwellers per day has more than doubled to 115,000 (Barrett 1994:25).

The essays in this book flow out of the concerns that are integral to these realities. Readers of general urban literature

---

Harvie M. Conn is professor of missions and director of the Urban Missions Program, Westminster Theological Seminary, Philadelphia, Pennsylvania. Please see the contributing authors section for more information.

will hear echoes of past studies—community and kinship, immigration, religion, and poverty. Those accustomed to church growth literature will also hear these themes welded to an evangelical vocabulary not unfamiliar to them—theology of mission, witness and evangelization, contextualization, incarnation. Added to them are interests not always associated in my mind with church growth thinking—injustice, systemic structures, and urban infra-systems.

The past

In one sense, these essays do not represent a new direction. They come at the end of a particular wave of concern for the city that is already decades old. They are part of a more recent Christian concern for the city that traces its roots to the fifties and sixties, the growth of the urban Black and Hispanic constituencies, and America's "white flight" from an urban center to a "suburban captivity" of the nation and the white church.

Shaping the background to early thinking in this wave was the long-standing anti-urban bias characteristic of general Western scholarship (White and White 1962). It focused on the city as the place of crisis, of the erosion of values, of the segmentation of personal life (Karp, Stone, and Yoels 1991:3-44). Urban studies in sociology and cultural anthropology were beginning to question this bias (Conn 1987:20-22). But this research filtered too slowly into the church's urban planning.

The church and the city: The early stages

Within this Christian community of the fifties and sixties there were sharp divisions in perceptions of the city. Many turned to a definition of urban mission too reminiscent for some of the agenda of the social gospel movement on sociopolitical change. Harvey Cox spoke for many when he sought to turn urban pessimism into optimism and baptized "secularization" as urban blessing, not bane (Cox 1965).

By 1960 almost every major denomination had a staff
member or department for urban mission and it could
list a number of churches, parishes, and programs that
were principally led by White personnel, usually male
clergy, in predominantly Black or Hispanic areas of the
major metropolitan areas (Younger 1987:31).

Between 1962 and 1975, 27 action training centers were
born in 22 large U.S. cities, states, and regions, to help the
church cope with issues of empowerment, urban social
change, and transitional communities.

The bulk of White evangelical sentiment on the American city during this time moved, meanwhile, in another
direction. Increasingly withdrawn logistically from the city,
frightened by the social upheaval of the decade, and wary of
what it perceived as a mainline church concentration on the
wrong agenda, its traditional roots in pietism focused on
evangelism. Its church planting attention turned heavily to
the suburbs (Conn 1994, chapter 6).

The church and the city: Transition

The seventies and eighties brought changes for evangelicals in significant directions. McGavran's call for reaching the city began to touch the lives of some who saw its
potential. Roger Greenway was one of the earlier voices to
see its possibilities: "The rapidity of world-wide urbanization," he predicted, "demands a reorientation of missionary
strategy in which church workers, both foreign and national,
catch the vision and share the responsibility" (Greenway
1972:243). He merged his Reformed theological commitments with a modified church growth paradigm to survey
mission strategy for Latin American cities (Greenway 1973a)
and the urban challenge of the U.S. (Greenway 1973b).

Overall, however, the inner circle of church growth
strategizing—led by Fuller Theological Seminary's School of
World Mission—did not respond quickly to echo concerns

like those of Greenway. Early invitations to urban evangelism (Wagner 1971:179-197) were received skeptically because of the growing emphasis on "holistic evangelism" that questioned the prioritization of evangelism isolated from social transformation (Wagner 1981:90-109).

Support for that symbiotic relationship, recognized by many of the essays in this book, came largely from elsewhere. America's "Young Evangelicals," radicalized by the civil rights movement of the sixties, by the dynamic of a vibrant Black church, and by a repentant spirit toward their own racism, pressed the conservative wing of the evangelical church for a wider understanding of gospel mission. Third World leaders like René Padilla and Orlando Costas challenged the 1974 International Congress on World Evangelization meeting in Lausanne to face more seriously the social and cultural dimensions of evangelism.

In addition, the Lausanne platform began to provide a more global dimension to earlier urban concerns fixed on the U.S. Continuing discussions in the erected Lausanne Committee for World Evangelization moved even further in an explicitly urban direction.

The 1980 Global Consultation on World Evangelization held in Pattaya, Thailand, structured a mini-conference called "Reaching Large Cities." Out of it came a follow-up program oriented to world-class cities. Its coordinator, Ray Bakke, focused on process not program. He has traveled extensively to gather church leaders in the world's major cities to pray and dream about macro-strategies. Within four years, 86 cities had hosted Lausanne-initiated and World Vision-sponsored discussions (Bakke 1984:20-21).

Pattaya's strong emphasis on unreached peoples drew mixed reviews. Some still seemed confused by the concept; others, like Bakke, may have been more skeptical of what they understood as McGavran's homogeneous unit principle (Bakke 1987:138). But ultimately Pattaya's message was to prevail. The global city and the unreached people concept belonged together (Conn 1991:3-5).

Lausanne II, held in Manila in 1989, further reinforced the urban dimension of holistic mission. Called by one commentator "an immersion into the urban labyrinth," the gathering served as a platform for dialogue and consultation "oriented specifically toward urban mission" (Escobar 1990:22, 24).

The present

The essays in this book appear against this backdrop. In continuity with the recent past, they reflect a more global dimension. The cities of Kenya, India, and Mexico are among those examined here and examined on their own terms. The writers have made efforts to avoid the overlay of the American industrial city, a pattern of study that has confused urban studies in the past. Whether they have succeeded altogether we leave to the judgment of the reader.

One finds here also an enthusiasm for the city that appears to have left behind to a great degree the anti-urban polarizations of past studies. McGavran's gift of optimism to missiology has not been lost in the plethora of urban challenges that past writers addressed as "problems" or "crises."

Here, too, past skepticism over "holistic evangelism" seems to be fading. These pages wrestle with evangelization and church planting as they are affected by questions like injustice, marginalization, and urban structures. It is, after all, what one would expect when contextualization issues are taken seriously in a setting as complex and challenging as the city. Will the global city provide the contextual instrument for fulfilling David Bosch's prediction of an emerging paradigm shift in the theology of mission for our day (Bosch 1991:368-510)?

New directions

At least two new ingredients also enrich this evangelical mix and, with other writings, may signal a new turning point in urban mission studies.

1. Previous mission studies have followed earlier academic interests in focusing on urbanization—the process of a demographic shift as a population acculturates to urban ways of life. It was an expected direction in view of traditional missiological concerns in the Third World. Massive urbanization has characterized that World, especially in the last half of the twentieth century (Barrett 1986). And a growing segment of the Christian community has become increasingly sensitive to the change (Conn 1993a:326-332).

   This collection of essays begins to move beyond such concerns. In some of these pages the reader will begin to hear another word: urbanism. The focus now turns to the city as a way of life, an evangelical agenda of study seldom explored until now for many reasons (Conn 1993b:97). Will we continue to speak of urbanism more as a place than a process, more as a static, negative paradigm shaped severely by too much attachment to the Chicago models of an industrial past? Or will we start to think of urbanism as a process, its structural forms, roles, and images shaped by our faith commitments either for or against God? Urban missiology cannot neglect the connection of "religion" to urbanism. These essays begin to struggle with these questions.

2. These essays are preliminary exercises in an urban hermeneutic that is much needed. That is, they seek to link the urban horizon of the biblical text and the contemporary urban horizon of Los Angeles and Mexico City, Nairobi and Madras.

The writers employ new tools from the social and behavioral sciences in this linking process. The academic disciplines of urban anthropology and urban sociology, relatively new to the scholarly world, add their wisdom—as well as their misdirections—to our search. These are not instruments to arouse our suspicions; all truth, whether discovered by theologian or urban sociologist, historian or urban anthropologist, comes from God. Urban missiology looks for the proper hermeneutical proportions in the mix. These essays are an "in progress" cookbook effort at searching for the right recipe.

Future directions

Like any experiment in hermeneutics, this collection will leave new avenues to consider, a new agenda to be shaped out of the questions it poses and the answers it provides. That is no more than what any stimulating book should do. The last chapter of this book offers for your consideration some suggestions for future paths to explore.

I see a question flowing out of the center of this symposium: What is the connection between a theology of mission and the new reality we now face in the cities of our world? Exactly how seriously will the future make that connection? More specifically, what fundamental role will urbanism as a quality of life play in future discussions?

Cultural anthropology and sociology have recognized the urban as a variable serious enough to create new sub-disciplines. Urban anthropology and urban sociology were born in recognition of the importance of that connection. Will a theology of mission do the same?

Will we see in the future a theology of mission in the city or a theology of mission for the city? The first choice, I fear, will use the city as the setting in which a theology of mission is operative, but does not see the city as a fundamental variable. The second choice will see the city as a fundamental part in the design of a theology of mission. In the first, "urban" will become an adjectival addendum, adding little to the basic, radical understanding of a theology of mission. In the second, "urban" will be a definitive category, part of a new core that will create a new sub-discipline, urban missiology.

We already have in print samples of the first option. May this volume take its place as part of the new search for the second. Ralph Winter heralded the challenge of the cities as one of the fifteen most significant challenges for tomorrow's mission (Winter 1991:48). Will its challenge touch our theologies of mission as well as our strategies?

Preface

Charles Van Engen

SIRENS BLARED, fires raged, and fear gripped all of us as the riots of Los Angeles eclipsed our lives during those terrible days of May 1992. These events were not what we had envisioned when a dozen of us planned to gather as a doctoral seminar to reflect about God's mission in the city. We even had to postpone a couple of meetings because of the trauma of those days.

We have passed the first anniversary of the fires, yet the horror, the questions, and the sadness of those days hang like thick fog around us. Today is Thursday, August 19, 1993. The headline of *The San Gabriel Valley Tribune* reads "Reliving the Riots: Victims' Horror Stories to Emerge as Trial Begins in Denny Case."

Although little seems to have changed in Los Angeles, the members of our seminar have changed. Our understanding of the complexity of the city has grown. Our sense of dependence on a God who must be bigger than the corruption, oppression, and alienation of Los Angeles has deepened. Our perspectives beyond easy "fix-it" solutions that come today and are gone tomorrow has lengthened. And our appreciation of the unique contribution that each one in our group has made to our understanding of the issues involved in God's mission in the city has broadened.

This book involves a search for understanding, and a prayer for greater wisdom and deeper insight into the unbelievably complex nature of today's megacities. It is born of a deep, shared conviction that Christians can no longer ignore the enormity, complexity, and urgency of urbanism. The foremost agenda of the church's ministry and mission into the next century will need to be ministry in the city. We can no longer turn our backs on the city. In a recent feature article in *Time*, for example, Eugene Linden emphasized the urgency of humans and their governments facing the issues of the city. He wrote:

> In the coming years, the fate of humanity will be decided in the [megacities]. Faster than ever before, the human world is becoming an urban world. Near the end of this decade, [humankind] will pass a demographic milestone: for the first time in history, more people will live in and around cities than in rural areas (Linden 1993:31).

Some say that by the beginning of the next century the Los Angeles metroplex will spread from San Diego to Santa Barbara (about 150 miles), and from the Pacific Ocean to Palm Springs. The enormity of this context is made even more difficult to grasp because of the ethnic, linguistic, economic, religious, historical, and political diversity that it entails. So this book represents a search for a way to ask the questions, rather than an assurance of having found any answers.

The substance of this book

The substance of this work constitutes the product of more than sixteen months of reflection, investigation, group study, and mutual enrichment by a group of doctoral students in the School of World Mission at Fuller Theological Seminary. All of the participants are involved in various ways and to varying degrees in issues of urban missiology. The publication of the findings of this group has two complementary purposes: one deals with theological content, the other with theological method.

First, the personal experiences of the authors form the basis for the stories in this book. These stories are given as examples of a search for contextually appropriate theological themes that we must investigate and articulate in the creation of a theology of mission for urban missiology. The themes highlighted in this book are in no way meant to be exhaustive or complete. Rather, we offer them as illustrative cases. They are meant to raise consciousness and stimulate the readers to explore for themselves the creative and explosive possibilities that flow from a theology of mission arising out of the reality of life in the city.

Second, the theological and missiological reflection on the stories is meant to demonstrate to the readers a particular methodology for doing theology of mission in the city. This method entails a profound hermeneutical encounter with the reality of each story that searches for an integrating theological and missiological theme in the story. It then goes on to develop the deep-level meanings and their implications for mission in the city.

Essentially, we have been searching for a way to respond to a challenge given by Harvie Conn about midway through our time together—a challenge to explore ways to integrate theology, urban studies, and contextualization in a theologically informed, holistic, and transformational theology of mission for the city. As Conn said it,

> Contextualization requires that we connect the normative biblical horizon that provides divine meaning with our contemporary urban horizons. It calls for "a critical discernment of the text's inner meaning and then a

translation of it into our own culture" (Stott and Coote 1980, 315). A contextual mission theology then, by definition, adds a third horizon to the task—that of the one to whom we translate the text in gospel witness. Out of this linking of three horizons (message or text, messenger and responder-in-context) comes a theology of mission for urban missiology (1993b: 97).

Why read this book?

This book is written for pastors, seminary students, missiologists, and informed members of congregations involved in ministry in the city. Adult congregational study groups in churches would profit greatly from the stories, the reflection, and the methodology, since these may help shape their own theology of mission for their city. Using this work as a text will enrich seminary courses in missiology, contextual theology related to the city, issues of urbanization, and the challenge of urban ministry. The stories and format build on matters of wisdom and life-enrichment that are broader and deeper than what the reader may have received through a formal education.

This volume is also unique. Although it will interface with a number of other related fields of inquiry, its multi-disciplinary methodology, its breadth of diversity in terms of contexts, and its depth of insight into each story is meant to reflect as closely as possible the actual way in which urban missiological reflection happens in real life. Thus, it builds a uniquely interdisciplinary methodology that draws from various other bodies of literature, yet weaves them together in an adapted case study approach that differs from—but closely complements—the related fields from which it draws. The works mentioned in the bibliography offer a guide the student may use to investigate further the theme or themes emphasized in each chapter.

A number of persons were instrumental in the success of the seminar and the subsequent publication of this book.

We would like to acknowledge the role of Paul Pierson, dean of the School of World Mission at Fuller Theological Seminary at the time of the seminar. He strongly encouraged us to begin meeting and pursue our hunches, even though this type of process was unusual in our setting. Subsequently, Dudley Woodberry, present dean of the School of World Mission, continued to lend strong support to the project.

In terms of the preparation of the manuscript for publication, we would like to extend a word of appreciation to Edgar Elliston, who made the initial arrangements with Mission Advance Research and Communication Center (MARC) of World Vision International, for the publication of this book. We are very grateful to Nancy Thomas for doing much of the editing and proofing of the manuscript, and want to thank David Sielaff and his staff in Fuller's Word Processing Office for the excellent work in typesetting the manuscript. We are especially indebted to John Kenyon and World Vision International for their willingness to publish this volume. We have deeply appreciated their valuable help and support in this venture.

Pasadena, California
December 1993

Introduction

Jude Tiersma

Today is Saturday, not just any Saturday, but that space of time between Jesus' death on the cross on Friday and Resurrection Sunday.

Saturday. Surely that Saturday in Jerusalem must have been a despairing day. Jesus was gone, the one in whom the disciples had put their hopes and dreams. Crucified. The cursed death of a criminal, yet an innocent man. Certainly this was the "most unjust event in all recorded human history" (Newbigin 1972:18).

The Saturday between Good Friday and Easter began to take on new significance for me after the "social quake" that shook my neighborhood and other neighborhoods in Los Angeles in the spring of 1992. I remember that for many of us, the most difficult time was the weeks following the initial days of unrest. The first days there was a certain excitement, and no doubt we were still in a state of shock. Military helicopters, National Guard, curfew, major cleanup efforts, lots of immediate attention kept us too busy to feel much the first week. Then, suddenly, it was as if everything was supposed to "get back to normal." Except that the swap meet, which we passed daily, was in ruins. Our young friend Miguel's bicycle was gone—confiscated in police

1

raids in our apartment building, when anything that looked new and had no receipt was taken as possible stolen property. Everywhere were signs of devastation. The pain inside had exploded into the streets, and could not be so easily contained. The media was already speaking of signs of hope, but that hope had not yet been kindled in the hearts of those who lived in the devastated areas. I remember that I found myself surrounded by a deep blanket of despair, overwhelming me at every turn. Easy answers only deepened the despair. Today is Saturday—the day between death and resurrection. (April 1993, personal journal).

IT IS NOW a full year after the fires. It is the Saturday before Easter. Los Angeles again holds its breath, on edge, waiting, watching, wondering as the jury deliberates. Will the jury release the verdicts today? Tomorrow? What will be the consequences if the police officers who beat Rodney King are set free? Will the city burn as it did a year ago? Has anything changed? Have we learned anything from the spring of 1992? Many are asking, along with *Time* magazine, "Is the City of Angels going to Hell?"

We gave birth to this book during those months after the Rodney King beating trial and the outrage over the verdicts. A group of doctoral students at Fuller Theological Seminary's School of World Mission had been preparing to meet as a seminar with Charles Van Engen, coming together to discover and learn an appropriate theology for an urban missiology.

Our first assignment was to share a story that reflected our various ministry contexts and our concerns within each context: venues as diverse as Nairobi; South Central Los Angeles; Tijuana, Mexico; and the culture of Christian organizations.

Scheduled to begin with the spring quarter, we had only met one Friday to share our stories when we had to postpone our next meeting due to the civil unrest that shook not only Los Angeles, but also neighboring cities like Pasadena, sending shock waves throughout our country. Many of us lived and worked in the areas that were most devastated. In this setting, the group grew to become a safe place to share the tears, fear, anger, and confusion that accompanied the events of spring 1992. We prayed—for each other and for our city.

What began as a group of students became a community, with our hermeneutic reflecting not only the person who was doing the writing but also the rest of the community. Those of us who grew up in this country appreciated deeply the insights of our brothers from India and Kenya.

Together we began drawing out the themes in each story, looking at each particular context, then rereading the Scriptures, allowing the new insights not to determine but to inform our reading of the Scripture. We returned repeatedly to the urban reality, asking, "What then is the missional role of the church in the city?"

Some of us, like many urban practitioners, have been immersed in the grassroots level of ministry, and our eyes have not seen beyond the sidewalks of our neighborhood. Others have been involved in the city from a more macrolevel, a broader planning perspective, striving to see the big picture but not necessarily in touch with the heartbeat of particular neighborhoods. Both perspectives are needed. James Vigil's theory on double marginality helps us understand why gangs are on the increase. But the statistics on how many gang-related deaths took place a few months ago take on a face when we've eaten watermelon with Manotas the day before he is shot by a rival gang.

The stories were changing during the seminar (as were we!). They are part of stories not yet finished, and they raised questions to which there were no easy solutions. Easy answers cannot satisfy difficult questions, for easy answers come without struggle. Several years ago I took part in a prayer march to end the drugs in MacArthur Park. I remember the tension of wondering if I should be sitting on a park bench or standing with those who had come to pray. One woman carried a sign that said, "Jesus is the answer." A homeless woman saw the sign and approached her, passionately yelling, "Where were you when I lost my job and couldn't pay the rent and ended up on the streets? Where were you when they took my babies away because I couldn't provide for them?" The message was clear. With little classroom education, this woman knew at a gut level that answers are not helpful unless they come through the difficulties, and are struggled through in community.

Another person of a different gender, class, and ethnicity—Lesslie Newbigin—has made a similar observation:

> The answers to great questions are not obvious. They are not shouted at us, or written up in the sky. We cannot find them by buying an examination guide in a bazaar. We have to take risks if we are to understand the really important things. We have to look, to listen, to ponder, to reflect, to experiment and to ultimately take risks—to risk our very selves. The answers to great questions have to be struggled for (1972:4).

We invite the readers of this book to join us in asking the questions. It is time to reflect on our stories. It is Saturday—the Saturday between Good Friday and Easter Sunday.

PART ONE

Approaching the City

1

What does it mean to be incarnational when we are not the Messiah?

Jude Tiersma

THE STORY

FATHER GREG BOYLE—G Dog, the "homeboys"[1] called him—has left the *barrio* (Spanish for "neighborhood") he called home for the past six years. As a Jesuit, he was required to take a year of spiritual retreat, after which there was talk that he would return. But his superiors in the Jesuit order decided to send him elsewhere.

Father Greg became well-known for his life and work among gang members. His parish in East Los Angeles, Dolores Mission, counted eight gangs within its boundaries. When he arrived, Father Greg began walking the streets,

---

Jude Tiersma lives and works in a Hispanic immigrant neighborhood in central Los Angeles as part of the Cambria Community, Innerchange. Please see the contributing authors section for more information.

befriending the young men, becoming a father figure who extended grace and unconditional love to them. In time, he earned their trust and their love.

Anyone who met Father Greg knew of his deep commitment to and love for the members of the various gangs, like Cuatro Flats and Mob Crew. How much pain it caused him when he had to bury one of them, an ordeal he went through 26 times in his six years there. Many times he grew discouraged and weary, wondering if his presence was making any impact.

But even in his exhaustion he carried on. He had fully expected to return to the eastside after his sabbatical, a place where he said he wanted to grow old and die. So he too was heartbroken to learn that he would not be returning.

Now the community surrounding Dolores Mission is learning to adjust to life without Father Greg. The programs he helped to start—such as Homeboy Tortillas, a small business that employs gang youth—continue. But the people miss his presence. Gang warfare increased after he left, and with it the sense of despair that things would only get worse.

Some in the neighborhood believe that the only solution is to have Greg Boyle come back. Some even drafted a petition requesting that the Jesuits reassign him to Dolores Mission. Others, however, believe it is time for residents of the neighborhood to take more ownership of their lives and their community. Father Greg himself has never felt or said that he was indispensable. But no one denies that the authority he earned and the love he showered on the young gang members was a source of hope for a life beyond their world of gangs and poverty.

The story isn't finished yet. Dolores Mission is a parish with much dynamism and life, a community on a journey. What does the future hold for Dolores Mission?

REFLECTING ON THE STORY

This story illustrates the difficulties facing almost all those who choose to enter urban mission incarnationally.

When we speak of incarnational mission, we speak of a theology on the way, of accompaniment (*del camino*[2]—on the way), of walking alongside. It is a theology of those who are not from the periphery but, knowing that Christ died "outside the gate,"[3] have chosen to identify with, to walk alongside, those the world has cast aside as unimportant. In the context and writing of urban mission, those not originally from the city who choose to live among the people of the city—usually among the economically poor—often use the idea of incarnation.

Manuel Ortiz, in "Being Disciples: Incarnational Christians in the City," states, "Our Lord broke through the barriers between history and eternity to be with us. He underwent all the physical and emotional experiences of a Jew in first century Judaism" (1992:85). Likewise, when we choose to cross barriers into another class and culture, we choose to undergo the physical and emotional experiences of our neighbors, identifying with them in their struggles and joys.

Is incarnational mission the right idea?

A key element of incarnational mission is this identification, of being present with people. According to William Pannell, "The challenge to empower the poor begins with presence" (1992:50). Christ modeled a sustained relationship with persons.

John Perkins prefers the term "relocation" for those who choose to move into areas of economic need. Relocation is the starting point of his philosophy of ministry, followed by redistribution (of resources) and reconciliation (1982). Perkins believes that we can develop healthy communities in two ways: either through indigenous leadership development or through committed Christians and their families liv-

9

ing in communities of need. "The importance of our physical presence in these communities cannot be overstated, whether it means moving to them for the first time, coming back, or just staying put" (1993:1).

Although Perkins doesn't believe that relocation is for everyone, he does believe many more are called than are willing to make this sacrifice. Some try to water down the ideal, claiming that relocation is a matter of the heart, not location. Perkins replies, "But I'm glad that Jesus didn't just relocate his heart. We are all grateful that he came to earth in the flesh" (1993:12).

Perhaps the reverse is also possible: geographically relocating, without the heart of the incarnation, without having a ministry of presence. What makes a person or ministry "incarnational"? What does it mean when we as human beings become incarnational, following in the steps of Jesus, God incarnate?

David Bosch, citing the incarnation as the first of six major salvific events, reminds us that Protestant churches have had an underdeveloped theology of the incarnation. It was liberation theology, he says, that has led the way in viewing the Christian mission in terms of the incarnation, the human Jesus who "wearily trod the dusty roads of Palestine where he took compassion on those who were marginalized" (1991:512-513). Liberation theology has emphasized the incarnation. And since we also find much of the suffering and oppression that provides the context for liberation theologies concentrated in our cities, it is not surprising that we should find the theme of incarnation there as well.

The dangers of the incarnational approach

The concept of incarnation is at once significant and potentially dangerous. It is significant because the gospel does not exist in a vacuum but must be incarnated, "fleshed out" anew in each context. We know that when God had a message, he sent a messenger, his own son. Likewise, we are privileged and honored to be God's messengers, God's ambassadors.

But the concept of incarnation is also dangerous. Although we are called to follow Jesus, we are not the Messiah, and Jesus did not call us to be messianic. We have recently seen in Waco, Texas, how dangerous it is for mere mortals to think of themselves as the Messiah. David Koresh is an extreme example, but there are those within city ministries who set themselves up as the saviors of the city, the rescuers of the homeless, the shelter for refugees. Some of us recognize these dangers within ourselves. Perhaps the challenging urban context even attracts certain personalities that thrive on crisis and saving others.

Another danger accompanies the incarnational approach. As we become neighbors in a neighborhood and begin to share our lives, we discover the joys and treasures of life hidden in neighborhoods forgotten by most of the world. But as we become immersed in life and open our hearts, we discover not only the treasures, but also the tremendous suffering, inhumanity, and evil that seem to surround us on all sides. Sometimes we can even become overwhelmed, and the despair around us begins to take over within us.

Awareness of the dangers, however, should not keep us from acknowledging the transformation that begins to take place when someone like Father Greg pours out his life in a barrio of young men desperate for the love and limits of a caring father. Many of the young men will never be the same after experiencing a relationship with a compassionate adult who didn't give up on them, who loved them unconditionally.

READING THE CONTEXT

The Dolores Mission Parish is the poorest parish in Los Angeles. Most of the residents speak Spanish as either their first or second language. Historically, East Los Angeles was the site of the zoot suit riots during World War II. In a rampage of racism, military men raided the area, beating and killing Mexican American men, and raping the women.

Although racism is more subtle now, Latinos are still significantly under-represented in most professions and in city government. As they compare themselves to the dominant culture of the city (in terms of who holds the money and power), many in this parish feel that their skin color and poverty marginalizes them.

James Vigil's study of East Los Angeles gangs shows that this double marginality is a major factor behind gang involvement (1988). Father Greg often spoke of the anger and despair among the youth. Many have little hope that even a small portion of the American Dream can be theirs.

We can say this is true of many neighborhoods in our cities, as the gap between rich and poor continues to grow. We saw in Los Angeles last spring one of the results of what can happen when large numbers of people believe they are marginal to the systems of the city. As one person phrased it after the civil unrest, "L.A. is a boiling pot. The lid blew off for three days, but the pot is still boiling."[4]

A person such as Father Greg, who moves into a neighborhood in East Los Angeles, can be a bridge between worlds. Father Greg spent many hours advocating for the local youth within the court system, and helped start an alternative to the school system for gang youth. People sometimes criticized him for identifying too much with the homeboys, rather than cooperating with the police.

The city can be vast, complex, and overwhelming. Perhaps this is why many urban workers focus their ministries in one area. For urban workers, a tension can exist between the location of their heart in one particular context, and the need to see the bigger picture into which their piece fits. Father Greg chose to focus on one subgroup—gang youth—

although he understood the systems and structures that contributed to the poverty and despair in his barrio.

One result of the seemingly endless need in the city is the high rate of burnout among urban workers. This is especially true of those whose ministry is incarnational, because there are no natural boundaries separating work from the rest of life. While this integration of life and work is part of the appeal of incarnational ministry, it can also take a toll on physical, emotional and spiritual health.

In East Los Angeles and many inner city neighborhoods, the overriding theme seems to be a deepening, deadly despair. There are signs of hope, but for many that is not the substance of their lives. Too often this utter hopelessness and anger explode into violence in the streets. Increasingly, this tide of violence is not limited to our inner cities, but we find it throughout the urban metroplex.

REREADING THE SCRIPTURES

Two Scripture references are often used as the biblical basis for incarnational, relocation ministries: Philippians 2:5-8 and John 1:14. Jesus, even though he was God, emptied himself and became like us. The Word became flesh and tabernacled among us. A lifetime of reflection can only increase the wonder and mystery of this event.

As I have reflected on what incarnational mission is and is not, I have taken a new look not only at the above-mentioned Scriptures, but also at the life of Jesus as revealed in the Gospels. Even though we are not the Messiah it seems we attempt things that even Jesus, though he was God, did not attempt. Or we attempt them without the time of waiting, preparation, and prayer that Jesus felt he needed.

One helpful insight comes from the story of Jesus at the pool of Bethesda (John 5). Here Jesus heals one of many disabled people. One. Only one. Certainly there were many more who needed healing. The Gospels tell us of some peo-

13

ple whom Jesus touched and healed, but he left many untouched. The overwhelming needs around him did not drive Jesus. His mission was not to touch and heal every person, but to be obedient to his Father. Today we do well to follow in his steps.

A friend of mine was remembering a Hindu festival that he and I attended in Nepal. There were lines of people with every kind of ailment: withered hands, bent backs, massive facial disfiguration and many deformities such as we rarely see in this country. From such a mass of humanity, how would Jesus know whom to touch? How are we to know?

The need is not the call

In addressing this question, Robert Linthicum states that the need is not the call. The city is full of human pain, and we cannot begin by responding to the needs that may pull our heart strings. The things that tug at us may be more of a reflection of our own unresolved needs than the call of God. How do we find that call? According to Linthicum, "As our fellowship with God deepens, the Lord will reveal the call" (1991a:238).

If we allow the desperate need of the city to be our starting point, it will not take long before we are completely overwhelmed. This is perhaps the key to how Mother Teresa has continued so many years in such difficult work. In a television interview several years ago she was asked, "How did you receive your call to serve the poor?" Without missing a beat she replied, "My call is not to serve the poor. My call is to follow Jesus. I have followed him to the poor. But if he called me to the rich, I would go to the rich."

Likewise, we see in the Scriptures that his union with the Father was central to the life of Jesus. John 14 speaks beautifully of this intimate relationship. To know Jesus is to know the Father. Jesus is in the Father, and the Father is in him.

John 5:19 develops this relationship further: "I tell you the truth, the Son can do nothing by himself; he can only do what he sees his Father doing, because whatever the Father does the Son also does." Apart from God, Jesus could do nothing.

The same is true for us as urban workers; we must also participate in what God is doing. We do not bring God's reign into the city. God is already there. He invites us to join him in his activity. In humility we must realize that we will never have all the answers. We cannot meet all the needs. We are not the answer. The ministry belongs to God, not to us.

If we truly understand this, the tendency to see ourselves as the rescuers of the city, to be messianic, will diminish. A secret of the Christian life is learning to trust God, depending on him. Yet as incarnational Christians, one of the greatest dangers we face is that we create dependencies not on God but on ourselves and our programs. We must never forget: there is only *one* Messiah.[5]

The story of the bleeding woman in Luke 8 also gives us some insights into the ways of Jesus. Like many of us, Jesus was a busy man, on his way to carry out an important task—in this case the healing of the daughter of a leader of the synagogue, a man with power in his society. Desperate and too ashamed to address Jesus, the woman reached out to touch his robe. We know she was immediately healed.

But have we considered why Jesus bothered to stop? After all, he had healed the woman, he had accomplished the task. And he was in a hurry. This woman was but one in the crowd. Perhaps that is the point. Jesus wants to meet this unknown woman. He desires a face-to-face encounter, not an anonymous healing. He knows that the years of shame she had endured were not cured when she touched his robe. Her secret has to come to the light so that her soul could find healing. She needs to meet the Messiah. We hear the compassion of Jesus as he says to her, "Daughter, your faith has

15

healed you. Go in peace" (Luke 8:48). Imagine—a few moments before this woman had been afraid to show her face! Now Jesus affectionately calls her "daughter" and draws her into the family of God.

Protestant Christians have spent many years debating which takes precedence: ministry of word or ministry of deed. But whether Jesus used words, deeds, or both (the mode of mission), his means were always the way of love and compassion, as the story above demonstrates. We can serve many meals in rescue missions (deed) or preach sermons to people in parks (word) but both can too easily become merely tasks we must complete. To be incarnational is to follow Jesus in his compassion and love. This involves the being of the person involved in ministry, not just the doing of missional tasks.

In looking at the life of Jesus, Viv Grigg points out that Jesus spent thirty years learning Aramaic and Jewish culture (1984:52). In contrast, our society values instant results. How many years are we willing to devote to "growing up" in the city and learning a new urban culture? Perhaps if all urban missionaries and workers new to the city had a significant time to listen and learn, if they adopted an attitude of openness, we would see fewer paternalistic ministries that ultimately disempower people.[6]

Absence is also part of ministry

Perhaps most striking is that even though Jesus spent 30 years growing up in his world, he only spent three years in intentional ministry with his disciples. What would have happened to the disciples if he had stayed? Would Peter have become the rock on whom Jesus could build his church? Would the disciples have gone on to accomplish what they did?

In the fourteenth chapter of John, Jesus speaks of his leaving. He often spoke of his time to depart, and attempted to prepare the disciples for his absence. In this passage, Jesus makes it clear that he must leave so the Holy Spirit, the Spirit of Truth, the Comforter, may come. Again in John 16:6-7 he says, "Because I have said these things, you are filled with grief. But I tell you the truth: It is for your good that I am going away. Unless I go away, the Counselor will not come to you; but if I go, I will send him to you."

Henri Nouwen in *A Living Reminder* speaks of these verses:

> In his absence a new and more intimate presence became possible, a presence which nurtured and sustained in the midst of tribulations and which created the desire to see him again. The great mystery of the divine revelation is that God entered into intimacy with us not only by Christ's coming, but also by his leaving (1977:42).

Nouwen goes on to say that absence, or leaving, needs to be as much a part of our ministry as presence. "We have to learn to leave so that the Spirit can come" (1977:45).

This has tremendous implications for incarnational ministries. If we do not know when to be absent and leave room for the Holy Spirit, we may give the message that we are somehow the answer, instead of pointing to Jesus. As Nouwen so well phrases it, we may be *in* the way, rather than showing the way.

Despite his active life, we often find Jesus drawing aside to spend time with God. In Mark we read that he got up early in the morning to pray. Before the cross, he needed to go to Gethsemane, where angels came and ministered to him. Learning to find silence and solitude amidst the noise of the city wilderness is a challenge indeed. Jesus knew himself well enough to know he could not live by bread alone (Luke 4). Do our active lives reflect the same reality?

New Mission Insights

The idea of incarnation, of walking with and dwelling among people, of identifying with their sufferings, is essential for mission in the city. A theology that looks in from the outside, that sees the sin and wants to go in and rescue the city, is inadequate. American Christians still need to learn much about this, especially in this country where we live with a denial of death and pain.

Accompanying others may mean confronting our own suffering and weaknesses. More profoundly, if we cross the barriers into the world of the oppressed, we may have to ask a hard question: Why do large groups of people in our cities carry so much more than their share of shame and suffering? Incarnational mission will most probably mean abandoning our own physical, emotional and spiritual comfort zones.

While incarnation is Jesus' entry point, the Scriptures do not end there. It seems that there are ministries in our cities that, albeit unintentionally, act on the premise that this is the end of the story, that the main purpose is the walking alongside. While there is a sense of hope that comes with this accompaniment, this knowing that we don't walk alone, reducing the incarnation to only "being" is less than what God intends.

Hopelessness in our cities is rooted in a sense of despair that nothing will ever change, accompanied by a sense of powerlessness to cause needed changes. Some change may take place through presence alone, but we cannot leave it at that.

God broke into human history through the incarnation not only so that Jesus could walk with us. Rather, it led to the most significant event in salvation—and human—history. The incarnation led to the suffering and death of Jesus on the cross and his triumphant (not triumphalistic) resurrection.

In a sense this seems obvious. But I know from my own life, and from observing others around me, that the city constantly denies and negates the life and power of the resurrection. We are called to walk alongside, to "dwell among" in our cities, but always with our eyes and hearts on the cross and the resurrection of our Lord. We must be people of compassion who say with Jesus, "O Jerusalem, Jerusalem!" and be willing to weep for our city as Jesus wept over Jerusalem. We must be willing to listen to the stories of pain and brokenness, but as we embrace the pain we must also remember that the cross is no longer in darkness, but we now see it in the light of the resurrection.

The crucial matter of hope

This crucial matter of hope came powerfully to me when the jury announced the verdicts in the Rodney King beating case. Most of us will remember when we first heard the "not guilty" verdicts. Certainly it was a mistake—the evidence seemed so clear. My young Latino friend said it well: "I'm so angry, Jude." I sensed his despair as he continued talking. "Before the verdict, I had some hope that the system might work for us. Now I know it never will."

It took nearly 24 hours for the rioting to reach our neighborhood. We were not prepared; we had not anticipated this. As I spent the next few days absorbing, listening, being there, I was overcome by a despair such as I've rarely known. Deadly despair. Paralyzing. And with it the feeling of being completely powerless. It felt like the Saturday before the resurrection. Would hope or beauty spring from the ashes? The media spoke easily of the signs of hope, but they came from the outside. My neighborhood hardly seemed a hopeful place.

Some are asking, "Is there hope for the city?" Maybe we should ask, "Is there hope in the city?" Cheap talk of hope deepens the despair. If hope is the anchor of our souls, then our city was adrift, myself included. I had no energy or desire to take part in a big cleanup. As I wept, grieving over

19

the city, my only comfort was that Jesus had wept over his city, Jerusalem. Was it possible that he was also weeping over our city—over the deep wounds always there, now suddenly exposed? Raw. Open. So many living in shame, without dignity or recognition of full humanity. The looting and rioting and subsequent police raids stripped away more of the humanity.

It seems that so often what we as Americans call hope is more an optimism that comes from our denial of pain, suffering, and death. How do we truly embrace the suffering of the cross and still live in the hope of the resurrection? How do we live in resurrection hope without denying the intense pain in our world?

Jack Pantaleo, after writing of Jesus' sacrifice and death, goes on to say, "Let's face it. Death had been done before. Anyone can die. Jesus revolutionized creation because he had the nerve it took not to remain dead. . . . The hardest thing we can do is not to die, but to live, and to live abundantly in joy" (1992:8). In many parts of our cities, it is easier to choose death than to choose life. Only in the power of the resurrection can we choose life. Only through the hope of the resurrection can we overcome despair.

The principalities and powers

There are times, however, when the darkness of the principalities and powers seems to overwhelm us. Whatever our theological orientation before we move into the city, it will not take long to become aware of a depth of evil we perhaps have not encountered before.

To some extent we can explain suffering and despair in purely human terms, and speak about them without much embarrassment. But eventually there comes a time of confrontation with evil, of something so menacing, horrifying, and bone-chilling that we dare speak of it only under the protection of the cross of Jesus. Although Christians from various theological traditions interpret this evil differently, there is a growing sense among many that there exists a dimension in the city far greater than human sin can explain. How do we withstand the powerful forces (powers) in the city that try to blind us to the life-giving power of the resurrection?

Some authors have written at length on this subject from various perspectives. Thomas McAlpine gives an overview of various ways we can face the powers. He also mentions other authors who have written on this important subject (1991). In looking at incarnational ministries, it is important to note that the very act of intentionally moving into a neighborhood is an act of spiritual warfare. Light dispels darkness. Those who desire that their deeds remain in the dark do not want the light. So those who relocate can expect resistance to their presence.

The wise words of C. S. Lewis are a good reminder that we are not to overestimate or underestimate the power of the Evil One (1963). Jesus did not focus on demons or the things of Satan, but he dealt with them when it was necessary. He knew where his authority came from. We do not need to live in fear, but we should also not be naïve about the powers that may seek to destroy us. We must change our vision of the power of the resurrection over the principalities and powers from an abstract concept to a living reality.

One essential point in dealing with the principalities and powers is to realize how weak we are when we stand alone. To stand firm we must stand together. As we stand together, accompanied by the presence of Jesus Christ, we can reflect on the role of community in our context.

Robert Lupton speaks of this in one of his newsletters. In the early years of his ministry, he spent much time earning the trust of 15 youths from a "low-hope" environment. He mentions all the wonderful things that can happen in such a relationship. In time most of the young men also became followers of Christ, although he was unsuccessful in his efforts to involve them in a church body. As they entered their late teens, things began to unravel as the responsibilities of life set in. One by one he watched them drift away. Two were killed, two received life sentences for murder, four are strung out on drugs, two are homeless.

> It is good to build programs for urban youth; but it is best to build communities where healthy families are fostered and children are valued. . . . It is good to introduce young people to Christ; but it is best to invite them into the family of faith that will walk with them through the passages of life (1992).

MISSION ACTION

A definition of mission for the city *must* include not only the transformation of individuals, but also of the city itself. It must include the gathering of people into the church as a faith community, not only into an individual, personal relationship with Christ. Incarnation is not the end of mission, but the mode, or the means. We can do both word and deed ministries without the spirit of the incarnation.

I've heard sermons preached in MacArthur Park and seen meals given out at a rescue mission without any relationship or connection from human to human. What are we communicating? When God had a message, he sent a person, a person who never treated people as objects of his words or deeds. In the story recorded in the Gospel of John, we see that the woman at the well not only met Jesus and was forgiven, but also became an agent of mission. In our cities, those who have been victimized will gain a new identity when they see that God can use them as agents of transformation in their own neighborhoods.

Mission in the city must deal not only with people's feelings of powerlessness but also with the injustices and evils that contribute to the powerlessness. We must also be cautious not to increase feelings of powerlessness by only "doing for" people. Community organizer Saul Alinsky followed an iron rule: "Never do for people what they can do for themselves."

Whether our particular ministry is involved with church planting or community development, this should also be our guideline. To do otherwise is to continue in paternalistic, messianic patterns that ultimately disempower people. Do we know when it is time to be absent, when to leave? Do we know how to be present without dominating?

The concept of incarnational ministry refers to ministry carried out by individuals. But what does it mean for a church to be incarnational in the city? What of a church that is located in the city but has no relationship to the city? Or a church that has relationships that move in one direction, only providing services to the people of their neighborhood?

What kind of church should a church in the city be?

Robert Linthicum addresses this question when he speaks of three responses of the church to its city: the church in, to, or with the city. In the first instance, the church sees itself *in* the city, but does not identify with the community around it. We can see it as a fortress. The second response is for the church to see itself as a church *to* the community. Here the church does get involved, but it is the church deciding what the community needs and providing services based on those perceived needs. It may see itself as the savior of the community. The third response is the church *with* the community. We could call this the incarnational approach of the church in the city. "When the church takes this third approach, that church incarnates itself in that community. That church becomes flesh of the people's flesh and bone of the people's bone" (1991c:9). The church becomes a listening and learning church as it identifies with the people. The church itself becomes a partner with the community.

23

We might add one other type of church in the city—the church *of* the city. Especially among immigrant groups, there are churches of the poor, indigenous to the community, already rooted in that context. In time, these churches may face the same choices. Do they relocate to a "nicer" environment, or do they stay where they were first planted?

RETELLING THE STORY

Crossing the Los Angeles River into East Los Angeles, a group of young people come marching over the bridge, carrying banners. "Stop the violence." "Justice for All." "Comité pro Paz en el Barrio." My heart warms as I see them, for the barrio they are from is none other than Dolores Mission. As I round the corner down Gless Street, the new building for the Dolores Mission Women's Daycare Cooperative greets me. Homeboy Tortillas has expanded and has a new building.

Leonardo informs me that the base community groups are doing well. Yes, they miss Father Greg.[7] But the people of Dolores Mission have been reclaiming their neighborhood for several years, and continue to do so. The involvement of the Group of Mothers stands as an example to other neighborhoods in Los Angeles. And to those who wonder if change is possible in our barrios, Dolores Mission shines as a beacon of hope.

NOTES

1   "Homeboy" is the word gang members use when referring to fellow gang members. In the last few years, it has been used to refer to one's "buddy" or close friend, whether or not one is in a gang.

2   See John MacKay, *The Other Spanish Christ* (MacMillan, 1993).

3   "Outside the gate" is a reference to Orlando Costas' book by that title (Orbis, 1982).

4   It is worth noting here that during the civil unrest of spring 1992 that left much of Los Angeles in ashes, East Los Angeles was left untouched.

5   Carmen Renee Berry, in *When Helping You Is Hurting Me: Escaping the Messiah Trap* (Harper, 1988), deals with this topic in depth from a psychological perspective.

6   Dr. Betty Sue Brewster and her late husband Tom refer to three roles of the incarnational missionary: learner, story-teller, intercessor (class notes, "Incarnation and Mission Among the Urban Poor," Fuller Theological Seminary). These three roles are a very helpful way to move beyond paternalism in a neighborhood.

7   Father Greg has since returned to Dolores Mission. He is much rested after his sabbatical. When asked recently how he survives in such a difficult environment, he replied that he's learned a few things over the years. "I've learned that I'm not God. I'm not Jesus. I can't always be there. God uses me, and the rest is up to him."

2

Structures, injustice, and insensitivity: Who is the neighbor, anyway?

J. Timothy Kauffman

THE STORY

A Los Angeles Christian asked Jesus, "What must I do to inherit eternal life?"

Jesus returned the question, "What is written in the Law? How do you read it?"

The Christian answered, "Love the Lord your God with all your heart, and with all your soul, and with all your strength and with all your mind; and, love your neighbor as yourself."

"You have answered correctly," Jesus replied. "Do this and you will live."

But the Christian wanted to rationalize, so he asked Jesus, "And who is my neighbor?"

J. *Timothy Kauffman* was a pastor and urban church planter in Germany for twelve years. He teaches pastoral formation, urban studies and leadership as an adjunct professor at several institutions. Please see the contributing authors section.

In reply, Jesus said, "A certain young Anglo male stopped at a red light in his big-rig at Florence and Normandie. He was on his way to make a delivery. While he was sitting there, an angry crowd pulled him out of the truck and threw him to the ground. There in the middle of the street the mob attacked him, beat him, and left him to die. The first group that should have helped him were the enforcers of the law. They were conspicuously absent. The second group that could have helped him was the press in a helicopter overhead. They could have sounded their sirens immediately. Seeing a story, however, they just let their cameras roll until the man was almost dead. Then they hurriedly left the scene.

"About that time, a young African American male, watching this tragedy unfold on television in the safety of his home not far away, had compassion on the young white man. Risking his own life, he left his home, faced down the mob and helped the young man back into his truck. Emboldened by his courage, several others also came to his aid. Together, they drove the white man to the hospital where they were later told that if they had arrived one minute later, the young man would have died.

"Which was a neighbor to the man who fell into the hands of the angry crowd: the law, the media, or the African American?" Jesus asked.

The Christian answered, "Those who helped the young man."

Jesus told him, "Go and do likewise."

REFLECTING ON THE STORY

LIKE MOST Los Angelenos, I sat in horror and watched the civil unrest after the jury had vindicated the police officers in the beating of Rodney King. It arrived in my living room through the latest journalistic "live television" technology. The city was already beginning to burn. Then, without warning, the story recounted above began to unfold before our eyes. We instantly added terror, fear, and revulsion to our anger at the verdict. These emotions rushed over us in waves. As the world gazed transfixed, the truck driver, already on the pavement, was beaten until he lay motionless. It did not seem possible he could still be alive. This could not be happening. It seemed almost like an instant replay of the Rodney King case that had ignited the conflagration.

Then, without warning, the television helicopter crew showing us the horror fled the scene, leaving us to agonize about the truck driver's fate. The police were nowhere to be seen. My only thought was, "I have just participated in and am somehow a co-conspirator to murder." My soul felt dirty.

Later we heard the heroic story of how truck driver Reginald Denny's life had been saved. These incidents parallel both in content and intensity the parable of the Good Samaritan. The difference was that Jesus was telling a fictitious story; the story about the truck driver was real.

Structures and parallels in the stories

The neighbors in my story are different in substance from the priest and Levite in Jesus' parable of the Good Samaritan. But they are similar in kind. In Jesus' parable, the priest and the Levite were not just individuals, but also represented major social structures in their society.

In Jesus' parable, the first person who should have helped the victim was the priest. Priests exercised the structural role of protecting and preserving the Jewish culture and values of Jesus' day. In contemporary society, both the print and the broadcast media are major players in the formation and protection of societal values.

The second person to walk by—the Levite—was related to the priest. Although both were descendants of the same tribe, the role of the Levites differed from that of the priesthood. Since the Levites were laity, they performed subordinate duties at the temple (Moulder 1986:964). They also

29

held a majority of the seats in the permanent Sanhedrin. So the Levites bore a major responsibility in the administration of justice (W. Smith 1967:347). Law enforcement in society today represents the first and most immediate structure in the administration of justice. But in my story, the police didn't even show up.

Embodied in their respective representatives in both stories, the structures failed to respond to the needs of individuals.

Contemporary values have secular sources

Notice that in the contemporary story, secular structures have replaced the religious providers. Why has this happened? Is it because the church has become complacent and lost its credibility and relevance as a leader in setting societal values? Could it be that the state, having become secularized, has usurped the position of helper and protector? Has the sheer size and complexity of the need to help and protect citizens forced this change?

Whatever the reason, it is a reality the church must consider. We know Christians must be neighbors—but how? For the followers of Christ in an urban society[1] the story has come full circle. We too must ask Jesus, "Who is my neighbor?"

READING THE CONTEXT

Any urban society is a combination of systems[2] and structures. All cities have systems. Similar systems in different cities tend to look alike. These systems and structures work together to ensure the common good, i.e., to nurture, to transport, to protect, to educate, to inform, and so on. The dominant culture that founded each system gives it uniqueness and life.

In the same way, heredity and the socialization process act to form a person's values and unique personality. A structure's uniqueness is evident in cultural repositories

such as values, attitudes, collective knowledge, and procedures. And the system goes on to look after the needs, the
interests, the nurture, and the protection of its original
founding culture.

Whom do systems and structures serve?

Once in place, systems and structures look out first for
themselves and for those they were created to serve. Lyle
Schaller writes that the natural tendency of social systems is
to respond to demands for change by following normal procedures (1978:68). "Normal procedures" means business as
usual. When push comes to shove, these entities will protect
the dominant culture from those perceived as outside its
boundaries, or who threaten it from within. Thus, a denial of
impartial justice is likely.

Could it be that the true root of the neighbor problem
lies at the structural level? Historically, white males dominated the society that formed the structures in the U.S. Is it
possible that those structures still serve White male interests
regardless of who serves in them?[3]

If this is true, let me suggest that in my story the systems of law enforcement, justice, and the media—structures
that are supposed to protect citizens—were not really mis-
functioning. When we look at the riots themselves, the systems worked at the macro level—but only for the benefit of
those they were designed to serve. In the specific micro
level case of the truck driver, however, the systems failed
miserably.

Paulo Freire underscores this issue when he writes in
Pedagogy of the Oppressed:

> Any attempt to "soften" the power of the oppressor in
> deference to the oppressed almost always manifests
> itself in the form of false generosity; indeed, the attempt
> never goes beyond this. In order to have the continued
> opportunity to express their "generosity," the oppres-

31

sors must perpetuate injustice as well. An unjust social order is the permanent fount of this "generosity," which is nourished by death, despair and poverty. That is why the dispensers of false generosity become desperate at the slightest threat to its source (1970:28-29).

The bottom line in my story is that the structures were neighborly for some, but not for all. It took the extraordinary action of specific individuals to be neighbors to Reginald Denny. And as it was in Jesus' parable, ethnicity was also an issue in my story. The contemporary African American "Samaritan" not only overcame the stultifying effects of the structures, but also was willing to risk personal danger for the sake of a white man.

Are there any solutions?

It seems that there are at least two possible solutions to ensure that being a neighbor becomes the rule for everyone in our society. The first possibility is that we must change the structures. That would involve rethinking and restructuring the most basic and elemental understanding of who we are as a society. We must ask ourselves, "Who is really included?" But as we turn to U.S. history for examples, we find that it is not very positive about total social restructuring.

From the beginning of our republic, the prevailing metaphor describing the U.S. social make-up has been that of the melting pot. Yet as Glazer and Moynihan point out in "Beyond the Melting Pot" (1971:99), by as early as 1882 this metaphor excluded the Chinese, to say nothing of women, African Americans, or other non-European immigrants. The melting pot metaphor referred only to those who were members of the group that created the nation's structure. It did not challenge the original conception of the structure, and so may be one of the reasons why this outmoded metaphor still has life in our society.

In addition, the cultural equation has changed dramatically in contemporary Los Angeles. The kind of people for whom the structure was created has dwindled to around 20 percent of the population.[4] That means four people out of five feel that they are not sufficiently included in the structures. An erosion of unity occurs. Groups of people, including street gangs, practice the stakeout and protection of emotional, economic or geographic "turf."

When such atomization happens, an almost total loss of a sense of unity can occur.[5] When people do not commit themselves to being neighbors to one another, it is possible that atomization might become total in a city like Los Angeles.

There is also a spiritual crisis

Add to the systemic and bureaucratic limitation of governmental systems other value signals being sent to the cultural matrix of the U.S.: (1) Secret arms deals to hostile nations, (2) savings and loan scandals, (3) insider trading on the stock exchange, (4) employee theft, and (5) bounced checks in Congress.

This value crisis was not lost on working people on the streets of Los Angeles. Except for a few convictions, those in leadership in the dominant culture have either not been charged, were given light sentences, or pardoned. Those who do not belong are prosecuted to the law's fullest extent. In an interview with Janet Clayton, Cornel West underscores this value discrepancy in the enforcement of existing structures.[6] After decades of such repeated examples and personal experiences, hope of ever belonging fades and dies.

Spiritual poverty results when people lose faith or hope of any kind. In Los Angeles at least, many are drained of hope from the buildup of events over the years. It seems that anything short of a fundamental rethinking of who forms the dominant culture, the construction of inclusive structures, and the incorporation of all as fully vested participants in those structures will end in continued cultural gerrymandering and unrest due to disenfranchisement. Many people's lives and futures are tied to governmental systems that can or will no longer deliver self-determination or impartial justice. People are angry and frustrated. They not only feel powerless but also consider themselves at the mercy of systems that have their makers' best interests at heart.

The power of one

For these reasons, the only help for Rodney King and Reginald Denny was at the hands of individual citizens who were not afraid to act when the structures and systems failed to act as neighbors. Because one person was willing to be vulnerable, others who would not have acted were encouraged to become involved.

Was Jesus saying to us that if we would "Go and do likewise," we would also empower others to become neighbors? The lawyer who prompted Jesus' story of the Good Samaritan showed concern for thinking the right thought. But Jesus' interest lay in demonstrating the power of one person doing the right thing.

In addition, we could affirm that the young man who initiated Reginald Denny's rescue was not only a neighbor to Denny, but also to Denny's alleged assailants. If Denny had died, they would most likely have faced murder charges.[7] Denny now openly declares that he forgives his attackers. The story has come full circle. The person who needed a neighbor is now a neighbor himself. Can we find here a kernel out of which *shalom* for the urban society might blossom into reality?

REREADING THE SCRIPTURES

Whether religious or secular, structures are closely connected to being a neighbor. They can either help or hinder neighborliness. In his instructions to the children of Israel,

God set up several structures to protect the weak and ensure justice. I will examine them more or less chronologically.

The Decalogue

The first and most basic structure is the Decalogue. It defines the standard of what it means to be a neighbor for both the Old and New Testaments. In the Decalogue we find not only a religious but also a societal structure so profound that we can build civilizations on it. It addresses the use and allocation of property, respectful and faithful relationships, the honor of a person's name and reputation, and much more.

The first commandment in the Hebrew Decalogue includes the statement, "I am the Lord your God, who brought you out of Egypt, out of the land of slavery" (Exod. 20:2). Throughout the Pentateuch, Yahweh continually reminded his people that they must be kind to foreigners because they were also once aliens in a foreign land.

Cities of refuge

Yahweh gave the cities of Canaan to the Israelites as a gift (Deut. 6:10-18). The Levites received special cities. One of the Levites' functions was to preserve, transcribe, and interpret the law. Yahweh set aside six of the levitical cities as cities of refuge. These cities involved a structure that provided both Israelites and aliens living in Israel with justice in cases of involuntary manslaughter (Num. 35:15).

The Sabbath year and Jubilee

God also outlined an economic structure that assured the cancellation of debt and the equitable redistribution of land for his people. It was called the Year of Jubilee. Every fiftieth year all land was to be returned to the descendants of the original owners. Yahweh did not want to have any one family or class of people accumulate great fortunes over time. God will never absolve a nation that is content to allow some to have too much while others have too little.

In the Jubilee theology, God also provided a way to be neighbors to indentured servants and the land. Those forced for economic reasons to sell themselves into indentured servanthood were to be released after seven years. The land was able to regenerate and yield good crops because of the prohibition against planting farmland during the Sabbath Year (Exod. 23:10-11, Deut. 15:1-3). These observations help to provide a valuable Old Testament link between what it means to be a neighbor and the matter of social structures. God's structures mandated equity, compassion, and stewardship towards people and nature. They facilitated being a neighbor to those who had no voice or recourse of their own.

John the Baptist

John the Baptist provides an essential theological and structural link between the Old and New Testaments, particularly concerning the life and teaching of Jesus. John quotes Isaiah as both his legitimization and the major thrust of his message (Isa. 40:1-8). The metaphor he uses is a powerful statement likening the coming changes to a transformation of the very structures of nature:

> *A voice of one calling: "In the desert prepare the way for the* LORD; *make straight in the wilderness a highway for our God. Every valley shall be raised up, every mountain and hill made low; the rough ground shall become level, the rugged places a plain" (Isa. 40:3-4).*

In answer to the questions of the repentant and newly baptized concerning the ethical content of their new lives, John the Baptist replied in the best Old Testament tradition in Luke 3:10-14. According to him, the structural attributes of this new life included a willingness to share wealth, justice in law enforcement, and fairness in governmental structures.

When you read the appropriate passages in the Gospels, remember that the Roman army was corrupt and supplemented its income with extortion. Graft, payoffs, and greed were common in the tax collection system. John the Baptist called for each repentant sinner to be a revolutionary and swim against the tide in corrupt structures. Changed people must exhibit changed behavior in their respective systems.

Jesus speaks of new structures

Jesus practiced John the Baptist's admonishment by socializing with government officials and those deemed social outcasts by the existing religious structures. The Pharisees criticized him for eating and drinking with these outcasts. Jesus countered that his mission was to sinners, not to the righteous. He said that we must pour new wine into new wineskins, because the new wine will burst old skins. Jesus was not afraid of new structures. He was affirming that new truth needs new structures.

Then Jesus made a very curious observation: ". . . No one after drinking old wine wants the new, for he says, 'The old is better'" (Luke 5:39). He seems to be suggesting that those who had never experienced any benefits from the Old Covenant would accept the good news of the kingdom with joy. Those who were used to the old wine, however, would never want to switch. Therefore, the old structures would not be adequate to accommodate the new wine and we will need to bypass them in favor of new structures.

Jesus is the neighbor

A closer look at the Scripture passages above shows that Jesus put himself at risk with the religious establishment by extending the offer of the kingdom to those whom that very establishment considered unfit and alien. Yet an unconditional love only God could give saturated his offer

37

to those outcasts. Jesus was being a neighbor. His unflinch-
ing loyalty to them in offering God's Good News ultimately
cost him his life. Truly the low of society are exalted and the
high brought down. This is the substance of his call to the
church: ". . . As the Father has sent me, I am sending you"
(John 20:21).

The resurrection is the hope of all those who follow
Jesus' example. We could never have predicted the resurrection from an analysis of the past, or even a rational assess-
ment of the present. But viewed from this side of the event,
we experience the reality and power of the resurrection as
eternally present. The Law is now written ". . . with the Spirit
of the living God, not on tablets of stone but on tablets of
human hearts" (2 Cor. 3:3). The resurrection of Christ and
the power of the Holy Spirit's presence in the life of the
church anchors the new structure.

NEW MISSION INSIGHTS

The parable of the Good Samaritan goes to the very
heart of God's agenda for the people of his kingdom. It was
Jesus' answer to the question, "What must I do to inherit
eternal life?" (Luke 10:25). Normally, most Christians think
of a neighbor as the person they do something for, the person they invite to church. The neighbor is the other person.
But Jesus did not say the neighbor was the wounded man.
Jesus asked, "Which of these three do you think was a neighbor to the man who fell into the hands of robbers?" (Luke
10:36). The neighbor was the Samaritan. Gustavo Gutiérrez
asserts that the neighbor was not the wounded man: ". . . the
neighbor was the Samaritan who approached the wounded
man *and made him his neighbor*" (1973:111).[8]

Why is it that we confuse this issue? Why are the words
"neighbor" and "love," found in Leviticus 19:18, still subjects of such discussion?

The word "neighbor"

When faced with having to act, the lawyer in Luke asked, "Who is my neighbor?" Robert Brown helps us when he writes that by asking the question in that fashion, the lawyer redirects the discussion back onto safe territory. The question puts the lawyer back in control of the discussion. Now that defining the neighbor is the issue, an academic exploration can take place. The "lawyer, his own life-style now exempt from scrutiny, can do brilliantly in the ensuing verbal exchange. It is the kind of terrain on which lawyers excel" (Brown 1984:107). Jesus is pointing out to the self-righteous lawyer that "being good in the traditional, legalistic sense was not at all the same thing as loving God or loving one's neighbor" (Hoyer and McDaniel 1990:329). Jesus was telling the lawyer and subsequent followers, ". . . go and act like a neighbor" (Hoyer and McDaniel 1990:326; see also Gutiérrez 1973:198).

The word "love"

Jewish scholar Abraham Malamat suggests that the second half of the Great Commandment is not a command to love as we would love God, wife, children, or even ourselves. He carefully exegetes comparable usages of the Hebrew word in the Torah. Based on his research, he proposes that other meanings for the word "to love," could be "to be of use to," "to be beneficial to," "to assist or help" (1990:51). A translation of Leviticus 19:18 might then read, "You should be beneficial or helpful to your neighbor as you would be to yourself" (1990:51).

This exegesis helps clarify any discrepancy between the commandment itself and Jesus' interpretation of it to the lawyer. It also turns our attention away from the myopia connected with needing to love ourselves before we can love others.

Important parallels in the parables

In both Jesus' and the contemporary parables, we see several important parallels: (1) an injured person, (2) the irrelevance of ethnic differences and rivalries, (3) the failure of those from whom one should have expected help, (4) the challenge to act courageously when existing structures leave people out, and (5) the inconvenience and vulnerability the neighbor takes upon herself or himself to help. Jesus' question lingers in our ears, "Who was the neighbor to the man who was attacked?"

Being a neighbor often means putting myself at risk to come alongside persons who need my help (Luke 5:30-31; 7:34; 15:1-2). The forces at work within any urban society seem to discourage being a neighbor. The immediacy of danger and the very real fear of death tend to snuff out our good intentions. It is the power of Christ's resurrection through the Holy Spirit that empowers his disciples to be neighbors.

In Jesus' conversation with the Los Angeles Christian in our story, the Christian asks Jesus, "What must I do to inherit eternal life?" Jesus answers, "There are people who are on the road of life. They are beaten, stripped of everything, and left to die. They are children, homeless, imprisoned, mentally ill, unemployable, working poor, single parent families, immigrants, HIV positive, and many others. Go and be a neighbor."

MISSION ACTION

What can the people of God offer when society's structures do not function for everyone? Where do the people of God begin to be a neighbor? What is the church's role in an urban society?

Go and be a neighbor

With a few exceptions, the church in urban society has adopted a fortress mentality and embraced one of at least two approaches. The first is that of a large middle-class church that offers broad-ranging programs for middle-class families. Such churches attract middle-class families from smaller churches that cannot compete with the larger churches' excellent programs. These larger churches are eth-nically inclusive, but their socioeconomic target group shuts many out. They grow while the smaller churches become old and die. Nevertheless, the larger churches may also die out if their growth remains dependent on transfers from smaller churches, or if they eventually cannot meet the demands of their constituency.

A second approach is the smaller church with very few human and program resources to attract a cross section of their neighborhood. These smaller churches experience rapid change around them. In their attempt to survive they too often lose their energy and enterprising spirit. The result is that such churches also fail to take the initiative.

Unless churches become neighbors to the socioeco-nomic, ethnic, immigrant, and other diverse urban subcul-tures, they will become anachronistic. They will minister to a dwindling minority and eventually see values foreign to Christianity become the norm in their neighborhoods.

The church's first call is to be reconciled to God through Christ. A second and equal call is to be reconciled to each other by accepting personal and collective responsibility for the common good of both the household of faith and society at large.[9]

> Cooperation with the liberative and redemptive action of God, therefore, decisively shapes the ways persons seek positions, use resources, and make themselves available in the domains represented in the creative and governing action of God. Put most simply, it means an active, generative, initiating love for those whom God loves, which transvalues images of power, value and success and which is ready to spend and be spent

41

in God's work of fulfilling an inclusive commonwealth of love (Fowler 1984:92).

The "neighbor" churches are those that take the initiative. They transcend the values that they encounter by ministering together with God in redemptive partnership.

In the power of the Holy Spirit

In the Book of Acts, the secret to the living out of Christ's ministry in the church was the presence, the power, and the guidance of the Holy Spirit. The first Christians gladly lived out the mandates of the Old Testament, because external pressure was no longer the basis for the Law of God. The indwelling person of the Holy Spirit now internalized God and his presence.

The church in urban society desperately needs a new Pentecost to burst forth from behind its locked doors and fortress mentality, and rediscover a new spiritual community. It was through the power of the Holy Spirit on the day of Pentecost that the disciples overcame the language barrier. The ministry of the Holy Spirit prepared Peter for the destruction of ethnic barriers (Acts 10). All through Acts, not just in chapters two through four, we find many demonstrations of socioeconomic diversity in the church (2:42-45; 4:32-37; 6:1-6; 9:36ff.; 13:1; 16:12ff.; 21:26; 24:17).

Class, gender, and color blindness

There is also a connection between being a neighbor and (a) practicing what it means to love one another as Christ loves us, (b) no longer perpetuating ethnic, gender, and economic discrimination, and (c) rediscovering being part of a community of faith, where there is truly no longer a distinction between "Jew or Greek, male or female, slave or free."

The segregation of neighborhoods along ethnic, social or economic lines is often the enemy of the biblical concept of neighbor. Don't churches limit their ability to be a neighbor when they insist on moving to a more homogeneous area or on ministering to a traditional constituency? Churches that practice true equality can become a symbol to urban society of what it means to be a neighbor.

Salt, light, and leaven?

Society has always been corrupt. John the Baptist taught his disciples that being a neighbor means being honest in a context of dishonesty. They were to be generous with the little they had in a culture that valued greed. Their signature should be gentleness, caring, and compassion, when all others were increasingly callous and violent. Neighbors are not always well liked, but they are salt, light, and leaven. They model what it means to be in redemptive partnership with the urban society.

The churches of the suburbs representing homogeneous cultures have become complacent and dependent on safety, comfort, and convenience. Our study of the ministry of Christ tells us that being a neighbor means being willing to live with danger, hardship, and inconvenience. Salt, light, and leaven lose themselves in the process of being neighbors—and so undergo transformation.

New congregational structures

Thirty years ago David Moberg pointed to the way congregations may function as social and structural bridges between individual values (honesty, respect, friendship, compassion for the weak, and self-integrity) and the public sphere (1984:52-187). More recently Roozen, McKinney, and Carroll analyzed *Varieties of Religious Presence* in their study of ten congregations in Hartford, Connecticut. They affirmed that "relatively few institutions can 'mediate' effectively between society's megastructures and individuals, but congregations are clearly among them" (1984:17).

43

Lesslie Newbigin supported this view when he spoke of "the congregation as hermeneutic of the gospel." "To be faithful to a message which concerns the Kingdom of God, his rule over all things and all peoples," Newbigin affirmed, "the Church has to claim the high ground of public truth. . . . The primary reality of which we have to take account in seeking for a Christian impact on public life is the Christian congregation" (1989:222, 227).

If congregations are to be mediating structures between Christian values and public life, how can this happen in the city? What would congregations of those who have chosen to be neighbors look like? Are the present structures adequate to penetrate urban society, or are they old wineskins? Robert Linthicum writes,

> The model of the church that presently exists in the cities of the First World is based in that world's rural past. That model is of the parish church—a congregation set in the midst of a small locale and assuming spiritual and pastoral care over that community (1992:111).[10]

Structural differentiation[11] may be necessary if the church is to serve the needs of society. We need new or modified structures that encourage the neighbor lifestyle. That such structures are essential is now clear. Robert Wuthnow, for example, has concluded that

> Spirituality begins to move people toward being compassionate only when a threshold involvement in some kind of collective religious activity has been reached. . . . Once [a] person is involved in [an organized religious community], then a higher level of piety may be associated with putting forth effort to help the needy (1991a:13).

Linthicum mentions networking, community organization, coalition building, leadership development, and an

44

evangelism of respect as some structures that are working (1992:111-121). One possible structure that could incorporate much of the above is a community-based house church that uses the "ward heeler" approach.[12] Churches could develop such a structure with attributes quite consistent with being a neighbor.

Envisioning a new structure

If the church is to be viable in the city, it is time to think creatively about its structure. Let me suggest a scenario.

First, a group of Christians would choose a geographical area and a home in that area would become the center of activity. An essential element of the philosophy of ministry would be that every person living in the neighborhood is included as a potential member. Because the grassroots ministry would be continuous and inclusive, the effects of inevitable change would become a part of the nature of the faith community.

Second, the most important initial activity of the members of the house church would be to spend time in the neighborhood. They would converse, get to know people, and ask about the community's needs. If appropriate, the spontaneous meeting of needs might take the form of prayer, showing sincere interest, and identifying with the people and being their neighbor.[13] This kind of involvement is similar to the slow first steps of community organization. But the house church members would make a conscious effort to prepare fertile ground for the Holy Spirit to work in the hearts of people and gather them as a viable faith community in their neighborhood.

Third, relationships would be built over time. New friends would be invited to attend the house church. The Bible would become a living book. The church would become relevant to the daily realities of the people, and an invitation to accept Christ would be given. People would

45

work on personal and mutual needs. They would give aid and support to one another. The faith community would face collective needs and solve them through collective prayer. Where possible, the people would take action by consensus.

Fourth, the people would use available resources to bring change to their lives. When larger problems affecting the greater community[14] become known, the house church would either initiate or seek ways to become part of a wider discussion.

Fifth, the house church would grow like an organism whenever possible. It would include an adjacent geographical area in the network. A new house church would be planted with a small number of key people from the original house church and some who live in the adjacent area. Over time, the proliferation of house churches would cover a significant number of neighborhoods. They would maintain contact with each other and network for larger projects and corporate celebration. Tithing would be taught. The savings in building and personnel costs would make funds available to help meet needs in the specific and greater community. The house church community would use significant percentages of these savings for helping others. The maximum size of each house church would be such that all members could continue to be a part of the decision-making process for non-routine items. The development of people and the community would have priority over relief projects.

Sixth, relationships would form the basis for the structure of the house church. These relationships are not "warm fuzzies." They are hard-fought and won on the streets, in the yards, the bars, the homes, and the apartments of the neighborhood with the sweat of prayer and brow. Resulting partnerships bring to life (a) true reconciliation and redemptive relationships with God and each other through Jesus Christ,[15] (b) empowerment that celebrates freedom and a zeal to empower others, and (c) encouragement for the urban society and its structures to follow the example of the community of faith.

In spite of the obvious difficulties and problems of such structures, the church could again become relevant to the lives of people in the city through these newly viable congregations. These congregations would take seriously the mandate given them by Jesus: "As the Father has sent me, so send I you." His words to the lawyer remain his standard for his church today: "Go and be a neighbor."

Christ's call includes not only a call to repentance, but also a call to reconciliation. He sent his church to be a neighbor to all people, people who mutually empower each other, in turn, to become neighbors. As the church grows, it should always enable more and more people to become neighbors.

Being a neighbor is a deliberate choice

Lest we confuse the sins of the structure with our personal responsibility, we need a reminder[16] that individuals create and perpetuate structures.

> . . . even though Jesus was telling a story, he was still talking about reality. Psychological research tells us that, strange as it may seem, people really do act in the ways he described. Knowing this, Jesus presented his story in such a way that people could find themselves in the story and thus make the story their own (Hoyer and McDaniel 1990:332).

The neighbor in my story disregarded the fact that the structures were not acting as neighbors. Through his action, others also were inspired to become neighbors. His courage unmasked the dysfunction of the structures. For each person, being a neighbor has an infinite variety of meanings. However it manifests itself, being a neighbor is always a new story. It always requires a decision to act. A neighbor ignores ethnicity and the structures that divide. A neighbor

47

intentionally chooses to be there for the sake of the other and in doing so challenges the structures and may even stimulate the structures toward change.

Ultimately, the question in the city is *not*, "Who is my neighbor?" The *real* question is, "Am I willing to be a neighbor?"

NOTES

1   Definitions of the term "urban" and "city" are many and varied. The author has, therefore, opted to use the term "urban society." An urban society consists of all human interrelated activity within any contiguously inhabited geographical area. This means, for example, that I also include within the scope of urban society what we normally refer to as "suburban." Due to the uniqueness of any given urban society, it is possible to speak of them in the plural. New York and Los Angeles are examples of two urban societies. This viewpoint has now become more widely accepted. For example, David Roozen, William McKinney and Jackson W. Carroll defined "urban" to refer not only to a central city, but also to an entire metropolitan area (1984:4).

2   The author is aware that systems have structures, but structures are not necessarily systems. In this chapter I will use the word "system" in a structural sense.

3   Those interests include the functions of nurturing, educating, financing, informing, protecting, and so on.

4   Los Angeles County population figures show the non-Hispanic white population at around forty-one percent. More than half of this figure are women.

5   Karen Grigsby Bates, "Shades of Black." In *Los Angeles Times Magazine*, May 23, 1993, pp. 22-24, 45-46.

This article by Bates will help to orient the reader in one stream of current thinking in the African American community. Her thesis contends, "As U.S. Blacks embrace a crazy quilt of backgrounds, their deepest roots lie in culture, not color" (1993:22). Some feel such trends further foster Black atomization. Others are adamant that they will not allow themselves to be categorized by anyone. They insist on claiming all their ancestry.

6   In an interview with Cornel West in *Los Angeles Times Magazine* of May 9, 1993, Janet Clayton quotes him as saying:

> . . . The hopelessness is often tied to a sense of rootlessness, no connections, no linkages. That's the cultural side. The economic side is when there's massive unemployment, when there's decrepit education, the very notion of there being some sense of possibility, opportunity, wanes.
>
> The combination of these produces a level of self-destruction we've never seen in this country. It takes a form of a cold-hearted and mean-spirited disposition toward the world, toward one's self. If one's self has no worth, then others have no worth. If one has no property, then other people's property has no worth.
>
> And so we see a kind of gangsterization of both spaces in which persons live but also in terms of how they understand themselves. And it reflects much larger tendencies in our society. We've had a kind of gangsterish mentality that's more and more pervasive. Oliver North could just do whatever he wanted to do, by any means necessary, to pursue his own little private agenda—even though he was in public space . . .

7   The story continues. The trial of Denny's alleged assailants is still going on as I write this essay.

8   With a few exceptions, most writers consider a neighbor to be someone for whom some kind of service or help is given. Gutiérrez and Brown are two exceptions who correctly point out that the Samaritan, and all like him, are the neighbors.

9   James W. Fowler, *Becoming Adult, Becoming Christian* (Nashville: Abingdon Press, 1984), pp. 84-92.

In the chapter entitled, "Christian Faith and the Human Vocation," Fowler addresses the subject of Christian maturity. He discusses Richard Niebuhr's thoughts on God's work in the world and the meaningful partnership of people through the covenant relationship. Niebuhr used three metaphors to describe this partnership: "God the Creator," "God the Governor," and "God the Liberator-Redeemer." The people of God in partnership with him, take initiative in each of these three areas.

Niebuhr spoke about these concepts in a lecture series at Yale. For a full discussion see James W. Fowler, *To See the Kingdom: The Theological Vision of H. Richard Niebuhr* (Nashville: Abingdon Press, 1974).

10 The author is aware that the parish model was also intended to serve a geographically, culturally, and often denominationally homogeneous community. Because of its static nature, the parish model historically has not responded well to change, particularly the rapid change of the urban society.

However, because of its strong orientation to place, the parish concept still has a great deal to offer. The recognition of its historical resistance to change is a significant first step in refashioning it. I will suggest an "inclusive parish" model, which deliberately includes all the people living in the neighborhood, as a first step in this direction.

11 Structural differentiation is a term that attempts to explain that urban society is becoming increasingly heterogeneous. In such heterogeneity, the traditional church structure alone is inadequate. To be a neighbor means to come alongside people so that they feel comfortable.

In *U.S. Lifestyles and Mainline Churches*, Tex Sample identifies three major lifestyle groups in U.S. culture. He names them the cultural left, the cultural middle, and the cultural right. According to Sample, the church can best reach each major group with different theological paradigms and church structures. Within each major group, he delineates at least three subgroups. Again, the ideal approach for each will differ. Even when culture seems to be homogeneous, based on traditional criteria, it may not be.

For example, the megachurch model reaches the middle and upper-middle classes. Yet the church structures doing the reaching are not all the same. Yes, there are traditional structures. However, "seeker-sensitive" churches aimed at Baby Boomers, who are also middle class, have a different structure. William Easum's book, *How to Reach the Baby Boomers*, is helpful in understanding this phenomenon. Multi-congregational structures are being developed to address the needs of churches located in neighborhoods where most of the new people are immigrants and do not yet speak English.

12   Tex Sample, *Blue-Collar Ministry: Facing Economic and Social Realities of Working People* (Valley Forge, Pennsylvania: Judson Press, 1984), pp. 133-149.

Sample uses the phrase "ward heeler" as a metaphor to describe pastoral ministry among blue-collar workers in the urban society. Mayor Richard Daley of Chicago used the term to describe the job of his most important political operative. The job of the ward heeler was to walk the streets of their wards in Chicago and ask questions of the inhabitants to discover where the needs were.

> The ward heeler knew who needed a half ton of coal, who needed a job, who needed help with a hospital bill, or whose taxes were overdue, and so on. The ward heeler knew where the trade-offs were and where a bargain could be struck that would meet the needs of disparate parties and turn them into a coalition. All of these things, of course, meant votes and power (in Sample 1984:134).

Both Sample and the writer are aware of the political and ministry downside to this concept. If a ward did not vote for Daley, for example, it could not count on receiving any help from the ward heeler or from city hall. Sample's objective is to draw from the concept to make application for the pastor's role in working class neighborhoods. The pastor builds horizontal not pyramid relationships by being both a giver and a receiver, on a *quid pro quo* basis. For Sample there would be two non-negotiables: the pastor's integrity and the gospel's message of salvation through Christ. In addition, love is always a given.

Sample examines this concept for its positive implications for pastoral ministry in the urban society. The writer suggests that by using the house church model, each member would walk the streets and build relationships and trust through accessibility. Tradeoffs for temporary action are only some of the many possibilities.

51

Using this process, the ward heeler concept would assist all believers in being neighbors to all the people in the community. Churches could implement this new structure as a community outreach ministry without being too disruptive of existing church structures.

13 In ministering one-on-one, we need to keep in mind that we are affecting entire families. Particularly in working class and poor neighborhoods, whole networks of relationships may be influenced. Latin America Mission's "Christ for the City" program has demonstrated the unusual power and impact of the kind of model I am describing.

14 By "larger problems affecting the greater community" I mean political, economic, or social issues, local or city-wide. The house church(es) would become involved in any issue that has import for those living in their community.

15 William Pannell, *Evangelism from the Bottom Up: What Is the Meaning of Salvation in a World Gone Urban?* (Grand Rapids: Zondervan Publishing House, 1992), p. 57.

Questioning a theology whose sole purpose is to multiply congregations or to defend the inerrancy of Scripture, Pannell states, "The outline is clear: Jesus intends nothing less than a new order, a new kingdom made up of new people, people reconciled to God and to each other."

16 John the Baptist's advice to his converts was that they, as individuals, were to be insurgents (salt, light, and leaven) within the corrupt structures of their society.

3

Shadrach, Meshach, and Abednego: The implications of religious pluralism in the city

Marsha Haney

THE STORY

RELATIVES AND FRIENDS of thirteen-year-old Curtis Walker gathered for his funeral at New St. John's Baptist Church on Wednesday, March 11, 1981. Curtis was the latest victim in a series of twenty slayings of children and youth.

On March 31, someone found the decomposed body of another child, a thirteen-year-old student, in underbrush. On April 19, the body of fifteen-year-old Joseph Bell was found; he was the twenty-fourth in a string of missing or murdered youth found slain in the Atlanta area in a 20-month period.

Marsha Haney is an ordained minister of the Presbyterian Church, U.S.A. (Greater Atlanta Presbytery). She has served as a pastor, chaplain and theological educator in Sudan and Cameroon. Please see the contributing authors section.

The tragedy of missing and murdered children left the city in a state of shock. "A simple child that slightly draws its breath, and feels its life in every limb: what should it know of death?" David Evans, a citizen of Atlanta, quoted these lines from Wordsworth, often repeated by his grandmother, a former slave. In this way he expressed the grief of most Atlantans concerning the tragedies.

Because the victims were innocent children, the sympathetic response was overwhelming, deeply affecting people across the U.S. and throughout the world. And given the racial overtones of this particular tragedy (all the missing and murdered children were African Americans), fear, frustration, and mistrust compounded the shock and grief.

What is the appropriate Christian response to tragedies such as this? They occur often within the urban setting. The police bomb a city block in New Jersey to drive out the MOVE cult. Riots and uprisings occur in Miami, Bedford-Stuyvesant, Chicago, and Los Angeles. Gangs in seemingly endless and senseless drive-by shootings commit repeated violence and killings, often involving the innocent. The repeated disenfranchising and abuse of minorities mock all the easy talk about diversity in the city. The bombing of the World Trade Center in New York City reminds everyone that in the city we live on the edge of chaos. Each situation involves a crisis of tremendous proportions—sociological, emotional, and psychological—that creates traumatic responses among the citizens.

The case of the missing and murdered children occurred in Atlanta, but it could have happened in any city. Many of us know of similar stories elsewhere. Like most large urban areas, the complexity of a multitude of urban problems and opportunities is interwoven in such a way as to fuel tension, distrust, anger, and even violence.

In the Atlanta incident, officials set up a special task force, and more than 300 police officers, volunteers, people from the Georgia Bureau of Investigation, and FBI agents took part in the search. While law enforcement did all it could toward solving the crimes, while the politicians called for peace in the city, the enormity of the problem began to touch the hearts of people across national, racial, ethnic, class, and religious lines. Each time someone reported another child missing or found dead, the frightened and worried citizens felt more helpless. Many offered to help. Thousands of persons sent money or sought personal involvement in an effort to heal the city and protect the children.

The religious community's response

In response, local people of all theological, class, racial and ethnic persuasions began to seek active ways in which to identify and stand in solidarity with those in the inner city who were most affected by the tragedy. Among the most concerned were religious persons from some of the mosques, temples, and churches. Realizing that the religious community needed to respond, and acknowledging that the problems of the city were too complex for any one group to address alone, some Christians sought to set up an ecumenical ministry to partner with others and seek a solution to the tragedy.

The Christian Council of Metropolitan Atlanta was identified as the religious organization best prepared—because of available means, priorities, networks, and linkages—to facilitate relevant Christian involvement in those inner city communities most affected by the crisis. The ecumenical strategy that emerged was one that brought volunteers primarily from concerned churches and specific communities together to form a partnership cluster. Each cluster consisted of four to five congregations of various theological traditions and from various geographic locations (suburban, urban, inner city), along with participants from

55

the communities (mostly low-income or housing projects) who covenanted to partner together to address particular needs identified by a community.

The structure of this ministry included a series of training sessions for volunteers to ensure that they effectively carried out the process of partnership. Knowledge of the urban area and its demographic factors, understanding of spheres of political and economic influences and how they operate, effective use of the city's resources, and sensitivity to the issues of racism and classism were among the urban concerns comprehensively included in the training.

What emerged over time were eighteen unique ministries, each determined by the nature and resources of the clusters, and influenced by their level of involvement with the people in each particular community. The people involved developed activities and programs ranging from weekly tutorial and recreational programs for children, community co-ops, entrepreneurial projects, teenage employment readiness, and advocacy programs.

The results of these cluster activities and programs can still be observed in some communities. Overall, the "Help the Children Project" was successful because it demonstrated that religious people care and can make a difference.

Religious pluralism in the city

A key concern emerged, however, regarding urban missiological implications. This concern often came up in particular relationships that were problematic for many urban Christians within their immediate communities. It raised the question of whether the Christian churches are willing or able to develop relationships with people of other religious faiths in a complex urban world.

The issue of concern is that of religious pluralism and its implications for urban mission. Churches are unsure of how to respond appropriately in the face of religious pluralism—even in a time of crisis—often diluting the opportunity for Christian witness.

What we saw in Atlanta was the inability of U.S. Christians to have positive relationships with persons of other religious faiths. This issue represents a relatively new challenge to the contemporary church in the cities of North America. For many Christians, this was their first exposure to the reality of religious pluralism in the modern city—and often they became "religiously" defensive. Many of the Christian volunteers were uncertain about their involvement in projects with volunteers from a mosque. Was this a Christian thing to do?

On the other hand, too often those Christians who chose active involvement did so with an attitude of superiority. A question that continually emerged had to do with placing limitations or boundaries on the involvement of Christians with persons of other religious faiths.

In response to religious pluralism, one congregation adopted a chauvinistic style of leadership that did not take seriously the feelings of the Muslims involved and created a distance and distrust in that particular cluster. This resulted in the church "using" the community, rather than ministering to it.

In yet another situation, the result was the complete opposite: Non-Christian religious members from the community began "using" the Christians because the Christians were afraid to offend the non-Christians. The partnering did not foster mutual respect and responsibility.

As a result, relationships between the Christians and other religious believers were often superficial. That is, although there were inter-religious partnerships, these relationships usually had little depth because many people tend to network or partner only in times of crisis. This is how caring and concerned religious persons and institutions end up abusing and using each other instead of working toward true partnership. The inability of Christians to engage in effective mission and witness within a religiously plural society is unfortunately not unusual. Urban missiology requires an examination of the churches' response to religious pluralism.

READING THE CONTEXT

Many people acknowledge that the city is multicultural and multiethnic, consisting of peoples of various languages, world views, traditions, and values. Often, however, many others do not see that the urban context also consists of a variety of religious traditions. Sometimes, as a result of crises that occur and conflicts that arise, the diversity becomes more noticeable.

It would appear that my story about Atlanta is not only about developing an appropriate Christian response to crisis in the urban context, but also calls for an examination of the relationship between Christianity and other religious faiths. At the heart of this issue is the meaning of humanity within the context of a pluralistic society. Because of the heterogeneous character of cities, the factors that contribute to conflict are numerous and the humanitarian responses are many. The gathering of large numbers of people permits other religions (and cults) to establish active and supportive subcultures, and to influence the majorities around them.

Christians in urban centers today cannot afford to ignore the presence of people of other religious traditions whose perspectives lie outside the bounds of the experience and historically specific tradition of Christians, especially in North America (Whitehead and Whitehead 1980:20). Too often, Christians in our cities are not even aware of their own church's cultural bias, or of the merits of other denominations, but instead assume a kind of spiritual superiority (Bakke 1987:48).Yet an understanding of other religious faiths that Christians encounter in the city is necessary.

While there is an American belief in the freedom of religious practice, many Americans display attitudes of fear and intolerance toward religious groups that hold views different from their own.

The urban area: Multiple religious movements

In 1985, there were reportedly 1,300 different religious groups in the U.S. (Melton 1985). Until very recently, many experts considered Christianity the only significant religion in which North Americans were engaged. Whether the church is aware of it or not, however, there are many non-Christian religious groups engaged in a multiplicity of missional activities in urban communities appealing to both the religious and social aspects of life.

It is time to ask a new question: How will the church in North America respond in an environment where it is one religion among many? As long as Christianity was seen as the dominant religious force, it could tolerantly ignore the others. But what is the attitude of Christianity in the face of religious pluralism?

The current understanding of religious pluralism allows for religious freedom to prevail. This includes tolerating other faiths within the rubric of Christian dominance. The expression of this pluralism usually means acknowledgment of other religious expressions to a certain degree.

This kind of tolerance by the Christian community comes from a sense of security in being the dominant group in society. It does not necessarily reflect an inner security. Therein lies a crucial issue of religious pluralism: Do the churches have the inner security and the understanding of what the church is called to be that it won't feel threatened by the presence, commitment, and action of other religious groups?

Because Christianity is the dominant religious community in the North American context, the security its size provides hides the church's vulnerability. However, the reality is that because we have never solved interdenominational issues, Christians fight among themselves. How then can the church make that quantum leap with more profound requirements—to relate meaningfully to other religious faiths? If Christians continue fighting with those who are within the household of faith, how much more will they struggle with those who are without?

In the cities of North America, specifically in the African American communities, Christianity is still a dynamic religion. But as a functioning religion, Christianity is no longer dominant—politically, socially, or economically, or because Christians are the majority.

Today the church cannot afford to be fighting within itself. And it will not survive by simply putting on a face of tolerance without a related inner transformation of its own intolerance. Instead, the church must be willing to define itself by a sense of vulnerability, rather than as the majority or the powerful. Questions of pluralism and integrity, issues of majority and minority, the search for cooperative ecumenical strategies, and the rights of all persons in the city call for the church's inner transformation so it can relevantly meet the challenges of today's cities.

The African American community: A case study

Religious pluralism is very real and active in the African American community reflected in my story, and in most large urban areas in the U.S. Currently, there are at least six identifiable generic religious movements among urban African Americans: (1) Judaism and ancient Christian traditions (Ethiopian Orthodox Christians, Ethiopian Hebrews, the Black Israelites, and the Falashas); (2) predominantly Anglo-Protestant and Catholic traditions and faith; (3) indigenous African American Protestant denominations; (4) Islamic communities (Hanafi, Sunni, Ahmmadiya's, and the

60

Nation of Islam); and (5) "New World" religious traditions and syntheses (Yoruba, Santeria and Vondun).

In addition, we can also find African Americans in many of the racially and ethnically pluralistic religions and cults such as Baha'i, Jehovah's Witnesses, the Unification Church, Buddhism, the New Age movements and cults such as the People's Temple and the Davidic cult. The African American community generally accepts this religious pluralism without question as an integral part of its community life. However, the African American church took notice and began to address this relatively new phenomenon because of the motivation, resources, and dedicated commitment by which persons of non-Christian religious faiths carried out their strategic missional activities, and their success in converting Christians, particularly to Islam. According to the Harvard *Encyclopedia of American Ethnic Groups,*

> African Americans are the largest ethnic group in America, second only to Afro-Brazilians in the Western Hemisphere and larger than any single ethnic subgroup in Africa. However, not their number but their minority status has governed the position of African Americans in America (Thernstrom 1980:5).

This definition has formed, and continues to shape, the African American world view and experience. It speaks to both the challenge and potential of the African American experience that, for instance, could produce two great leaders—El Malik Shabazz (Malcolm X), the Muslim, and Martin Luther King, Jr., the Christian. So it is very appropriate that theologian James Cone should bring these ministers together in his book *Martin & Malcolm & America: A Dream or a Nightmare* (1993). "The 'dream' and 'nightmare' images are used to focus their perspectives on America and to reveal something about the audiences to whom and for whom they spoke," he writes (1993:ix).

61

So when African Americans who have converted to other faiths give reasons for their conversion ("Because the Christian church represented a barrier to African American progress," or "As a cultural statement, recognizing our spiritual ties to Africa," or "Christianity is the oppressors' religion,"), we must realize that they speak from a particular sociohistorical reality. Additionally, some people attach themselves to non-Christian religions in their search for an authentic relationship with God through a religious expression that, they may say, "conforms with the truth that I have been seeking," "worships one God," "is a religion for all people, emphasizing discipline and morals," and "focuses on the family and the interconnectedness of all things . . . permeating all of life."

There is a third reason why African Americans are drawn to other religions, especially Islam. Immigrant and naturalized Muslims living within the U.S. have found community and common goals within the African American Muslim community. This has proven to be a mutually beneficial relationship.

Within the North American context, African Americans have desired the freedom to be treated with humanity—that is, to be judged and evaluated on their humanity, instead of constantly struggling for justice and a sense of dignity. Immigrant Muslims are sympathetic to their plight, perhaps because they too have had the experience of being stereotyped and discriminated against. They too have struggled against some of the same issues.

We see the clearest example of this in a speech entitled "Muslims in North America: Problems and Prospects," by Dr. Ilyas Ba-Yunus (1977). Well circulated throughout the immigrant Muslim community, it identifies four problems peculiar to Muslims on this continent. One of the problems identified was the need to support African American Muslims.

Slightly different but more pressing is the problem of those who have willfully accepted Islam lately. A very large portion of new Muslims in this society is of those who have been the objects of discrimination because of their color or race. We Muslims are more fortunate in the sense that we are color blind in our social relationship. It is the duty of the larger Muslim population to give support to their new brethren who are being discriminated against by the Whites because of their being Black and who are now further discriminated against by other Blacks for their being Muslims. Those who became Muslims lately have done so to solve their spiritual and also social problems and not for the sake of adding more to their already heavy baggage of difficulties. I am sure that, Insha Allah, they shall remain steadfast in Islam despite the growing discrimination because of their becoming Muslims. But, what is going to happen to their children? Then, our new brother has not just one but two problems. One is that of their continued low social-educational-economic status because of racial discrimination and the other is the problem of their children which they share with other Muslims in this society (1977:10–11).

Regardless of the motive, where else in North America have African Americans received so much human affirmation but from the Muslim community? The reality is evident in the cities of North America. At least among African Americans, they no longer perceive Christianity as the only viable religious option.

Crisis and religious pluralism

It is a missiological truth that during times of transition, turbulence, or crisis, people seek spiritual solutions. Missions-minded religious people of every religion, sect, and cult are aware of this.

The external crisis

On a national level, times of persecution and discrimination, civil disobedience, natural disasters, and other crises provide a unique opportunity for religious people of all persuasions to respond out of their convictions and bear witness to what they believe.

In *Megatrends* (1984), John Naisbitt confirms that while America is moving from an industrial economy to a new information-electronics economy, there is indeed a revival in religious beliefs. This revival, however, is one of multiple options, with no religious group claiming a significant portion of the growth (1984:269). Religious research shows that the strictest and most demanding religious bodies (Christian and non-Christian) are growing the fastest.

The internal crisis

In our cities people's lives often seem out of control, especially for those who are without the resources needed to have some influence over their lives. Rising crime, the collapse of urban infrastructures, declining educational systems, poverty, and other hardships help to produce feelings of anomie, frustration and depression among city dwellers.

Benjamin Tonna is aware of how the poor see their living conditions:

> In reacting to their condition of margination imposed by the urban system, they become convinced of the impossibility of success, at least as measured by the logic of the metropolis. Rather than fight against the causes of their status, they find themselves constrained to fight against despair. The result of this struggle is the culture of the stratum of the poor, a culture that is perpetuated and reinforced from generation to generation by reason of the early introduction of their children to adult life. Youngsters, following in the footsteps of their parents, cannot gain access to the opportunities offered by the city—schooling, employment, a position in the city

administration—in such a way as to derive profit from the advantages that the urban social intercourse could offer. According to Lewis, the lack of participation on the part of the poor, perpetuated by their weak organization among themselves and their strong fatalism, characterizes their culture by immobilizing it (1985:93).

This is certainly true of some persons of ethnic minority status, especially new immigrants to the city. We also need to consider factors of gender and race. Roger Greenway adequately summed up the hermeneutics of the context and the challenge it poses when he stated,

> One of the greatest challenges to Christian discipleship in the urban context comes from the inescapable encounters city people experience with other religions. . . . Christians are pressed daily to define what they believe and the source of religious authority on which they draw. Besides this, they are constrained to engage actively in the kind of religious apologetic that interacts with other religions, spells out the relationship between the Christian way and the many other ways people choose, and invites them boldly and winsomely to follow Jesus (1992b:40).

REREADING THE SCRIPTURES

We need to examine the missional role of the church within this religiously plural city. How to communicate the unique witness of Jesus Christ within the complexity of urban life is perhaps the greatest challenge facing the contemporary church.

In the face of violence and death, amidst feelings of hopelessness, powerlessness and frustration, and in an environment of racial and ethnic diversity, the church's call is to demonstrate a noticeable difference as it bears witness to the kingdom of God. But what does this mean today, given the multiplicity of religious outreach activities which, like Chris-

65

tianity, are expressions of and motivated by a sense of religious commitment?

It is helpful to remember that the Bible itself is a revelation that emerged over centuries of multicultural and multireligious influences. Not only that, but the Bible also views religious pluralism as a normal feature of urban culture, present wherever there is cultural diversity. The two—differing cultures and religious frameworks—often accompany one another. From the Bible, Christians can learn what it means to live in a religiously plural society. We find a biblical passage closely paralleling today's situation in Daniel.

Belteshazzar, Shadrach, Meshach, and Abednego

The story of Daniel and his three friends (Daniel 1–3) is an inspiring story from which to gain insight into faithful living in a religiously plural society, in situations of testing and turbulence. It is told against the background of the court in Babylon, and against a strong program of conforming the Jews to Babylonian culture and values. To inspire the suffering and discouraged people of God, the author illustrates how God empowered the faithful to be victorious.

We know that Babylon was a pluralistic religious environment because the author of the Book of Daniel used the word *Elohim*, with the article, to make a distinction between the true God of Israel and the false gods. Historians mention the statue of Sin in the temple of Ehulhul as a god the Babylonians worshiped along with Nebuchadnezzar's god, Bel (i.e., Marduk), the city god of Babylon, who was also then head of the pantheon (Isa. 46:1; Jer. 50:2, 51:44).

The author wrote the Book of Daniel to encourage the exiled children of Israel to maintain their loyalty to their faith and to endure under fire. The king gave Daniel and his three friends, displaced captives in exile, high positions in the Babylonian court. All four youths preached the same message of faithfulness to God.

This story is all the more interesting because of the change from their Jewish names to their assigned ones, showing an attempt to obliterate the name of the Jewish God. Their new names appear to be associated with the name of a pagan deity. The story of Belteshazzar, Shadrach, Meshach, and Abednego can teach us certain truths that are as crucial and valuable for life in the urban twenty-first century as they were for the second century B.C.

The passage in Daniel suggests that no matter what the circumstances, God constantly calls his people to reexamine their faith and rethink their commitment to the barest essentials of their relationship with him. Exposure to other religions can challenge and deepen our understanding of our own faith; that appears to have happened to these four Israelite men. Placed in a completely new context, God called them to respond to Babylon's religious context by conceptualizing anew their faith in him.

Similarly, our cities' religious pluralism challenges African Americans and other Christians to reexamine their world view and faith, searching for the most profound essentials of their relationship with God. As Walsh and Middleton have said,

> One day we will come to realize that our worldview is not the worldview of the Scripture; we see that it is not consistent with our confession that Jesus is Lord. Then we need either to deny our confession and look elsewhere, or to begin to overhaul our basic way of looking at life and living it (1984:39).

With this in mind, I can imagine my friends who were once Christian and are now Muslim saying, "One day we came to realize that our world view was not that of the church as we perceived it; we saw that it was not consistent with our understanding of God. So we chose to deny the church as we knew it, and to look elsewhere, and we found another way to look at life and live it."

67

New Mission Insights

Now the key questions the church must ask are these: Are we willing to readjust our world view so that it is consistent with the barest essentials of the biblical confession that Jesus is Lord? Are we willing (are we able) to overhaul our basic way of looking at life and living it?

Belteshazzar, Shadrach, Meshach, and Abednego had a similar decision to make. They realized that Nebuchadnezzar's world view was different from their own, but also that it was inconsistent with Israel's experience of the living God. Instead of choosing to deny their confession and look elsewhere, they made the decision to hold on to Israel's God and his way of looking at life and living it. Yet they did so by framing their faith in a way that was appropriate to their Babylonian context. This radical rethinking suggests several implications.

Humanity

First, Christians are called to respect each person—regardless of gender, culture, ethnicity, or religious persuasion—as someone created by God in the image of God, for fellowship with God. This speaks to the universal spirituality of humankind. The story of Daniel and his friends in Babylon is the story of how they seek the only security they have known—the security and comfort that God gives—and how they find it in one another, in the people of the same community. The primary issues in the story focus on the things that are common to humanity, the basics of life: A place to live, food to eat, access to knowledge and truth.

Daniel, the leader, is renamed Belteshazzar. One of the first things we learn about him is that, in spite of his captivity, his primary concern is for right living and doing the right thing, not as defined by those in power, but as he understands rightness and truth. All people of faith, regardless of the crisis they face or the circumstances facing them, need to cling to what gives meaning and purpose to life. Exposure to other religions can challenge and deepen our understanding of our own religious faith in ways that will help us see our common humanity.

Faith

Second, urban life itself is a challenge to faithfulness. The mood and tone of the Book of Daniel are an attempt to stop God's people from falling away. This is important because in times of testing and temptation, people tend to doubt God's presence and even God's ability to care.

Trust

What could have possibly made Shadrach, Meshach, and Abednego respond to the king by saying: "O Nebuchadnezzar, we do not need to defend ourselves before you in this matter. If we are thrown into the blazing furnace, the God we serve is able to save us from it, and he will rescue us from your hand, O king. But even if he does not, we want you to know, O king, that we will not serve your gods or worship the image of gold you have set up" (Dan. 3:16–18)? It was their trust in God, a God of compassion who had a history of caring for Israel in times of trouble.

This is a reminder to us, a call to live a day at a time and to trust the future to God. Fear of the future, fear of enemies (those who do not seek our welfare), and fear of the institutional powers that threaten to crush people are very real. But God is real, too, and more powerful.

Risk

Fourth, Daniel 1-3 is a reminder that religious faith is something that demands risk. Daniel and his companions took a big risk when they insisted that they be allowed to follow the commands of their faith. Like them, Jesus demonstrated courage throughout his ministry. He risked rejection

69

and even death on the way to resurrection victory. There could not have been a crown without a cross. So many urban people understand this and have taken huge risks, but few have recognized its profound importance in the journey of faith.

Making a difference

Our faith in the living God makes a difference. In the Daniel story Nebuchadnezzar himself came to say, "Praise be to the God of Shadrach, Meshach, and Abednego . . !" (Dan. 3:28). The faith of Shadrach, Meshach, and Abednego made a difference not only in their lives, but also in the king's!

The supreme test of a person's faith is that it makes a difference. Our faith makes a difference to us as individuals because it provides a solid transtemporal and transcultural foundation on which to reflect on the past, accept the present, and hope for the future. The fruit of our faith, however, should benefit others.

MISSION ACTION

What then is the mission of the church in the city? The goal of a church in an urban setting is a willingness to be overhauled—that is, transformed—even as that church ministers in the city. The ability to help the poor, to partner with others who show concern for God's people, and to serve God faithfully in the midst of pluralism is the fruit of a church that is willing to sacrifice itself to be present with those who hurt.

This may mean standing in the furnace of suffering. Today this may also involve a willingness to coexist with others, although we are no longer the dominant culture or the dominant religious faith. In other words, are today's urban Christians willing to minister in a religiously plural environment?

Which one of us who lives in the city has not at one time or another felt like the four exiled captives of Daniel 3? And yet God told them and all of exiled Israel to ". . . seek the peace and prosperity of the city to which I have carried you into exile. . . ." (Jer. 29:7). In spite of being strangers, aliens, refugees, and exiles in Babylon, they are still God's people—and called to seek the *shalom* of the context in which God has placed them.

We don't usually take the context of this verse seriously, for if we did we would not read it from a dominant position of influence and power. Instead, we would read it from the opposite perspective. Do we enable and encourage the exile to seek the welfare of our cities, or do we act as if we are owners of the city? Do we see the poor, the hungry, those who are different, as persons who may offer us friendship? Or do we, who don't bow down to the God we profess, expect these others to do so? Is the Christian church not in the position of the Babylonian rulers?

Not until the church understands itself and its calling to be God's people in a foreign land will it have the mercy necessary to stop persecuting those who have different beliefs.

Hope-affirming

It is not until the church transforms its understanding of itself and rediscovers what it means to be a sojourner and alien (the 1 Peter 2 perspective) will it be able to do urban ministry in the midst of religious pluralism. This puts the onus on the church to be faithful to its Lord, and the mission the Lord gave—to be willing to walk through the fire.

Part of the reason we are still playing the powerful and the dominant is that we are not willing to be a powerless community of hope. Our hope resides too often in our own dominance, and too seldom in our Lord Jesus. We refuse to be the remnant; we will not get in that furnace.

Does this mean that we do not have any message until we reach the necessary maturity? No, because if we transform our understanding of ourselves and our message, the message will move us to a maturity in hope that will allow us to transcend ourselves and become like Shadrach, Meshach, and Abednego, the sojourners. Then our message becomes one of sharing hope, from one sojourner to another sojourner. And this hope is never satisfied with the status quo. Rather, it is impatient for the transformation of this world, always seeking ways whereby God's will may be done "on earth as it is in heaven."

Love-sharing

True love-sharing is related to the need for the church to be in the urban community representing the liberating, compassionate, healing, and prophetic power of the God who meets human needs. Too often, Christian congregations in an urban community do not identify with or relate to the needs of the people within that community. Too often, our church polity, denominational agendas, and the unresolved issues of classism, gender concerns, and minorities (religious, linguistic, cultural, or ethnic) prevent the church from being as sensitive as it could be in addressing the pains and hurts of those near its front doors.

As a result, people tend to view Christianity as irrelevant or lacking integrity. They need to see the love of God incarnated, made real, not in the abstract. There must be radical renewal for the love of God to be made real.

An incarnational ministry must take the people and their culture seriously, analyzing the conditions that create oppression, injustice, and poverty. Humans cause these conditions, not God. Historically, the African American understanding of the Christian faith is that of standing in solidarity with people, sharing in their sufferings, and providing hope and prophetic vision.

Goalsetting and action-unifying

If it works for us, urban ministry itself moves us toward the goal of a willing, vulnerable church that proclaims in word and deed the good news of a God who creates and cares. This describes the direction in which urban ministry itself can form us.

Through hopeful, loving, and open envisioning of new goals and actions, the church in the city may discover partnering instead of manipulating and using. The church could learn what it means to be motivated by acceptance and by an open heart, instead of power and prestige. Open witnessing could be the result, rather than self-protection, deceit, and competition. This kind of ministry in the midst of urban crisis and religious pluralism would be part of how the church can become God's people in mission in the city.

RETELLING THE STORY

If the Christian churches that responded to the missing and murdered children of Atlanta had moved in the directions suggested here, how might it have been different in Atlanta in 1981?

The churches might have stimulated and helped each other to reconceptualize the gospel and their missional calling in the midst of cultural diversity and religious plurality. One of the greatest mission challenges confronting urban churches today is the reconstruction and enabling of new vision by providing an incarnational ministry, and forming leadership and discipleship in the communities where these churches are called to serve God. The desire to be renewed in spirit to love the people in our midst, to be willing to give ourselves to those who are perishing, and to sustain those who seek "Good News" in a world gone awry must be the motivation for the worship, witness, work and service of these churches.

73

When it comes to their relationships with God and with others, it is crucial that Christians find new ways to define themselves out of an understanding of what it means to be the people of God. The church must reexamine the quality of its relationships with people who are both inside (sisters and brothers in Christ) and outside (other human beings) the church.

Effective ministry amidst religious diversity

Like Shadrach, Meshach, and Abednego, Christians today must take seriously their calling to be change agents in both the private and public spheres of life, for to do so is to take God seriously. The churches must be willing to wrestle with the difficult questions posed by religious pluralism. "Is everything that is 'religious' thereby either admirable or desireable?" asked Bishop Kenneth Cragg (1993:2); it is a key question.

Particularly given the religious pluralism within the African American community, effective ministry today involves rediscovering a biblical theology of suffering (the Suffering Servant and example of Christ) and a hope that speaks to a pilgrim people called to transform the reality in which they may no longer dominate. Shadrach, Meshach, and Abednego were taken to a foreign land and had to learn a foreign way of life.

Primary, however, was their call by God—in spite of their circumstances—to act justly, and to love mercy, and to walk humbly with him (Mic. 6:8). This provides the basis for a call to a vision that urban churches today need to regain, particularly in training Christian leaders for service and witness in the midst of pluralism. Every Christian needs a theological framework for religious diversity and pluralism. This would include, as Richard J. Mouw points out, the need for interreligious dialogue and its implications for ministry in today's cities (1991:37).

Along with their social and political efforts, the churches of Atlanta needed to respond spiritually to the crisis of 1981. As Luke 4 makes clear, incarnational mission involves socio-political and economic change along with the transformation of our faith.

This type of ministry undoubtedly requires hard work based on a dedication of time, commitment, and prayer. The result, however, would be that more of the African American population would perceive the Good News as relevant and necessary, even in the midst of other religious voices. Also, church members and leaders would learn to hold the structures of the church accountable to the Good News of the gospel—theologically, culturally, and socially.

Christianity is not the opiate of the people, or a foreign faith ("White man's religion"), nor is it a tool of manipulation by the powerful of society. It also does not advocate "pie in the sky, joy when I die." Rather, in Jesus Christ the Christian message is about the Way, the Truth, and the Life leading to a God who desires only the best for African American and other Christians, to a God who really does care.

This challenges the church to see itself as God does, to see itself at the foot of the cross planted in the city. For it is there at the foot of the cross that we discover our common humanity, regardless of race or ethnicity, culture, world view, language, gender, or age differences. And it is in the risen Christ that African American churches can draw strength to claim God's promises for today, and hope for the future. Could such new vision, new faith, and new hope give us new words to speak and new actions to carry out among the children and their families and friends in our cities tomorrow?

PART TWO

Reflecting on the City

4

When we are dying in the city: Three sources of life

Mary Thiessen

THE STORY

I MOVED into the inner city of Los Angeles because I recognized that my experiences and skills could provide hope, a sense of belonging, and salvation for the children and teenagers I observed on the streets.

I was part of a team with World Impact, an inner city mission organization that had stated goals of round-the-clock availability. Our team consisted of young adults, most of us recent college graduates.

I envisioned meeting many needs through music, sports, games, crafts, teaching the Bible, and providing a family setting. And it was very likely that some people would become Christians through my ministry.

Mary Thiessen lived in the inner city of Los Angeles as a missionary with World Impact, where she served for eighteen years before beginning her doctoral studies at Fuller Theological Seminary. Please see the contributing authors section.

My assumptions were correct. By the end of less than a year my colleagues and I had begun Bible clubs for children and teenagers in five different neighborhoods around Los Angeles. I also directed a staff home where we hosted groups of children each weekend, and where by the first summer we had young women from the city living with us as assistants—for purposes of discipleship and leadership training.

Yet during my first year in Los Angeles, a series of unplanned events began to unfold. Neighborhood teenagers repeatedly broke our windows. All of our electrical items were stolen one Saturday morning while we were at Bible club—every iron, toaster, tape player, radio . . . gone. The home of the family who witnessed the robbery was set on fire. The pimp of this supportive family's teenage daughter burned her internally, and then shot and killed her three months later. The women in our household were threatened with dismemberment. A gang rape was planned against me. Gang warfare on our cross street killed four young men whose mother was a Christian. I cared for a nine-month-old baby for several days because his mother was arrested the night I was baby-sitting him. We counseled a girl whose father had sex with both her and their dog.

We responded to these events by listening, crying, praying, and always trying to do more to help. We believed that if the children accepted Christ while they were still young they could avoid experiencing many of the pains that surrounded them.

In subsequent years we responded to the educational needs by starting a school, to the deplorable housing by setting up an apartment for needy families, to the joblessness by establishing a business, to the physical needs by opening a thrift store, to the idleness by building a gymnasium, and to the anguish by being present in Christ's name. We continued the Bible clubs, and we added adult Bible studies. And a church was born.

Throughout the early years we enjoyed a great depth of community. We were a family. But as the crises multiplied, as we became aware of the depth of people's needs, as the complexities of a transient, multiracial neighborhood presented ever-changing challenges, as we felt compelled to maintain the programs we had begun, as our young people and adults grew in their faith, and as the needs of our staff changed, something vital to our health seemed to be slipping away.

We sought desperately to remain vibrant and to maintain a semblance of order. But the staff began to burn out, relationships grew tense, and differences remained unresolved. People from the city felt like recipients, the slow change disillusioned staff members, and conflict erupted. Many of my missionary colleagues left and the people in the city felt abandoned.

We had always taught that God was our highest priority and that health in the body of Christ took precedence over ministry. We believed that relationships were infinitely more important than projects, that *being* God's people was more important than *doing* God's work. But the projects and programs, the needs and crises, the goals and accomplishments, and the many financial demands—all these began to run our lives. We had meant the organization to be life-giving, but its people were dying.

How did this happen? Had we neglected something that resulted in this unhealthy condition, or had we lost something we once had? Had the city robbed us of vitality, or were we experiencing suffocation from some other source?

READING THE CONTEXT

I have had the opportunity to revisit my journey of the last eighteen years in search of the sources of suffocation. This revisitation also led me to seek out the sources of life, of refreshment, of vitality. I have recalled many remarkable characteristics of my friends in the city: the power of the human drive to survive, the exuberant celebrations of life, the strength of extended family support, and the lively expressions of inner creativity. I recall the many who became Christians, the deep healings Christ accomplished, the families God restored, and the new beginnings the Spirit created. I was awed again at God's visitations in the ordinary and the miraculous events I experienced.

I remember the deep joys of our committed Christian community: the intimate fellowship, the ecstatic worship, the unselfish servanthood, the creative celebrations, and the hilarious parties.

But I also recall the incredible power of oppressive forces to choke out the passion for life, the inordinate amount of suffering and sadness, the multiple layers of problems a single household often faced in a given day, and the draining pace of life in the city.

My experiences reflect only a portion of what my neighbors experienced—and unlike me they had not chosen to live in that neighborhood. They could not choose to leave and go home.

As I look back I recall the many nights I was awakened by screams coming from the home behind mine where prostitution and drug dealing provided the money the inhabitants needed for survival. How often I desired silence! I can still see the trash through which I had to navigate daily in the underpass on my way to the office and school. I will never forget the smell of urine and excrement in the alley between our schools. It made me long for freshness and brightness.

From time to time I replay the mental tapes of the murders. I repeat in my mind the testimonies of molestation or physical abuse. I feel again the loneliness of the neglected. At these times I remember how I wished my friends in the city could experience belonging and security. When I recall the sadness of young women who witnessed their mothers being beaten or who longed to know who their fathers were, I understand why I began to hate impurity and lack of commitment. I realize why we determined to protect our church from immorality and unfaithfulness.

When I remember the many times my house was robbed, my car vandalized, my friends accosted, and our lives threatened, I admit that at times I believed life's greatest gift must be safety.

And finally, when I think back on the poor education, the joblessness, and the poverty, it does not surprise me that I wished for greater productivity, for more success, for better time management—for everyone.

Oppressive forces choke out life

In this environment of physical, spiritual, mental, and emotional onslaughts, it is almost inevitable to respond to disorder by creating order, to crises by taking action, to neediness by providing resources, to problems by seeking solutions, and to chaos by imposing control. The conscious and subconscious tendency is to establish rules to ensure safety, to define doctrine to preserve purity, to set up programs to enhance productivity, to insist on schedules and reports to guarantee success, to build buildings to offer visible proof of change, to outline procedures to prevent failure, and to devise policies to prevent uncertainty and insecurity.

The bombardment against the senses invites the building of walls of self-protection, shutting down the deep emotions, living almost solely by will, obedience, and intellect. It is no wonder that individuals and organizations in the city move ever so subtly toward survival, rather than transformation; toward the exclusion of those who threaten and endanger them, rather than to the gospel of inclusion and belonging; toward clearly defined programs and projects

83

that they can control and measure, rather than to building intimate relationships that seem so illusive.

When missionaries and ministries suffer the same suffocation as those around them, is there any possibility of regeneration?

Order versus disorder

In a recent mission class Chuck Van Engen challenged me to pursue the life-giving possibilities that could overcome the suffocating forces I had experienced. Intertwined in the delightful discussions of God's passion for life as demonstrated in Luke and Acts he shared two painfully convicting observations.

"Too many churches and mission organizations," he said, "respond to organizational decline by restructuring rather than by seeking revival. The frequent pattern in organizations is from the vision of a *man* or *woman*, to the beginning of a *movement*, to the formation of a *machine*, and finally to the establishment of a *monument*."

This direction from an original God-inspired vision or dream to eventual death is not deterministic or inevitable—it is a sociological tendency. How can we replace the slow death of mere preservation with an experience of ongoing dynamic revitalization?

How does a God of order create structures that allow for ongoing growth and development? How can God break in with creativity and the miraculous? How can we embrace both the organization and the organism, the structures and vibrant fellowship, the institutionalization and dynamic growth of the church in the city? How can we respond to destructive disorder without creating confining order?

I do not mean to say that order is intrinsically wrong, or that disorder would characterize a dynamic mission. A look at the Scriptures quickly reminds us that God is a God of order and design. He makes plans and carries them out. He ordained the rhythms of nature, of work and rest, of life and death. Families, nations, and the church are instruments of security and order: their structures provide a framework that give protection, provision, and purpose.

Scripture also teaches that self-control is a fruit of the Spirit (Gal. 5:23) and that a person of knowledge and understanding maintains order (Prov. 28:2). Paul firmly corrected disorder in the church due to the careless use of the Spirit's gifts (1 Cor. 14:33, 40). But order alone is not life-giving. Order is vital, but it does not produce vitality.

Gradually, the Spirit has led me to seek those things that infuse life, not merely prevent death. I turned to the Scriptures and to God in search of life, of resurrection in the midst of death. How can missionaries and mission structures become vehicles for the life of the Spirit in the city?

The presence of God through the Spirit gave me personal rejuvenation and life-giving breath for the city and its mission organizations. I have been drawn back to my original call and vision. And in this search I discovered that Luke offers us three sources of life for ministry in the city: the presence of the Holy Spirit, the exercise of concerted reflection, and God's unexpected interventions.

REREADING THE SCRIPTURES

As Luke tells it, Jerusalem and Antioch (two significant urban centers of that time) experienced visitations of the Holy Spirit that provided the foundation for all subsequent church history. These visitations also forever transformed Jews and Gentiles alike. The Pentecost occurred in a city and the first Gentile church began in a thriving metropolis.

The Spirit was the initiator of mission. The Spirit preceded those who carried the gospel to new centers, creating a hunger for truth within Gentiles who were losing their lives through immorality and ritual prostitution in the mystery cults. The Spirit prepared legalistic Jews to accept a

85

gospel of freedom offered by the resurrected Jesus. Spirit-filled believers, like the Cypriots at Antioch, recognized the racial inclusiveness of the Spirit. And men like Barnabas were humble enough to observe and submit to what the Spirit was already doing in these complex urban centers.

Could the stories of Jerusalem and Antioch inform our mission activity in Los Angeles, and provide hope for urban mission in the cities of today's world?

The Holy Spirit and urban mission

How does the Holy Spirit breathe life into suffocating cities? How does this breath become a powerful wind in our midst? Luke teaches us that the Holy Spirit mediates the presence of Jesus, empowers us for ministry, and creates community.

The Spirit mediates the presence of Jesus in the city

The arrival of the Spirit in Jerusalem was the fulfillment of the repeated promises of Jesus: ". . . I will be with you always . . ." (Matt. 28:20), and "I will not leave you as orphans; I will come to you" (John 14:18). The disciples were not alone in the city—the resurrected, death-defying, victorious Jesus was always with them.

The Spirit in us today is proof that the resurrected Jesus is alive, that he is with us, that he desires to produce life. This living Jesus wants to transform, regenerate, heal, save, illuminate, and comfort, just as he did when he walked among us in the flesh. Where there is death, darkness, and dehumanization, Jesus says, "It is not the healthy who need a doctor, but the sick. . . ." (Mark 2:17). Jesus is present in the city, by his Spirit.

When I was a missionary in Los Angeles, the Spirit mediated the presence of God to me on many occasions. Often the Spirit ministered to me through the Word, through my brothers and sisters in Christ, and even through a vision. But I was not always aware of the Spirit filling, enfolding, surrounding, and comforting me and those suffering around me. Maybe I failed to experience this constant nearness of the Spirit because I closed down my deepest inner self. My own pain and my inability to accept the intensity of the pain around me caused me to encapsulate my emotions to quiet my inner fears. I no longer relished the mystery, the ambiguity, and the complexity of God's creative presence.

Awareness of the deep inner work of the Spirit is difficult when running from job to project, from program to crisis, from family to neighborhood. When we no longer enjoy God's intimate presence in our souls, we merely tend to respond to others' wounds with cold action. My self-protection and fear locked out the presence, grace and love of Jesus. How we need the Holy Spirit's life-giving breath to blow through the dryness of our souls!

The Spirit empowers us for ministry

Peter's boldness and courage immediately demonstrated the fulfillment of Christ's promise, ". . . You will receive power when the Holy Spirit comes on you . . ." (Acts 1:8). The same Peter who denied Christ, who slept instead of prayed, and who fled in fear now preached boldly to thousands in the hostile city of Jerusalem. He gladly endured imprisonment for the sake of Jesus Christ. Even the unbelievers testified that what they saw in Peter was no ordinary power (Acts 4:13).

The temptation in urban mission is to fall back on human energy when responding to human need. Why is this so? The pace of the city and the preponderance of needs work against receptivity from the missionary. Moving ahead of the Spirit's timing and responding with human solutions where only the power of the Spirit can perform healing quenches receptivity to the Spirit. Innumerable human efforts cannot accomplish what the Spirit's power is able to do, because the Spirit uses supernatural means to minister to people.

The book of Acts is replete with records of signs, wonders, and miraculous healings (2:43; 3:1-10; 4:23; 5:12; 6:8; 8:4-8; 16:26; 20:10; 28:8) all done in the city by the Spirit in the name of Jesus. Visions, dreams, and angelic visitations often give direction or insight to the believers or to those seeking salvation (10:3-6; 16:7; 18:9; 22:17-21; 26:19).

I will never forget our neighbor, a young mother struggling with alcoholism and nearly crippled with arthritis. God spoke to her through two visions. She received the second vision on what the doctors believed was her death bed after she overdosed on pills. When the Spirit miraculously healed her she recognized the fulfillment of these visions and responded by joyfully leading many others to the Healer. No human power can save life and restore the wounded and broken among us. That is the work of the Holy Spirit.

The Spirit creates community

We cannot help being touched by the relational force of the Spirit-filled community that came together after Peter's sermon on the day of Pentecost. The new converts loved God and each other. They were no longer in bondage to their possessions. They gave up independence and self-existence. They shared their homes and food not only with their friends and families but also with the needy. They reveled in prayer and worship (Acts 2:42-46). They enjoyed favor with the people and ". . . the Lord added to their number daily those who were being saved" (Acts 2:47).

This new community began with a demonstration of inclusiveness that is profoundly foundational for urban ministry. When the Spirit came, people from fifteen different geographic locations ". . . heard them speaking in [their] own language" (Acts 2:6). Aramaic-speaking Jews in Jerusalem (Acts 4:23-31), converts in Samaria (Acts 8:14-17), a Gentile centurion of the Italian regiment in Caesarea (Acts 10:24-46), and Hellenists in Ephesus (Acts 19:1-7) experienced subsequent visitations by the Spirit.

Although the disciples may not have grasped the significance of the multiplicity of languages that people understood on the first Pentecost, the Spirit makes this profoundly clear through Peter's encounter with Cornelius. In Acts 11:18 the Jerusalem Christians confessed, ". . . God has even granted the Gentiles repentance unto life." The Spirit underscored with indelible ink that there were to be no distinctions based on race, status, background, age, or gender. The Spirit fell on all.

When recalling the incredible diversity of languages, ethnic groups, cultures, economic status, and customs I experienced in Los Angeles, I also recall the confusion, differences, conflicts, unmet expectations, and challenges that this diversity brought. It is imperative that a missionary to urban centers deeply understands the message of Pentecost concerning the equality, unity, value, and dignity the Spirit demonstrated toward all people in giving birth to the church. Only the Spirit equips, humbles, reminds, and graces us to live together as one body in the midst of our complex diversity.

We need forgiveness and reconciliation in the midst of this diversity. Openness and communication are mandatory. We must discuss and embrace differences. We should study and creatively celebrate histories. Time allotted for understanding each other *is* Spirit-filled mission because it is through these times that the Spirit validates and empowers each person. Even Paul had to return from productive missionary travels to attend a conference that would ensure that the church did not lose the Spirit's unmistakable emphasis on racial equality (Acts 15).

Reflecting and remembering the vision

A second way that provides ongoing health for urban ministries and city dwellers comes through deliberate reflection on and intentional recollection of God's mission and vision. To reflect means to ponder, to consider, to meditate, to contemplate, to turn one's thoughts back on past experiences, to carefully bring to mind.

The Scriptures invite us to *"remember* your Creator" (Eccles. 12:1), *"consider* your heavens" (Ps. 8:3), *"meditate* on [the Book of the Law] day and night" (Josh. 1:8), "do this . . . in *remembrance* of me" (1 Cor. 11:25), and *"ponder* what he has done" (Ps. 64:9). Scripture tells us that "everything that was written in the the past was written to teach us" (Rom. 15:4), and "these things occurred as examples" (1 Cor. 10:6). I have counted over 308 Bible texts that call us to remember, to recall, not to forget.

Apparently the exercise of reflection profoundly affects us as the words of God penetrate our souls to purify, heal, comfort, and direct. The lessons from the past lead to self-understanding and enriched relationships with others. The memory of God's works produces hope and confidence in his continued involvement in our world. Reflection seems to have a unique importance for urban missionaries and for the oppressed.

Reflection prepares us to receive

Times of reflection create the necessary space in our minds and emotions to receive God's presence, wisdom, hope, and assurance. Through reflection we rest in his forgiveness, healing, and grace for ourselves and then for others.

Urban missionaries know the sense of urgency and the frenetic pace of the city. They need a sense of dependence and patience to live in the Spirit. Perhaps the greatest lesson of Pentecost lies in the obedience of the 120 as they waited and prayed until the Spirit came.

According to the Gospel of Luke, many of them had watched Jesus, or had known that Jesus waited and prayed before his own baptism (3:21-22), before and after times of ministry (4:42; 5:16), before choosing the disciples (6:12), and before teaching (9:18, 28-29; 11:1). He prayed for his disciples as his death approached (22:32), and the night before the crucifixion (22:41-44). Because the disciples remembered Jesus' life, they obeyed his command to wait and pray. They recognized their dependence on God. They were not self-sufficient. They unashamedly proclaimed that they did all healing and miracles by and through Jesus, and they made decisions after hearing from God. This spirit of trust stemmed from their times of listening to God's Spirit speaking within them.

I recognize anew how crucial it is in urban ministry to wait on God so we can spend time *receiving* what he has for us instead of asking him to bless what we plan to give. We must wait on God so we can *accept* the gift of patience as we catch a glimpse of his timetable, *understand* his plans for righteousness and justice, be *filled* with his power for ourselves and for the powerless around us, and *breathe* in rest for our restlessness.

My spirit resounds with my Mennonite colleague who recently wrote an article entitled, "The Spiritual Poverty of the Anabaptist Vision," where he says:

> Until we can think and talk as passionately about receiving and being as we do about strategizing and doing, until we get as passionate about praise and prayer as we do about social-political analysis, we will remain spiritually impoverished (Dintaman 1993:6-7).

We enhance *receiving* and *being* through prayer, meditation, keeping a journal, walking in creation, singing, studying, listening to each other, observing—in other words, by reflecting. Several godly persons have challenged me to practice "centered praying," the simple discipline of waiting for the Spirit to initiate the agenda for our time together. This practice and various methods of keeping a journal[1] have proved both restorative and empowering for me.

Reflection prepares us to listen

As we learn to listen to the Spirit, we also learn to listen to others.

Times of reflection provide the opportunity for us to hear what the Holy Spirit is saying to us about each other, to listen to our inner selves, and to listen to the deeper meaning behind the cries of our neighbors.

Just as Barnabas took time to observe what the Holy Spirit was doing in Antioch, we must also adopt an observant stance if we hope to recognize the signs of life, the working of the Holy Spirit around us. Stepping back to reflect allows us to take note of the Spirit's gifts to our companions, gifts the Spirit desires to use as a source of energy and refreshment for the whole body in ministry in the city. The Spirit's gifts are messengers to us, telling us what God is choosing to do among and through us.

When we take time to reflect together we learn to hear each other. We grasp God's call and vision in our sisters and brothers, thereby feeling in them God's longing heart for the city. We simply cannot capture many of these deeper truths and inner longings through asking others to fill out forms, submit their suggestions in memos, or give us a call if they get a good idea. We pick up on those things that excite others as we spend time in reflection together.

Just as the Holy Spirit often communicates through a still small voice, so we must also listen to those on the periphery who hear a different cry than the majority. The powerless and marginalized are invaluable in God's design. It is often these voices that warn us when too much order and control drain us of vigor.

Recently, a student colleague from India who was also part of our urban theology seminar said, "Poverty is to have no reflective skills." At the time I sensed an immediate connection between this truth and my growing conviction that "Poverty is to have no words for your pain."

In times of reflection we not only find words to describe our experiences and emotions, we also learn the meaning of those words and in them we find the meaning of our pain. I was unable to resolve the grief in my life until I found the words to describe the unfulfilled dreams I had for those who were killed, the sense of loss I felt over what was no longer mine, and the anger I saw within myself when I heard of abuse and violations.

This self-understanding led me to care more honestly for others. I wonder how much of the violence and abuse in the city stems from the absence of words for the inner rage produced by experiences of prejudice, oppression, and rejection.

Too often others have attempted to describe and interpret the experiences and inner thoughts of those in the city. Instead of listening to and inviting persons from the city to tell their stories, to share their insights and observations, to express their hopes and desires, researchers, visitors, and even missionaries have been guilty of describing the city and its people from the perspective and with the words of the outsider. It is disempowering to hear one's pain described by another, particularly if the true meaning is lost in the process.

David Augsburger's comments concerning Paulo Freire's definitions give us further insight to this issue. He writes,

> "Dialogue is an encounter between people" (Freire). . . .
> An encounter between persons who name and own a private world and seek to impose it upon others is inimical to dialogue . . . genuine encounter is difficult when there is a power differential between the persons or parties. When all power and authority flows one way, it is impossible (Freire 1970:76). . . . Dialogue and hierarchy are contradictory (1986:39).

It is as I listen and then reflect on what others have expressed that I begin to understand. I contribute to the

93

ongoing tragedy without this understanding. Apart from reflection I merely compound the problems of the city.

Robert Linthicum warns that while we are searching among the city's problems for those that we are to address, it is very likely that "what will tug at our heart strings will be those needs in the world that are projections of hidden problems or issues within ourselves that we have never resolved" (1991a:238). He asserts that "discovering our inner selves is strategic because only as we come to know our inner selves truly can we discover what . . . it is we project upon others" (1991a:238).

Several things need to occur within urban ministries if we are to tap into the power of reflective skills.

First, we must prize the development of these skills enough to set aside the necessary time needed for personal and group reflection. Those missionaries who practice reflection will empower others to reflect.

Second, all educational opportunities should include the building of these skills. Our Bible studies, schools, support groups, counseling services, and even church retreats provide natural opportunities for developing skills in reflection. Those who do not become involved in discovering, selecting, and expressing their inner stirrings will permanently view themselves as recipients and beneficiaries. They will not be empowered and will not recognize how much they can contribute to the healing of their families and neighborhoods.

Reflection helps us recall the vision

A third task of reflection is the intentional recalling of God's mission and call. Throughout the Old Testament, God called his people to remember why he had chosen them, what their mission was to him and to those around them. The stones of remembrance, the repeated discourses in Deuteronomy, the extended feasts and memorial celebrations, the lengthy repetitions of history in the Psalms, all

94

express the significance of remembering their purpose for existence—to love God with all their hearts and their neighbors as themselves.

A primary purpose for remembering was so that their experience in slavery and redemption would evoke compassion and generosity toward the alien, the fatherless, and the widow (Deut. 24:18, 21). They could fulfill their mission only by remembering their origins.

They were not to focus merely on self-preservation, to become territorial, or to ensure only their own safety and prosperity. They were to be channels of God's blessings to the nations. God issues these mandates to urban missionaries as well.

Recalling our vision and mission will give discernment for decision-making concerning such issues as the addition of new programs. Taking care to include biblical values in the foundational vision and purpose statements of our organization will provide invaluable checkpoints for us. For example, we must abandon or recreate any activity that devalues or demeans its participants. Harry Boer presents this convicting challenge:

> In Christ ends are not more important than means, ends are not more basic than means, ends do not in Him occupy a higher level of reality or enjoy a larger measure of divine sanction than the means that ought to be employed to reach them. . . . The means determine the end because the means are the end in process of becoming. The missionary means we employ are an expression of the now present kingdom of God. Clearly, the manifestation of the present kingdom ought not to stand in contradiction to the kingdom that will one day be revealed in its perfection (1961:207).

The incessant pull to respond to immediate and urgent needs and dangers tempts urban missionaries not to take time for frequent evaluation. The temptation to respond too quickly and to bypass listening for God's call can lead to programs and projects that lack passion and power. Many hasty decisions fail to produce long-term healing and health.

Occasionally, new responses may be God's will for us, but they will fail to truly empower if we do not take the time to ask basic questions: How can we accomplish this goal with our neighbors? How can this project bring life to all its participants? Ray Bakke issues two warnings about this. He points out that "too often a new pastor rushes in with programs, and recruits students from nearby Bible colleges, first to supplement, and then to replace local people who cannot measure up to the requirements and expectations of the program" (1987:93). He also says that

> Pastors are often too impatient to wait for gifts to emerge as God gives them. They rely instead on recruiting the particular gifts that they think God needs for their church. In fact, the congregation can almost always provide whatever is needed for ministry in their own particular situation—the real difficulty is convincing them of their own power to act and make decisions for themselves (1987:94).

Taking time to consider God's call may clarify that he wants to use others to meet those needs for which we are not equipped. We must network with others in the city for God's blessings to penetrate the city and the existing mission structures.

This call to return to the original vision does not mean that we need never exercise faith and move beyond what seems manageable or was our initial plan. However, when we make the decision to take on new challenges, the new opportunities must become the vision and product of the heart of the community. We drain life from our staff when we simply impose on or demand additional responsibilities of them. The community must decide to move forward in faith because all will carry the weight of the decision.

Some urban ministries establish a schedule in which staff members work for three months and then take three weeks away for reflection and evaluation. Others deliberately build in a blend of ministry and reflection on a biweekly or monthly basis. For example, they require staff members to take three days every two weeks or six days every month for reflection at some place outside the city.

Reflection and remembering are life-affirming. They teach us to celebrate life. Too often we hear urban ministers say, "Well, at least we're keeping them off the streets." When preventing death preempts celebrating life, we die a slow death.

God's unexpected interventions

Another way that God often brings life to urban churches, communities, and individuals is through the redemptive use of crises. God sometimes visits us in unexpected ways and at unexpected times to ensure that his work is accomplished.

God intervenes so he can redeem

Throughout Scripture we read of how God redemptively used seeming tragedies and evil. The stories of Joseph, Esther, Ruth, Job, and David remind us that God can transform and even use crises precipitated by dysfunctional families, hateful siblings, natural disasters, racial and cultural oppression, untimely deaths, wars, and murders to fulfill his purposes, and even to bless his people.

Can God use evil for his redemptive purposes in the city? I have witnessed dramatic restoration and redemption in the city. I have known those who suffered severe family pain—incest, physical abuse, and rejection—who could say with Joseph, "You intended to harm me, but God intended it for good to accomplish what is now being done . . ." (Gen. 50:20). I have walked with persons whose power to overcome bitterness and assume costly positions reminded me of Esther. No doubt they felt a kinship with Esther whose people also suffered racial prejudice and were destined for ethnic cleansing. With Esther, they could affirm that they may "have come to [their] position for such a time as this" (Esther 4:14).

Others, immigrants and widows whose families suffered multiple deaths, could stand firm like Ruth and declare, "Your God [will be] my God" (Ruth 1:16). Those whose losses and illnesses seemed unfair to any observer have said with Job, "Though he slay me, yet will I hope in him . . ." (Job 13:15). And God's words to an adulterer, murderer, and inadequate father—to David, ". . . a man after [God's] own heart . . ." (1 Sam. 13:14) gave comfort to some whose guilt and shame threatened to drain their lifeblood.

I must confess that although I see these redemptive interventions now, I did not always recognize them then. Nor do I fault those who cursed, "Why did I not perish at birth, and die as I came from the womb?" (Job 3:11). Sometimes we would cry with our neighbors, "Confuse the wicked, O Lord . . . for I see violence and strife in the city. . . . Malice and abuse are within it. Destructive forces are at work in the city; threats and lies never leave its streets" (Ps. 55:9-11). And when asked, "Can a mother forget the baby at her breast and have no compassion on the child she has borne? . . ." (Isa. 49:15), too often we answered, "Of course she can!"

This does not negate the fact that God did intervene. He heard the cries and he responded. This gives us hope that he will continue to respond in future times of evil. Remembering these past redemptive actions helps us not to become numb and lifeless in the face of suffering.

Crises provide the opportunity to act redemptively

At times tragedies are God's call to us to minister in new or more effective ways, to recognize the opportunities, to find his grace to represent Christ in a different way. In the Book of Acts, Luke records God's interventions to which the early church responded in life-affirming and dynamic ways. The famine in Jerusalem provided the opportunity for partnership in ministry (11:27-30). The martyrdom of Stephen resulted in cross-cultural evangelism (11:19-21). The injustice felt by the neglected widows led to restructuring in the church (6:1-4). A vision from heaven, timely visitors and the visitation of the Spirit to Cornelius and his household attacked racial prejudice (chapter 10). An earthquake led to the conversion of the Philippian jailer and his family (16:16-34).

Robert Tannehill summarizes Paul's trust in God's interventions by saying,

> Such trust is supported by a perception of God as a God of surprises, indeed, a God who works by irony, who can use even opponents of the mission to move the divine purpose forward. The mission must work within limits, yet God repeatedly breaks out of these limits in ways that surprise both the church and its critics. Faithfully serving in mission while trusting in a God whose exact moves cannot be anticipated is a part of the ongoing struggle of faith (1991:3).

Incarnational ministry in the city must constantly remain in touch with God to discern his desired response. I recall the day four children in our Bible clubs begged us to help them. A bus collision had hit their mother and they were going to be split up into different foster homes.

I remember other times that called for our response: When fire destroyed the home of one of our neighborhood families, when gang members "marked" (selected for shoot-

ing) our neighbors, when three children were going to be
sent to live with a father they had not seen in twelve years
because their mother was evicted from their home, when
three children were freed from a cult and wanted to enter
our school even though they had not attended school for
several years. Each time God enabled us to prepare a safe
place for the people involved.

We must not forget that even the bombardment of
tragedies—the murders, overdoses, drug abuse, incest,
neglect, poverty, and robberies—can be opportunities for
redemptive response. As we invite others to join us in God's
powerful presence during times of pain, God can transform
the tragedies into times of intimacy and belonging, hope and
comfort.

Organizational crises

Sometimes God intervenes with crises when urban
mission organizations lose their vitality, when programs and
projects replace relationships, when structures leave no
room for the Holy Spirit, and when control squelches
growth. Although not all organizational crises are God-
given, God offers to use these as sources of renewal.

Painful setbacks such as the sickness or death of staff
members, financial instability, burnout, disagreement among
workers, departure of personnel, and even immorality or
destructive accusations can become God's tools for renewal.
God can use such problems as calls to reorder priorities and
reorganize schedules.

God's interventions often lead us to genuine humility,
vulnerability, greater dependence on him, and deeper trust
and usefulness. He can use unforeseen and unplanned events
to cause us to look beyond our present plans and programs.

God can demonstrate his power to remind us of our
powerlessness, to expose the shallowness of our answers
and solutions, and to call us to tear down the walls built by
our confining rules and definitions so he can build others

100

through a living community. God also intervenes through the miraculous, creating new life and unexpected surprises. We do well to remember Paul Hiebert's insights in *The Good News of the Kingdom*:

> Missions must be rooted, therefore, in prayer and the leading of God. We should make plans and use strategies, but these must always be open to sudden and total change as the Lord of the Harvest issues his commands. The history of missions is full of the serendipities of God. We labor long and hard, and see little results. But suddenly there is a great harvest outside our program (1993:160).

When our policies and procedures limit the Master of mission, he may demonstrate that we cannot contain or control him. These miracles lead to the recognition that this is his work and he will accomplish his purposes. In every crisis the Spirit encourages us to ask, "How can this tragedy truly produce life?"

Discerning the intent of God's interventions

How can we know if God is calling us to restructure, to renewal, or to both? How do we know when God is calling us to respond with action to new needs and opportunities? We will discern God's divine intentions as the life-giving Holy Spirit mediates the presence of Jesus to us, empowers us and creates true community among us.

Our regular times of reflection and scheduled times of remembering will equip us to hear God, each other, our own inner call, and the cries of the city. Only then will we be ready to respond to God's ongoing interventions in the spirit of the greatest intervention of all times about which he said, ". . . I have come that they may have life, and have it to the full" (John 10:10).

RETELLING THE STORY

One of my treasured memories, albeit a painful one, illustrates well how God used all three of the above-mentioned means to bring life in the city.

Our private missionary school policies were carefully designed to provide excellence, to protect our teachers from overload, and to produce success and holistic development in our students. One policy stated that we could only accept students who could perform at their expected grade level, according to their age. We had no special education teachers, and had found that placing students with younger students jeopardized their self-esteem.

One day in June, our ministry director asked me to take Ernesto, an eight-year-old, into our school. Ernesto's parents were gang members. His father had hanged himself in jail. Ernesto had lived in a car with his mother for much of his life, and had never attended school.

Ernesto had recently moved in with his Christian grandmother. Some of his cousins were in our school. Our organization's director was convinced we should at least give Ernesto a chance. I desperately wanted to accept Ernesto but the policies clearly excluded him, and I was then the director of the school.

I listened, I prayed, I asked God for a sign, a miracle. That afternoon I received a call from a teacher in South Dakota who wanted to assist us for the summer. I interviewed her on the phone. She came within the week. This allowed us to assign our personnel so we could invest time and energy in Ernesto. It also gave me support for my decision, should anyone criticize me for breaking policy.

We gave Ernesto our best teacher. He absolutely loved school—he blossomed. He did everything right. I spoke with his teacher frequently. On Thursday of his second week I visited his class. He seemed happy and very cooperative but I saw again that he was clearly unable to perform at his

102

expected grade level, and he was big physically. "Just one more reason we shouldn't have him in a class with younger children," I thought. But we all loved him. What would we do after the summer?

The next morning someone awakened me and told me that Ernesto was dead. He had eagerly gotten his school uniform ready and had gone to take a bath. The light bulb that was attached to an electric cord from another room hung on a nail above the bathtub. It fell into the bath water. Ernesto was electrocuted.

I didn't know whether to rejoice or sob. He had suffered enough in his short life that heaven seemed most inviting. But he was a dear child with great potential.

His grandmother said that the last ten days of Ernesto's life were his happiest. He had often told his family to read the Bible like we did at school. We arranged for a free funeral. His aunt and cousin accepted Christ during the service.

God gave Ernesto life! Ernesto gave life to many others—to his family, to me, to our school, to our organization. He continues to be a reminder that life-giving sources are available when we are dying in the city.

NOTES

1   I have found *Pain and Possibility: Writing Your Way through Personal Crisis*, by Gabriele Lusser Rico (Los Angeles: Jeremy P. Tarcher, Inc., 1991) is an excellent aid for effective journal-keeping.

5

Do good fences make good neighbors? Toward a theology of welcome for the urban church

Kathryn Mowry

THE STORY

IT WAS 9:15 on a Sunday morning. In the heart of Los Angeles, God's people gathered for fellowship before the worship service. Children of many nationalities, dressed in their brightly colored Sunday best, scrambled over playground equipment. Their parents chatted over coffee and doughnuts in a sunny courtyard dotted with park benches, bushes, and trees.

The bars of a black wrought iron fence separated this bright space from the street. Through those bars, on the

Kathryn Mowry has served as an associate pastor in two multi-congregational urban churches in transitional communities. She is the associate director of the Bresee Institute for Urban Training in Los Angeles. Please see the contributing authors section.

other side of the street, a homeless man watched the gathering. He must have been there for a while by the time I noticed him, in between cheerful greetings and "How was your week?" conversations.

I gathered doughnuts and coffee cups and slipped out through the gate and across the street to eat with the man. His name was Bill. Although he gladly accepted the doughnuts, he would not accept an invitation to come in. Some well-meaning person, concerned with the safety of the children (and possibly the safety of her own purse), had already chased him away.

Up close, Bill looked even more sad and lonely. On his yellow, weather-beaten cheek, a tiny tattoo of a teardrop added to the pathos of the picture. In the language of the streets, the teardrop was a proud statement that he had served a term behind bars. Now Bill sat there on the curb, and the bars he looked at were no longer those of the prison that locked him in, but those of the church that locked him out.

I talked to Bill for a while and told him about food distribution times during the week and our computer referral system that could help him find work and housing. But somehow I knew damage had been done, that my offers were empty, and that all of our giving to Bill could never make up for what God's people had kept from him.

READING THE CONTEXT

In today's cities, many neighborhoods and communities are undergoing very rapid ethnic, social, economic, and religious change. The churches in these transitional communities face a number of options. Many churches decide to find new homes in the suburbs instead of dealing with the constant change. Some stay but maintain a "fortress mentality" and die a slow death from irrelevance. Still others stay and decide to change with the community. It is the latter that sets the context for this story.

For those congregations that decide to stay and change, still more options remain about how they will define themselves and their mission in the community. An ongoing effort to survive often parallels the effort of forging a mission in a changing environment. Sometimes fences, both literal and figurative, provide the means for a congregation to do both. The fence becomes a way to preserve the congregation's safety or sanity, as its mission becomes one of inviting community members to come inside for brief periods of receiving handouts or services.

It seems that one trend for such urban congregations is that the "mission" becomes social involvement while the "church" remains limited to a fellowship of urban missionaries. This is not a typical fortress mentality. Churches provide food distribution, and housing and employment programs to reach out to the stranger, but the church continues to struggle at the point of extending community to the stranger. Many urban churches have reached out through elaborate and costly programs, but a fence of professional distance remains. They have not allowed the stranger to be one with them.

The need for good fences

Before we too quickly condemn the church behind the fence, it is important to understand the need for fences in a changing urban context.

In the city there are very real reasons why a church might put up a fence around the property. Drug needles are in the bushes. Human excrement is on the lawn. There is a constant need to replace security lights smashed by the homeless because the light keeps them from sleeping. There are safety and insurance concerns for the children who attend school on the property each day. These are the realities, even for a church with a great concern for its homeless neighbors. Considering these issues, a fence around its prop-

107

erty becomes more than a "keep out" sign. A fence may actually enable a congregation to use the space inside more redemptively.

Beyond literal fences, however, there are other more significant fences that congregations in transitional communities may construct. These figurative fences may tell us even more about the felt needs of the congregation. Churches may build fences to protect the nurture of long-term members, the facility, the traditional worship style, the rights of old-timers to leadership positions, and even the rights of the members to worship without being joined by anyone who might make them feel uncomfortable. All of these fences reflect a profound resistance to change that is often subconscious.

To understand a congregation's felt needs for these fences, it is important to understand the cumulative effect of change in the urban context. Individuals in the city often find themselves in a state of overload, but without a clear sense of purpose that can help them cope. When all around them is changing, long-term members of urban congregations often cling to their history in an attempt to find stability and identity.

There is something that is right about fences in an urban context. What is right about them is their accurate portrayal of the congregation's psychological needs.

Suspicions about fences

A poem by Robert Frost says, "Something there is that doesn't love a wall." On that day when I sat with Bill on the other side of the fence, I began to develop a new aversion to the invisible walls or fences that surround my church. I realized with dismay that as a church we had given our best efforts to help Bill and others like him during the week, but we had failed to extend our most transformational resource: our being together.

I do not have to look beyond my own life to know that I respond best not when I am given choices, but when I am chosen. But where was the experience of being chosen here? Our benevolent kindness did not go far enough. We offered food and referrals during the week, but on Sunday we let fear keep us from offering more. I wonder how many times of shared laughter over coffee cups does it take to make up for one time of standing in a food line holding a number?

Yet with fences in place between church and mission, the church can continue almost indefinitely with a flurry of well-meaning activity and without stopping to assess the fact that little real transformation is happening on either side of the fence. Fences not only protect, they also minimize our opportunities for growth-producing encounters with those who are different from us.

I suspected another problem that day as I sat with Bill on the other side of the fence. I noticed this problem primarily because of the diversity that was inside the fence. There were Koreans, Filipinos, African Americans, Mexicans, Salvadorans, and whites—all enjoying fellowship with one another, giving and receiving. It wasn't Bill's ethnicity that kept him from finding a welcome. Here was a barrier more difficult to cross than ethnicity: socioeconomic level. Because Bill had nothing, we perceived him as someone who had nothing to give. Worse yet, we perceived him as someone who might take what little we had.

I realized that day that we did not know how to welcome. We did not know how to receive the stranger into our fellowship in a transformational way. We did not know how to reach out across economic boundaries. Somehow I think we sensed that to truly welcome, to choose the person in need as a brother or sister, would mean risk and inevitable change for us. My struggle with these issues led me to a new reading of the Scriptures. What does it really mean to welcome the stranger?

REREADING THE SCRIPTURES

From the day of Abraham's call the mission of the people of Israel was to bless all the peoples of the earth (Gen. 12:1-3). God commanded the Israelites to welcome the stranger in their midst and to provide refuge for the sojourner as a means of blessing other peoples. Christensen (1988), Keifert (1992) and others have written about this call and its implications for contemporary urban ministries.

What seems especially relevant to our story is a parallel theme we often overlook. To welcome the stranger, God often called the people of Israel to become strangers and sojourners themselves.

God called Abraham to leave his home and go, not knowing where he was going. In Genesis 12-18, we see Abraham vacillate between schemes for self-preservation and living out his role as sojourner. Abraham's ability to be faithful as a sojourner was critical to his success or failure in blessing the nations. He failed whenever he tried to escape the vulnerability of the sojourn through self-preservation or conquest. To be a blessing to the nations (the strangers), Abraham had to embrace the vulnerability of becoming a stranger himself.

> What a curious inversion—taking feelings of estrangement that we normally try to get rid of and calling them positive signs of vocation instead! By this logic, the need to feel at home turns out to be idolatry, because it involves finding our security in position and place rather than in dependence on God. If we live in God, we will find ourselves on pilgrimage; we will be taken to alien places where we are strangers and estranged. Only when we acknowledge that "you can't go home again" will [we] be on the road to faith (Palmer 1981:63).

Again and again, we find this "curious inversion" marking the people of God. In Egypt, the descendants of

110

Abraham were oppressed because they were strangers. Their delivery from Egypt and the subsequent forty years of wandering in the wilderness marked the formation of the pilgrim community that came to be known as the people of Israel.

In the two liturgical ceremonies of Deuteronomy 26:1-15, we see that the people of Israel recalled their experience of being strangers as the basis for both gratitude to God and hospitality for the sojourner among them. Two central understandings that undergird Israel's welcome of the stranger emerge from these ceremonies: The understanding that Israel's welcome must flow from the heart of a stranger, and the understanding that Israel profoundly knew God was its host.

The heart of a stranger

Exodus 23:9 (RSV) says, "You shall not oppress a stranger; you know the heart of a stranger, for you were strangers in the land of Egypt." As translated here, the Hebrew word for "heart" is *nepesh*. Paul Hanson says that we should understand *nepesh* as "the deeply personal knowledge derived from close involvement with the other person" (1986:46). The people of Israel had this deeply personal knowledge from their own experience. Their motivation to serve the stranger in their midst came to a large degree from this experiential knowledge.

The theme of vulnerability and intentional displacement for the nation that would be a blessing to all peoples continues with God sending Israel into exile. In the New Testament, we find this theme again with the persecution and scattering of the early church. In both these situations, with the people of God already suffering as strangers, God called them to make their position as sojourners even more intentional and more proactively missional (see Jeremiah 29 and 1 Peter 1:17). They were to settle in and seek the *shalom* of the city where God had placed them.

111

The intentional displacement involved in the welcoming task stands in direct contrast to building fences of self-preservation. One cannot work for self-preservation and maintain the vulnerability necessary to welcome the stranger. Besides, self-preservation is pointless, for only in becoming the stranger will we find our own wholeness. This theme becomes especially important for the church in the city.

> Thus the church stands apart from and against society neither to preserve its own purity nor to provide an escape from the tensions of exile, but rather so that we may find the very purpose of our lives as we seek the *shalom* of the cities where God has placed us as servants (Webber 1984:29).

God as host

Beyond its painful knowledge of oppression, Israel also had a deep experiential knowledge of God's grace. A constant grateful remembrance of the Exodus event punctuated Israel's worship rituals. Indeed, Patrick Keifert (1992) shows that the entire shape of Israel's worship tradition was a reminder that Israel was the guest of the Lord. God was Israel's host. His grace called for gratefulness, and gratefulness called for the welcome of the stranger.

When God's people forget God's grace and the knowledge of God as host, there results an inability to welcome others. Jesus says to the Pharisee who silently observed while the sinful woman anointed Jesus (Luke 7:36-50),

> *Do you see this woman? I came into your house. You did not give me any water for my feet, but she wet my feet with her tears and wiped them with her hair. You did not put oil on my head, but she has poured perfume on my feet. Therefore, I tell you, her many sins have been forgiven—for she loved much. But he who has been forgiven little loves little (7:44, 46-47).*

The Pharisee had not even shown Jesus the common courtesies of hospitality. Jesus implies that the Pharisee had been forgiven little, and therefore, loved little. A person without a fresh experience of forgiveness, who does not overflow with gratitude for deliverance, cannot welcome others. The Pharisee could not receive the woman's gift. He saw himself on a higher spiritual plain. All of these factors become barriers to his welcoming either the woman or Jesus.

For the older son in the parable of the Prodigal Son (Luke 15:11-32), the issues appear to be the same. Again, Jesus directs the parable to the Pharisees who accused him: "This man welcomes sinners and eats with them" (Luke 15:2). This must have been a high compliment to Jesus, who understood his mission to welcome the stranger. Jesus paints a picture of the Pharisees as he tells the story of the older brother in the parable. The older brother felt he deserved a higher status for his good behavior. He was not grateful for his father's generosity to his brother. The implication is that the older brother, although he never visited the far-off country, also never really came home to the father. He, therefore, lived in resentment instead of gratitude. And without gratitude, it is impossible to welcome others.

> There is always the choice between resentment and gratitude because God has appeared in my darkness, urged me to come home, and declared in a voice filled with affection: ". . . You are always with me, and everything I have is yours" (Luke 15:31). Indeed, I can choose to dwell in the darkness in which I stand, point to those who are seemingly better off than I, lament about the many misfortunes that have plagued me in the past, and thereby wrap myself in my resentment. But I don't have to do this. There is the option to look into the eyes of the One who came out to search for me and see therein that all I am and all I have is pure gift calling for gratitude (Nouwen 1992:80).

113

The realization that all we have is "pure gift" has important implications for the church that would minister to the stranger in the city. If we believe that we own anything, the urban context will encourage us to hold tightly to it, to put it in a safety deposit box, or to build a fence around it. But if all is grace, we can welcome the stranger in gratefulness and freedom. Only a profound knowledge of God's grace can empty our hearts to create the space necessary to welcome another.

Reciprocal hospitality

We find hospitality demonstrated in the new community that the Holy Spirit formed with the birth of the church (Acts 2). But here is a hospitality that bears little resemblance to the ways in which we use the word today. This was not a sentimental or soft hospitality, but one that brought radical sociological and spiritual unity.

The Book of Ephesians clearly states that God's mission is a unifying mission. God's ultimate purpose is to unite all things in Christ (Eph. 1:9-10). As the agent of the kingdom, the church must take up this unifying purpose. If by welcoming the stranger we participate in God's unifying mission, it is important that we understand the nature of the unity into which we are to welcome the stranger.

In Ephesians 4:1-13, we see several characteristics of the unity God has called us to. First, this unity is based on many unities: the unity of one body, one Spirit, one hope, one Lord, one faith, one baptism. This is a radical equality. Second, the prerequisite to this unity is a spirit of lowliness, meekness, patience, and love. Third, our unity is tied closely to the use of gifts within the body. The body needs all the parts to be complete or "one."

Radical equality

A radical leveling happens in the unity of the church. There are no hierarchies, only differing roles and gifts. All

114

who are part of the church come through the same door. There is only one Lord and only one way to enter his kingdom: by faith. The sacrament of baptism itself is a leveling symbol.

As we realize and practice our radical equality in the kingdom of God, it has the same effect as the alcoholic's admission at the beginning of each Alcoholics Anonymous meeting: "Hi, I'm Rhonda, and I'm an alcoholic." This is the kind of understanding with which we must come to the oneness of the body of Christ: "Hi, I'm Kathryn, and I'm a sinner saved by grace." Only this knowledge permits me to be free to be one with others.

A spirit of humility

Ephesians 4, Romans 12, and Philippians 2 all speak of the necessary attitude for true oneness or unity. The spirit of humility described in these passages seems to be a hurdle in learning to be the unifying people of God, especially when ethnic diversity or socioeconomic barriers are an issue.

The calling forth of gifts

Those who are gathered into the unity of the church must not only be built up by the body, but must also participate in building up the body with their gifts. In Ephesians 4, Romans 12, and 1 Corinthians 12, a discussion of various gifts quickly follows each description of the unity of the body.

The passages emphasize that the Spirit gives each person a gift to be used for the good of the others. It is the use of such gifts that enables a person to experience the equality and mutual sharing necessary for "oneness."

The implications of calling forth the gifts of others may startle churches with established ministries that tend to do things "for" people. But if we truly extend community to strangers by calling forth their gifts, we will become recipients of their ministries in our midst.

> There is no unity with Christ or his people unless we
> serve. This is why the exercising of gifts is important. It
> enables us to serve, to give of ourselves to another. This
> is how we find out what oneness in Christ is about.
> When you are moving out in faith to serve another,
> there comes a oneness within. It makes of your words
> unifying words and of your deed a unifying deed.
> There is no Christian community not rooted in service,
> and no Christian service not rooted in relationship
> (O'Connor 1968:40).

We cannot fully allow a person into the community or
give them a chance to be "one" with us until we enable them
to serve the community. As we come to understand this truth,
the implications for urban ministry are astounding. Not only
do we need to minister to the poor, but we also need the poor,
the homeless, and those of different cultures to have the complete body of Christ. We need the gifts that the homeless person, the bag lady, and the recent immigrant bring.

> I need the poor? For what? The question exposes my
> blindness. I see them as weak ones to be rescued, not as
> bearers of the treasures of the kingdom. The dominance
> of my giving overshadows and stifles the rich endow-
> ments the Creator has invested in those I consider des-
> titute. I overlook what our Lord saw clearly when he
> proclaimed the poor to be especially blessed because
> theirs is the kingdom of God (Luke 6:20) (Lupton
> 1989:6).

The unity we find demonstrated in Acts 2 and described
in Ephesians 4 involves a profound sense of our radical
equality in Christ, a spirit of humility, a calling forth of the
gifts of those we would serve resulting in mutual ministry
and transformation, and an understanding of the need for
every part of the body of Christ. When we define in this
way the unity we seek, welcome takes on a different shape.

MISSION ACTION

Our story reveals a paradigm in which giving forms the basis for ministry in the community. Congregations have built both literal and figurative fences, so that they separate giving completely from the place where they do their receiving (inside the fence in exclusive community). Charles Van Engen has described this distinction as a separation between "church" and "mission" (1991). Mission becomes located somewhere "out there." Churches of all types, rural or urban, face this problem. The struggle becomes especially noticeable, however, in the church in a transitional community.

The reflection on the Scriptures showed us that we need a theology of welcome to tear down the fences that have come to separate "church" and "mission." Properly understood, welcoming presents us with a new paradigm in which we cannot separate mission from the church community.

This definition of welcome requires a paradigm shift for us. We usually understand the word "welcome" as something we extend when we give to someone. As we read the Scriptures, it becomes clear that welcome is about giving and receiving. We have understood welcome as the opening of the door of our home to a guest. Biblical welcome, however, is the welcome by an intentionally displaced person so he or she can embrace the stranger. In true welcome, both parties are strangers, both parties give to the community, and both parties become transformed. Welcome, thus defined, becomes a transformational process, initiating and expanding the community of the kingdom.

God's mission in the city is much larger than seeking the transformation of the poor or strangers. His purpose is to transform all the people of the city, including the people of God. God brings us together in the city for mutual transformation. The Spirit is changing all of us into God's like-

117

ness. This makes openness to change essential for the Christian who seeks involvement in ongoing transformation. Only in this state of embracing vulnerability and accepting change as a gift can a person begin to welcome others. The person who does not want to change cannot afford to welcome others.

Frank Alton shows how the "giving" paradigm neglects the transformation of the one who does the giving.

> Psychology helps us see how we project our needs onto others. True transformation confronts this tendency, and allows us to grow by facing our own neediness. . . . There is an activism which looks impressive, but which misses transformation because it focuses on only part of the problem (Alton 1992:2).

True welcome requires a willingness to be changed. For those who would minister in an urban environment, part of that change means voluntary displacement from the suburbs, from cherished worship traditions and music, or even from the sanctuary. To position ourselves for mutual transformation means that we must leave our comfort zones behind. We must step out to the place where we can meet strangers and allow them to teach us. As defined here, we can never welcome someone "to my place."

We can only move away from the self-protective giving paradigm when we have experienced God's grace and truly understand that part of his plan is to transform us as we are involved in the transformation of others in our community. When these understandings are intact, we will find the space in our hearts to work towards the intentional incorporation of the persons we once regarded as threats. Such intentional incorporation, however, requires careful guidelines and an openness to new structures for the church.

Guidelines for welcome

True hospitality or welcome cannot ignore the realities of the urban setting. Becoming the welcoming people of God does not mean that we lie down as welcome mats and allow people to treat us as they will. It does not mean that we tear down all the fences around church property, remove the bars from the windows, and let the city destroy us. Some churches hinder hospitality by completely separating themselves from the stranger, but the opposite extreme of openness may be just as detrimental to true hospitality (Christensen 1988:94,95). There is a tremendous tension between being realistic and being transformational in our welcome.

Jean Vanier introduces the community function of "double discernment" in determining how to welcome strangers. There are two primary questions, and we must discern the answers in community.

> Can we in the community give that person the peaceful space and the elements they need to be at ease and to grow? And then will they, so far as we can know them after dialogue and prayer, really benefit from the community as it is, and truly adapt to its minimal expectations? (Vanier 1979:268).

Sometimes the answer to one or both questions will be "no." The most hospitable response in this case is to state this clearly. A community cannot be the savior of all.

> But there is a way of saying "no", with compassion; there is a way of taking time, listening, explaining why the person cannot stay and offering suggestions where he or she could go. It is such a wounding experience to be turned away. We must remember that (Vanier 1979:268).

119

Two simple principles emerge that bring balance to the community's welcome of the marginalized stranger: Minimal conformity and maximal space for diversity. Vanier (1979:275) introduces the concept of "minimal conformity." The community must state its rules clearly from the beginning. When this occurs, people exclude themselves, without the denial of a welcome from the community.

Conformity does not go, however, beyond this minimal requirement in true welcome. We must allow maximal space for diversity. Palmer has criticized the kind of hospitality that makes us insist that the stranger become "one of us." "The essence of hospitality—and of the public life—is that we let our differences, our mutual strangeness, be as they are, while still acknowledging the unity that lies beneath them" (1981:130). The stranger must be "one with us" even if he or she may never be "one of us."

Often, however, our idealized notions of family, community, and intimacy can squeeze out heterogeneity. This leaves us without openness to the stranger and without the most effective vehicle for our own transformation and growth. To prevent this, we must look at new structures that enable welcome and mutual transformation to occur in the church in the city.

New structures for welcome

We must banish the idealized image of the church as one extended, intimate family if the church is to become a place of welcome and transformation. Peter Wagner has shown that the single cell concept of the church limits the number and variety of people who may be incorporated (1990). Our single cell idea of the church comes in part from the geographical parish concept of the church, with its roots in rural Europe. In the parish concept, the idea of one church for a whole community leaves little option for diverse expressions of faith. There is a holy place, a holy person, and a holy hour. Inherent in the parish concept is the unstated assumption that people will come to us and worship as we worship.

The concept of welcoming the stranger must take us beyond the parish concept to see our mission as one of extending hospitality to the stranger, even if that hospitality must take radically different forms from what we are used to. This in no way should diminish the sense of commitment to the community that many have associated with the parish concept. In our commitment to ministry in a geographic area, however, we must take into account that different needs will make different structures necessary.

Morning worship in the church sanctuary may not be the best place for marginalized people in the community to experience welcome and transformation. It may be equally true that morning worship in the church sanctuary may not be the best place for church members to practice welcome and experience transformation.

The intentional displacement necessary for true welcome must move church members beyond what is comfortable for them. For this reason, Palmer suggests that the church should become a kind of "halfway house between the comforts of private life and the challenges of diversity" (1981:28).

The idea of intentional "halfway houses" where both the marginalized and church members come together as strangers has great potential for reuniting church and mission and for encouraging mutual transformation. Implicit in the idea of a halfway house is that the parties meet with the understanding that the place belongs to neither. The halfway house by its name is neither here nor there. God is the host. Creating such intentional centers of hospitality may well be the first step toward tearing down many of the figurative fences that a congregation has constructed with its giving paradigm.

Church members must take care that they do not view these hospitality times as one more area of their ministry. This view takes us quickly back to a giving paradigm. As people come together in hospitality, all parties must enter as learners.

> The risk for people who leave one community to go into another is that they will arrive as adults and not as children. They will come to offer service. They already know what to do. I really wonder whether anyone can commit themselves in a community if they do not first live a period of childhood there (Vanier 1979:28).

Missionaries who are learning a new language and culture find this "period of childhood" approach to bonding in a new community to be highly effective (Brewster and Brewster 1982). The same principles could apply when God's missionary people in the city are learning to reach across socioeconomic barriers to bond with the people of their community. To some program-oriented people, time spent in hospitality will seem like a waste of time. Nothing could be farther from the truth, for every stranger comes bearing a gift. And *all* come together initially as strangers.

RETELLING THE STORY

It is difficult to retell the story at the beginning of this chapter because I am unaware of any urban congregation that practices this kind of welcome. Any retelling offered here, therefore, will be visionary and incomplete—and will likely appear simplistic and fuzzy. Yet we must begin somewhere to ask: What will the urban church look like if it maintained fences with open gates that allow for true welcome? If we envisioned the first steps of this movement toward new structures, it might look like the following:

It is 9:15 on a Sunday morning. In the heart of Los Angeles, the people of God gather for fellowship before the worship service. The gates of an outdoor patio area are opened wide onto the street, providing an open invitation to the community to join one of the groups around the patio tables as they enjoy coffee, doughnuts, and conversation.

Homeless men and women are interspersed with young adults from the community and older members of the congregation. The homeless are learning to be comfortable with these new friends. Others are learning to listen and to understand the new and strange responses to their habitual "How was your week?" question. There are still some uncomfortable awkward spots, but the grace of God moves in to transform such moments.

As 9:45 comes and worship begins, a young man stands and explains what will occur inside. He firmly states the community's basic rules for worship time, and then extends a welcome to all who can agree to the guidelines. Some enter to sit with their new friends. Some excuse themselves. No one objects to either response.

Some of those who leave wander to the park for a simple time of worship on the lawn. For them, the park service is easier than being cooped up inside for so long. But they will see their friends from the church later in the week, for many of them serve together on task forces that are creating small businesses and making plans for a drop-in hospitality center for the homeless. They talk excitedly about decisions their groups will be making this week.

The group on the lawn begins to worship in its own way—singing or just listening to praise choruses played on the guitar by one of the homeless men. As they celebrate the grace and deliverance that God is bringing into their lives, the expressions on their faces reflect newfound hope. One of the men has a tiny tattoo of a teardrop on his cheek. His name is Bill.

6

Planting covenant communities of faith in the city

Richard Gollings

With what shall I come before the Lord
    and bow down before the exalted God?
Shall I come before him with burnt offerings,
    with calves a year old?
Will the Lord be pleased with thousands of rams,
    with ten thousand rivers of oil?
Shall I offer my firstborn for my transgression,
    the fruit of my body for the sin of my soul?
He has showed you, O man, what is good.
    And what does the Lord require of you?
To act justly and to love mercy
    and to walk humbly with your God.
Listen! The Lord is calling to the city . . .
                    Micah 6:6-9a

Richard Gollings has served since 1982 with the Baptist General Conference in church planting in Mexico City and Tijuana, Mexico. Please see the contributing authors section for more information.

THE STORY

IT WAS the last year of my family's missionary term in Mexico City, after which we would move to Tijuana to plant a new church there.

Our mission church, *Nuevo Nacimiento*, had bought a house to use as a *templo* (church). We needed an *albañil* (a brick and concrete worker) to direct the job of enlarging the templo's sturdy concrete roof. We had arranged for a *maestro albañil* to help us, a man whose house we had helped to rebuild after the 1985 earthquake.

One day, two men appeared at the *templo* door saying that Don Jesús, the *maestro albañil*, had sent them. One look told us much about these men. They were small, with Indian features, rough, dirty clothing, and submissive demeanors. They came from an *ejido*, a government-organized communal farming village.

The Mexican government bought unproductive farmland and gave it to the peasants to farm as cooperative *ejidos*. Until recently, no one in Mexico could buy or sell *ejido* land. Because parents divide the land and give it to their children, each succeeding generation possesses less and less land. The typical *ejido's* crop fulfills only about forty percent of what its family needs. The peasant men migrate either to do underpaid farm labor on big Mexican or American agribusiness concerns, or serve as underpaid unskilled construction workers in the cities. With the *ejido* system, the Mexican government subsidizes Mexico's private agribusiness and urban development by maintaining a docile population of underpaid laborers.

The two men at our church door were yearly migrants to the urban construction industry. The *maestro* had sent them because they were good workers, were evangelicals, and had not eaten recently. Pastor Rubén immediately invited them in to share dinner. He gave them a free room in the *templo*, where his family also lived. He invited them to

126

participate in church activities. When we were able to enlarge the concrete roof, they assisted the *maestro albañil* in directing the job, with church members (and one *gringo* missionary) functioning as the unskilled labor.

As we got to know each other better, they told us a sad story. They were Pentecostal Christians. There was a small church in their village, but the members could not support a pastor. Whenever these two men came to Mexico City for work, they would go to Pentecostal churches requesting preachers to come to their village to hold meetings. But city-dwelling preachers of their own denomination—the stream of Christianity that is supposedly the most effective in contextualizing the gospel for the poor of Latin America—would not go out to the "interior" to minister to their village. Unlike Pastor Rubén, no pastor had ever invited them in for a meal, let alone have them live in his home rent-free.

READING THE CONTEXT

This story illustrates an aspect of the church's idea of community for both members and non-members of the "household of God."[1] When people seek an experience of true community, will they find it in the church?

In every society, humans crave fellowship in some form. In the Old Testament, the search for a sense of community took on a particular social and ethnic form in the people of Israel. In the New Testament—especially in the Book of Acts—the church takes shape as a unique type of community, based on Jesus' words, "All men will know that you are my disciples if you love one another" (John 13:35).

Evangelizing and transforming a city requires enlightened church structures—local congregations—more than dedicated, hardworking mission structures. Mission structures will minister to people, but church structures must be present for personal growth, community fellowship, and the incarnation of Christ's love.

The question before us is not, "Is Christian ministry directed to the formation of community?" Instead, it is "To what kind of community is Christian ministry directed?" I believe that to address in a practical way issues of ministry in the city such as those examined in this book, the local church must recognize that it is a community formed by the covenants of God.[2]

REREADING THE SCRIPTURES

God called and formed his people by his covenants. In Genesis 15:7-21, we see his covenant with Abraham, an unconditional covenant. In Exodus 20, we have the first statement of the conditional Sinai covenant. The rest of the Pentateuch explains what the covenant means and what God expects of his human partners. The entire Old Testament shows the people of Israel struggling with the implications of their unique covenant. The prophets rephrase the covenant and its stipulations in contemporary terms, fearlessly identifying and condemning the people's rebellion. In Matthew 26:26-28 and its parallel gospel passages, God extends the new covenant in Jesus Christ to all humanity. This new covenant is unconditional to those who would join in it, but informed by the detailed Old Testament definition of God's covenants.

We are more familiar with contractual relationships than with covenantal ones in contemporary Western society. A contract is a legal document. Its major purpose is to *limit* the responsibilities of the partners to one another. Whether it is between humans or between a human and God, a covenant *enlarges* the mutual responsibilities of the partners because it invokes and identifies a supportive and loving kinship between them. Trust is the basis for this relationship, not competing self-interest. Mutual trust and faithfulness to their promises determine and shape the actions of the covenanting partners.

In the act of the Exodus and in the Sinai covenant God assumed the role of the *go'el*—the "kinsman redeemer"—to Israel. Through his own initiative, God bound himself to Israel as his relatives and kin, assuming obligations to them and requiring corresponding attitudes and behavior from them. As God's kin, reflecting his nature was Israel's obligation. In its separateness for God, Israel would incarnate God's justice and compassion, and worship him alone.

The Pentateuch exhaustively explains how this would work in practice, and the rest of the Old Testament shows how both parties act through Israel's history to make mid-course corrections. Micah 6:8 succinctly expresses the requirements God places on those who would be in covenant with him. Israel's relationship with God brought about the people's relationship with each other—their community.

The united worship of God and the mutual demonstration of justice and compassion would cement the people to one another and to God. But the covenant relationship God made with his people also included and enabled community obligations to strangers and outsiders. Israel had to treat strangers with compassion and justice "for you were aliens in Egypt" (Exod. 22:21). It would be the gravest of contradictions for people whom God had redeemed and adopted to become themselves oppressors of the poor.

As Israel developed over the centuries and interacted with the surrounding nations and cultures, it increasingly mimicked its neighbors in the development of oppressive and unjust social and economic practices. Israel also divided its spiritual loyalties. In the Sinai Covenant, God made Israel's rulers responsible for maintaining the nation's ethical standards. Instead, it appears that they led in the nation's spiritual degeneration. Even Solomon built the temple with Israelite forced labor.

This drift and degeneration called forth the office and anointing of the prophets. The prophets strongly directed their messages at Israel's sins against their covenant with God and with their neighbors. One can see a "theology-on-the-way" recorded in the Old Testament. It shows a struggle over the centuries between those who sought to concentrate power in the hands of a ruling class while turning the faith increasingly into ritual, and those led by the prophets, calling the nation back to its original covenant obligations.

Even through Israel's rebellion, degeneration, and punishment, God further clarified the ramifications of his covenant. The Israelite nationalists saw the Babylonian conquest as their final punishment and humiliation. Yet Jeremiah 29:1-13 tells them that Israel's covenant relationship with God calls and enables them to undertake covenant responsibilities (those of community) with the Babylonians, the outsider pagans who were their conquerors.

Through the sacrifice and blood of Jesus, the new covenant is unconditional, as Paul explains in Galatians 5. But, again, it echoes the demands of the prophets in setting the expectations for those in covenant with God, as in Matthew 5-7.

In Matthew 18:21-22, Peter asks Jesus, "Lord, how many times shall I forgive my brother when he sins against me? Up to seven times [and then I'm off the hook]?" This expresses a contract mentality, limiting one's responsibility. Jesus responds, "I tell you, not seven times, but seventy-seven times [as many times as necessary]," expressing the true covenantal attitude.

In John 21:15-17, Jesus twice asks Peter, "Do you *agape* me?" Jesus was asking for covenantal love. But Peter responds, "You know, Lord, that I *phileo* you," promising a contractual love. Finally Jesus says, in effect, "Even if you only *phileo* me, still, feed my sheep," calling Peter to a covenantal understanding of their relationship.

Beginning with the image of a vine and its branches (John 15 and 16), Jesus gives perhaps the clearest New Testament explanation of what it means to be in covenant with God. He also explains that the covenanted human can live up to this covenant only because the Holy Spirit now lives in him or her.

READING THE CONTEXT

The most basic contextual fact is that power corrupts. As religions and churches become established by the power structures, the system tends to co-opt them. They end up either actively supporting the government and the powerful, like the Roman Catholic Church in Latin America, or passively supporting or permitting the status quo, like American Protestantism.

People have quickly watered down the concept of a covenant, especially in the religious realm. We bargain with the supernatural. This happened in Israel and now occurs in modern societies. We bargain for current and future benefits from God in return for minimal ritual acts on our part. It may mean doing certain good deeds or fulfilling religious obligations.

The following acts are valid transactions in Mexico: Getting drunk at the annual religious fiesta for your village or for the neighborhood's patron saint. Paying for a new paint job or for clothing for the community's idols. Paying the priest to do a ritual that placates the Virgin in heaven who then pays off God for you. Based on a medieval theology, this system justifies the old contractual arrangements and destroys the possibility of covenantal communities of trusting and loving faith.

In contrast to medieval (and Iberian) Roman Catholicism, the Reformation called Christianity back to its biblical and covenantal norms. These norms included personal faith, loving behavior, and a covenantal understanding of the church as a community of believers. This effort continued in the settlement of North America.

New England Puritans sought to extend the covenant to include the civil community. Baptists pulled away from the Puritans partly because of this issue, arguing that the biblical covenant community could only include those who joined it voluntarily. There was less concern in both communities with following a minutely defined body of doctrine. The sense of community with God and within the congregation as demonstrated by godly living and loving behavior was more important.

Although surprisingly few people joined in these covenant communities, many lasting social blessings came to the general population from the Puritans and Baptists as part of their covenantal sense of responsibility. As commerce strengthened the appeal of individualism, however, the church and the larger society weakened their focus on covenantal responsibilities and moved toward more contractual-style limited obligations.

Throughout the nineteenth century, Baptist churches—particularly on the expanding American frontier—used written covenants to guide their people in living up to their Christian calling. Some communities turned inward to focus on maintaining covenant purity, as others looked outward and led much community social action.

The twentieth century produced a frontal assault on the concept of the church as a covenantal community. The American cultural value of individualism-above-all has crippled the Christian's willingness to submit to the discipline of a covenantal community. The fundamentalist-modernist wars in the U.S. left evangelicals afraid to involve themselves in "social gospel" ministries.

Mexico has its own radical individualism and "insider-outsider" separation. Also, American missionaries of an earlier age founded and continue to inform the attitudes of Mexican Baptist churches. After moving to Tijuana, I discovered that ministry in Tijuana involves living in the midst of divisive forces representing all the above perspectives. Whether from the U.S. or from Mexico, whether Protestant or Catholic, each viewpoint seems to militate against the search for covenantal community in Tijuana.

What are some contemporary models of church community and ministry that will help us develop the local church and its ministries in the desired direction? We can see the thinking and action of a contemporary urban Christian ministry being laid out along a continuum, as in Figure 1 below.

Figure I: Doing and being in urban ministry

A ⟵——————————————⟶ B

To do	To be
Outward	Inward
Materialism	Evangelism
Political struggle	Spiritual struggle

For a church living and working within its own context, "A" would include liberation theology, incarnated in the Roman Catholic base ecclesial communities that have grown in some parts of Central and South America. These communities exist because of their common struggle against the political, social, and economic powers that oppress the people. The members of these communities support one another morally, and struggle together to attain political, social, and economic goals.[3]

These communities demonstrate that Latin Americans, even the poor who are accustomed to being severely limited by authoritarian structures and culture, can find in Scripture and in committed communities the motivation and strength to address the needs of their society. This church model, however, too easily becomes a virtual mission structure (a sodality), existing primarily because of its sociopolitical and economic usefulness for change. While true spiritual transformation can result, the group's mission focuses mostly on the sociopolitical and economic realms.

In Tijuana, we can observe an instantaneous, easy, uninvolved version of purely socioeconomic action ("A" in the continuum—see Figure 1, page 133) in the many U.S.-based churches that come down briefly to build houses, distribute food and clothing, maybe hold a quick evangelistic meeting, and then immediately return to the U.S. These U.S.-based churches do not think in terms of follow-up for seekers and converts, or of forming partnerships with Mexican churches for mutual strengthening, much less of long-term covenantal relationships that foster solid community.

Position B (see Figure 1, page 133) is "body life." This is not simply old-fashioned evangelical church as usual, focused only on evangelism and worship, preaching against personal sin, and avoiding political entanglements. Ray Stedman (1972) and later Peter Wagner (1974) developed the body life concept some time ago. The focus is on the spiritual end of the continuum, but with the members exercising their gifts to reach out in evangelism and active ministry to the physical and spiritual needs of community members.

A danger in the body life focus is the development of what Peter Wagner has called "koinonitis." Wagner describes it this way:

> Koinonitis is a [church pathology] caused by too much of a good thing . . . Fellowship, by definition, involves interpersonal relationships. It happens when Christian believers get to know one another, to enjoy one another, and to care for one another. But as the disease develops, and *koinonia* becomes koinonitis, these interpersonal relationships become so deep and so mutually absorb-

ing, they can provide the focal point for almost all church activity and involvement. Church activities and relationships become [introverted and self-seeking, rather than oriented toward mission in the community] (1979: 77, 78).

So "koinonitis" (or the inflammation of the koinonia) involves an overemphasis on internalized fellowship to the point of a loss of interest in, and compassion for, those outside the group. The openness about personal things and the egalitarianism of Stedman's body life ministry go against the grain of self-protection and competition evident in Mexican Protestantism. Yet we have seen committed caring, deep sharing, and powerful ministries of intercession develop in congregations in Mexico City and Tijuana that modeled covenantal community.[4]

Mexican evangelical churches generally demonstrate an introverted exclusivism that approximates a fortress mentality. Historically, this can partly be explained by Mexican cultural factors, the anticlerical Mexican government prohibiting social ministries by the church, the militant hostility of the Catholic church (Mexicans who consider it their Catholic duty still persecute, beat, and occasionally murder Mexican evangelicals out of love for the Virgin), and the competitive and divisive attitudes of U.S. and Protestant missionaries of an earlier generation. Rather than excusing the lack of covenantal community, this history should make more urgent the call to the development of covenantal community in our urban churches today.

A true covenantal vision

A truly covenantal vision and lifestyle in a church would combine the best of both of the continuum's poles (see Figure 1, page 133), yet would transcend the contractual level. Concerning "doing," the covenantal community would understand its calling and commitment to action for

135

Figure 2: Being and doing in covenant in urban ministry

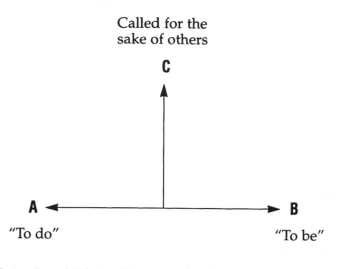

Called for the
sake of others

C

A ⟵ ⟶ **B**

"To do"   "To be"

"Being" and "doing" in covenant (covental community):
- "Full covenant"
  - Community with outsider
  - Holistic
    - Evangelistic and cultural
      mandates

holistic blessing of the nations who do not yet know Jesus
Christ. Concerning "being," the people of God would profoundly know that God calls them to be in covenant with
him and with each other as a community with a God-given
purpose, as shown in Figure 2 above.

Greenway and Monsma (1989) can help us with this.
They point out four key aspects of urban ministry modeled
by Paul and his coworkers. First, they taught a clear, concise
doctrine of Jesus Christ, of judgment and salvation. Second,
they described a moral system of behavior for the discipline
of new Christians. Third, in organizing local churches, they

promoted a high level of cohesion and group identity centered in a common confession. Fourth, the church experienced active fellowship—even amid persecution—giving it an atmosphere of growth, witness, and ministry.

> Without a thorough teaching ministry, the Antiochan believers would not have matured into the kind of people their critics dubbed "Christians," and no urban strategy today can be expected to produce great fruits unless it includes in-depth instruction in the Scriptures, Christian life, and discipleship (Greenway and Monsma 1989:37).

An example of this is John Perkins of Voice of Calvary Ministries. Perkins returned to his hometown of Mendenhall, Mississippi, with the purpose of evangelism and church planting. Yet contrary to much urban ministry (including ours in Tijuana), evangelism preceded and empowered social action. Perkins did not start with outside funds or workers. Those whom God raised up as converts in Mendenhall became the backbone of Voice of Calvary ministries.

> Evangelism creates the committed people, the concern for the needs of people and the broad community base from which to launch social action. Social action, in turn, fleshes out the Lordship of Christ, reaching people's spiritual needs through their felt needs and developing an indigenous economic base for the work (Perkins 1976:221).

Evangelism and church planting remained the priority. But as the church developed as a community covenanted together under Christ, the Christians also recognized their covenantal responsibility to address the problems of their neighbors.

Mission action

If a local church were more convinced of its identity as a special community formed by its biblical covenant with God, how would it minister more effectively to members and the larger community?

Scripture uses signs, story, and teaching to express, explain and model the concept of the covenant between God and his people. For a group or individual to exist in covenant with God, there are privileges (adoption, salvation, and empowering) and obligations (personal and group sanctification and ministry), particularly in the areas of justice, compassion and the worship of God alone.

God commissions a church to be salt and light to its population. It must demonstrate sanctification but also reach out into the community, to call people to the worship of the true God in Jesus Christ and serve with justice and compassion.

Charles Deweese calls for modern churches to write and adhere to covenants in the tradition of the Puritans and Baptists in America. Such a covenant would define behavior instead of doctrine and be informed by God's covenants in the Bible. Covenanting and the regular study of the meaning of God's covenants would militate against the individualism of today's Christians.

Clearly, we should not allow this covenantal relationship to become a new legalism. Instead, as in the case of the prophet Hosea, churches must base covenant on intimate, self-giving love that calls for the radical transformation of the entire covenant community (Deweese 1990).

Whether written or implicit, church covenants tend to become self-centered, anachronistic, and overly-specific boundary-setters. Just as Deuteronomy commands the king and people of Israel to read periodically, study and recommit themselves to God's covenant in its full meaning (including the people's covenant responsibilities toward the stranger), so the local church must repeatedly study the biblical covenants to understand and fulfill its covenant duties.

Christians would have to teach and model this vision of covenant community in evangelism, discipleship, and church teaching. They would have to teach and preach about it regularly in church and Sunday school. A curriculum like that of Shenk and Stutzman (1988) would help achieve this goal. The pastor must be convinced of its importance for the idea to take hold.

Traditionally, in Mexico a congregation looks for its pastor to be an autocratic leader. Part of the challenge would be for the pastor and the people to submit to a covenantal form of relationship, with pastor and people accountable to Jesus Christ, the Head of the church.

For now, it may be easier to inculcate the covenant community vision in newly planted churches than to cause such a radical change in established churches. This has been our experience in Mexico.

RETELLING THE STORY

The Lord called us to leave Mexico City and go to Tijuana. Because of those two humble brothers who appeared at our church door in Mexico City, the church there eventually developed a powerful ministry of intercession and action for the physical and spiritual needs of its city and neighborhood.

What we had learned in Mexico City helped us start fresh in Tijuana. Once there, we discovered that the situation in Tijuana had interesting similarities and relationships with the situation in Mexico City—in spite of the geographic and cultural distance. At least it did not seem so in the case of Paco. His story resembles the "Andrew connection" of John 1:35-51.

We knew Paco in Mexico City when we had helped his older brother plant a church there. He was a Christian, but

139

rather lazy and shiftless, with no passions beyond soccer. Soon after we settled in Tijuana, we received a letter from Paco asking if he could stay with us while he learned English, got a visa and moved to the U.S. We were not eager to reply.

One night, I returned to our house to find Paco on the doorstep! He lived in our home, got a factory job, and studied English. He also worked with me building houses in the El Florido area of Tijuana, holding evangelistic worship meetings, and doing pastoral visitation.

After living with us for a year, Paco returned to Mexico City and began to infect the youth of his home church with the idea that they could and should serve others. Before long, the youth group of that lower middle class church started work parties in their own neighborhood. Then they began to travel to small mountain villages to assist Baptist churches in construction, evangelism, and teaching. When the youth of a number of related churches from around Mexico met at this church for their annual retreat, they too spent the retreat ministering in social and spiritual ways to another poor church. This has become a tradition among these churches.

Paco's example served to energize his pastor brother to an enlarged vision. Later, that pastor, Miguel Altamirano, left a good position in Mexico City to move to the ugly outskirts of Tijuana and help us plant a church there. Paco accompanied his brother when they came from Mexico City, and now leads the youth of the Monte Horeb church in evangelism, discipleship, and ministry in the community.

In Tijuana, we planted a church in a migrant settlement by helping impoverished families build houses. The church that grew out of that ministry, Monte Horeb, and its pastor, Miguel Altamirano, carry out a number of servant ministries to their neighborhood, including house-building, relief distribution, and a Christian school. Experiencing ministry and seeing the Holy Spirit working in power through the congregation motivates the Monte Horeb church to lean more on Jesus and fulfill its part of the covenant.

Like the church in Mexico City, Monte Horeb is also learning that the church is a moral community, not just a voluntary association. A moral community's goals and gifts to its members are wrapped up in belonging, identity, transcendence, intentionality, and reciprocity. This is a covenant community of faith where people may hear the following confession:

> I *belong*. I am recognized as an integral part of a distinct community, and I make a difference.
>
> I am *somebody*. Those inside the community recognize me as someone special, someone important. To those outside, I have an identity in part because I belong to this group.
>
> My church is *bigger than you or me*. God formed it. It focuses on him and he empowers it. It has a long history, stretching around the world and back through history.
>
> My church was formed and exists for a *purpose*—to glorify God. God gave us our reasons for existing and they include caring for each other and for the world in his name.
>
> We have *responsibilities to each other and for each other*. I have received freely and I must give freely. My brother and sister and I are responsible to live up to the terms of our covenant with God and with one another. I will help my brothers and sisters and they will help me. My church will *nurture* me so I can grow through receiving and giving.

We can reach the goal of building churches as true covenant communities. As a part of its covenant relationship with God, the congregation can develop a commitment to the city. We have seen halting steps in this direction in both Mexico City and Tijuana. When people came into the shanty town of El Florido, Tijuana, asking for the Monte Horeb church, they reported that people on the street tell them, "Monte Horeb? Oh, yes! It is the church up on the hill—the church that helps its neighbors."

NOTES

1   See Lesslie Newbigin, *The Household of God: Lectures on the Nature of the Church* (New York: Friendship, 1954).

2   Cf. Paul D. Hanson, *The People Called: The Growth of Community in the Bible* (New York: Harper & Row, 1986).

3   Guillermo Cook (1985) describes the thought and work of base ecclesial communities in Brazil.

4   Jacques Ellul (1970) offers some interesting perspectives on the church in the city about this end of the spectrum. To Ellul, the modern city is antithetical to God and his kingdom. We cannot live without the city, but it taints all of us. Although the church must exist and work in the city, nothing of lasting good will come until Christ breaks in and remakes and redeems the city himself.

7

Family coherence and evangelization in urban India

Atul Y. Aghamkar

THE STORY

A YOUNG MAN knocked at my door during my first year of ministry in Nagpur, a city in central India. Shrikant was from a prestigious Lewa Patil community. His parents were well-placed middle caste Hindus with a closely knit family structure. Santosh, my younger brother, had introduced Shrikant to Christ while they were studying at the same school. Shrikant could not continue living with his family after his decision to accept Christ. That is how he landed at my door.

I welcomed Shrikant. Although I was a little surprised to see him, I gave him time to relax. To my amazement, he said, "I have thought for a long time about this, but now . . ."

Atul Y. Aghamkar ministered in two cities in central India with the Christian and Missionary Alliance, primarily as a church planter and pastor. Please see the contributing authors section for more information.

He paused and continued with determination, "I have decided to become a Christian." He indicated his desire for baptism. His decision delighted me. I was so overjoyed that I did not ask many questions. After a few days of teaching, I baptized Shrikant. We did not feel the need to inform his family members about his baptism. We believed Shrikant was an adult and legally could make his own decision.

When Shrikant's parents found out about his baptism, a chain reaction began to ripple through his extended family. His father, along with some elders from his community, came and forcefully removed Shrikant from us. They severed all of his connections with us and with other Christians. His parents and relatives expressed anger and antagonism toward Christianity and the Christian church. Shrikant's family and relatives joined in protecting him against a so-called "Christian attack." Consequently, this closed all the doors for communicating the gospel to Shrikant's family and relatives.

Shrikant was one of the first high caste converts I baptized in my early ministry. It saddened me to watch his family take him away. Reflecting on the incident over the next several years, I began to see that Shrikant's family was not really anti-Christian, nor were they explicitly resistant to the gospel (Aghamkar 1985:182). When a family member was being separated from them in the name of the Christian religion, they united themselves in protecting him and preserving the family's solidarity.

They considered Shrikant's decision to become a Christian without consulting any family members—especially the elders—a revolt and an insult. They could not tolerate the snatching away of a member of their family. For them it was an attack on their family solidarity. They could not tolerate either Shrikant's decision to become a Christian or our decision to baptize him without consulting his family members. Shrikant was an inseparable part of their family. As a result, we lost Shrikant, and his family and relatives became very hostile to the gospel. We created resistance to the gospel where initially there may not have been any.

READING THE CONTEXT

Traditionally, the strength of Indian society lies in the joint or extended family. According to Raghuvir Sinha, "The joint family in Indian society is altogether a different type of institution, which has evolved out of cultural and ethical traditions and prerogatives" (1993:22). Although joint family units differ from place to place, normally they consist of a number of married couples and their children living together in the same household, related by blood

"A joint family is a group of people who generally live under one hearth, who hold property in common and who participate in common family worship and are related to each other as some particular type of kindred" (Thomas and Devanandan 1966:vi). Indians place much importance on the family because it gives a sense of identity and belonging to a person. Sumithra and Nicholls are correct when they observe that

> Important decisions such as marriage and education are decided within the circle of the family of the local community. Decision-making is rarely a private act. The extended family of several generations gives a sense of identity and belonging both to children and to the elderly and in the accord with the biblical understanding of family . . . (1984:190).

Association with the caste system, however, adds complexity to the family in the Indian context. As explained by Sinha,

> An important aspect of Hindu society which has, in course of history, helped the joint family persist and

145

> which has also made it more intelligible and stable is its
> caste organization—one of the most complex systems
> in existence. Caste in India is, in fact, an extension of the
> joint family; it is an inclusive group of families having
> the same status and role (1993:21).

Although experts repeatedly portray India's caste system as a social entity, in reality it is an integrated part of traditional Hinduism. It has controlled Indian society for centuries.

In recent years, however, industrialization, secularization, and modernization are transforming Indian society. This is particularly true in urban areas. A modified extended family is emerging in urban India to meet the demands of the complex urban life. Here again, kin and clan play a central role.

Such structures may not look very traditional or formal, but they consist of a series of nuclear families joined as equals for mutual aid and functioning. These individual nuclear families, however, do not necessarily live together under one roof to form a traditional joint family. Members of kin and clan may be scattered in the city, living as nuclear units, but for all practical purposes they function as one large joint family.

Most urban migrants to the city seldom lose the feeling of belonging to a common home. Understanding this has tremendous implications for reaching urban families and triggering a chain of networking for the cause of Christ.

Urbanization is a worldwide phenomenon. Like the rest of the world, India is rapidly becoming urban. Urbanization draws millions of rural people into its fold. No matter how we look at India's cities, the fact remains that they are growing in number, size, and complexity.

No study of urbanization can neglect the part migration plays. "A discussion of urbanization in India, fundamentally is a discussion of net rural-to-urban migration"

(Punekar 1974:27). The growth of India's urban population during the past few decades shows a significant movement of people from rural to urban centers. Moreover, if this trend continues, almost half of India's population will have moved to the cities by the year 2000. Thus the whole migration phenomenon demands careful understanding.

Why do people migrate to the city?

People primarily migrate to the cities for economic reasons—to earn a living. India is predominantly an agricultural country. Most of India's agricultural land depends on direct rainfall. When there is little rainfall, drought displaces thousands of people, forcing them to leave their villages to find work in the cities.

Members of the lower castes and landless laborers compose sizable segments of those who migrate to the cities. In addition, partly because of changes in the traditional caste system, many landless laborers lose their traditional occupations and must seek employment outside the village. Thus most of the people who migrate to the Indian cities do so primarily for economic reasons.

Industrialization is considered a "pull" factor that attracts thousands of people to the city. Cities offer numerous options for employment, primarily in industry. Many educated and skilled people tend to move to the city. Bougue and Zachariah contend that ". . . in India the propensity to migrate to urban areas is much higher among literate and educated people than among the illiterate . . ." (1962:53). In recent decades, the significant growth of industrial centers in major cities has attracted millions from all over India. This is a major reason why people move to the city, where some kind of employment is normally available.

There are other reasons why people migrate to the cities. Disasters such as famine, flooding, and community unrest force people to migrate. The availability of better edu-

147

cational facilities, the allure of the mass media, and increasing freedom attract thousands to the city. Escalating unemployment in rural areas due to changes in the traditional caste system, and government policies related to land, labor, and minimum wages also push rural people to the city.

Who migrates to the city?

In most cases it appears that first-time migrants to the city are men. Often, family members or circumstances force them to leave their villages and make the move. For a time they maintain their families in the village and send money regularly. Thus they keep close connections with their families and clans in the village. After a time, these men either bring their wives, children, and siblings to the cities, or eventually get married. Normally, they marry someone who is from their own sub-caste in a nearby village and then they establish a household in the city.

In recent years, more rural people are migrating to the cities with their families and households. This is particularly true when there is large-scale famine, flooding, or rioting in the countryside. Those people who live in villages near major cities migrate to the city with their entire families because the expansion of urbanization absorbs their land and livelihood. Left with no possible means of support in their village, and having no other option, they take shelter in the city. Men, women, and even children begin a struggle for survival as they move into the city. Many women and children, then, must also work in the city.

Where do the migrants settle?

While understanding the patterns of migration, we must notice the patterns of settlement. India's major cities reflect dual structures. According to Brush (1962) there is a clear distinction between traditionally developed cities and the cities developed by the British. In traditional Indian

cities, the caste structure forms the basis for indigenous res-
idential patterns. Here high castes are centralized and the
laboring low castes are located on the outskirts. On the other
hand, the British section of the city, often called the "cantonment" or "camp," is usually pre-planned in a tight pattern
with a rigid hierarchy of status in which the highest ranks
live farthest from the center of town.

As migrants arrive in the city, they find no place in a
traditional city, where the caste system is the basis for the
settlement pattern. But settling down in a "cantonment" is
also difficult, due to its strict rules. Eventually, most of them
manage to find people of their own caste or clan and settle
down on the fringes of the city. As they arrive in the city,
migrants initially appear to be uprooted and dislocated. A
closer look reveals a different picture. When rural persons
migrate to the city, they do not come arbitrarily. In most
cases, they come to the city with some kind of initial contact.

Normally, the contact is either a close relative, someone
from the same clan, or a friend. This explains why one can
find groups of people from the same caste, language, and
village background in specific areas of the city. Monsma is
right when he says, "Networking relationships help people
to find work, provide clothing, shelter, and food when
needed, protect from destructive acts, provide help when
sickness or death strikes and fulfill mankind's desire for
social contacts" (1980:14).

Such kinship and caste pockets are found all over the
city. Trivedi calls them "Semi-Urban Pockets" (1976:4). These
pockets of typical rural migrants have a strong sense of community, and enable the migrants to keep in touch with the
village and their own caste community. So these pockets
process the continuous ebb and flow of rural migrants, and
assist in establishing and strengthening a web of relationships between families, clans, and castes.

What does the urban church do for migrants?

Traditionally, the Christian presence and activities in India are concentrated in the central part of the city. Most pastors expect newly arrived migrants, especially Christian migrants, to find a church and join the membership. Most of the people who migrate to the city, however, settle down at its fringes, and the churches generally find it difficult to leave their comfortable central location and move out to these people.

Some new independent churches occasionally move in and attempt to find rural Christian migrants from their own constituency and background. They establish initial contacts and follow-up with those migrants who show interest, inviting them to be a part of the church. Although the migrants appreciate these efforts, such initiatives normally do not consider the Christian migrants' non-Christian relatives and friends, who perhaps may show openness to the gospel.

Most migrants to the city have close contacts with their own kin and clan and they are often open to those who show interest and concern for them. Yet the church does not seem to be making use of these great opportunities. In fact, the church loses thousands of rural Christians as they move to India's large cities.

The city's complexity immobilizes many of India's urban churches and Christian leaders. Rapid urban growth puzzles them. Most of them are not well informed, trained, or equipped to take advantage of such opportunities. In many cases urban pastors are overloaded and on the verge of burn out. This makes them unwilling to do anything for those who are not yet part of their church. The urban church often perceives rural migrants as a burden and liability and, tragically, finds it extremely difficult to identify with them and accept them into the fold.

In addition, the church in India suffers from the lack of a wider vision. Most churches in the cities seem to have developed a maintenance mentality. They derive satisfaction from preserving the status quo. They show practically no interest in expanding their ministry beyond their own members. Internal problems, divisions, and litigation keep them so busy that they rarely stop to think of those who are outside the church. As a result, the church neglects most of the newly arrived migrants to the city.

REREADING THE SCRIPTURES

The Bible is a family book, and Christians cannot neglect its focus on the family. "When we turn to the biblical records, we shall discover that families feature prominently both as the recipients as well as the agents of salvation blessing" (Hian 1981:620). The Bible tells us how God took the initiative in establishing (Gen. 1, 2; Eph. 2:19), sustaining, and using families for the salvation of the nations. The terms "nation," "tribe," "house," and "family" have overlapping usage in the Bible (cf. Minear 1960).

The centrality of urban families in the New Testament

New Testament writers frequently used the Greek word *oikos*, translated in English as "house," "household," or "family." It is important to note that we find the New Testament usage of this word largely in urban contexts. Jesus and Paul recognized the importance of the family.

We come across several examples in the New Testament of whole families or households putting their faith in Jesus. In Luke 19:1-10, for example, we read about Zacchaeus and his household. John 4:53 tells us of the royal official and his household believing in Jesus. Paul concludes his letter to the Romans (Rom. 16) by sending his personal greetings to the households of Priscilla and Aquila, Aristobulus, and Narcissus. These households may have become Christian and thus were part of the church at Rome. Paul mentions in 1 Corinthians 16:15 that the household of Stephanas were the first converts in Achaia. 2 Timothy 1:5 indicates that Timothy inherited a godly family background.

Interestingly, almost all of these households lived in cities or large towns. Zacchaeus was from Jericho, Lydia was from Thyatira, and the household of Stephanas was from Achaia. The households of Aquila, Aristobulus, Herodian, and Narcissus were from the capital city of Rome. So in the New Testament we see the Christian faith moving from family to family, establishing its strong presence in the urban world.

Perhaps it is in the Acts of the Apostles that we find the most prominent example of urban family evangelism and church planting. We will do well to study the Book of Acts to find out how the gospel spread effectively along family lines.

Focus on the family in the Acts of the Apostles

Harry Boer observes that "Acts is preeminently a book describing a group approach in mission" (1961:163). Acts clearly shows how God brought several families and households to faith in Jesus Christ. Most of the cities that Paul visited were significant regional urban centers with a wide influence on their surrounding provinces. Paul basically focused his pattern of ministry on family units. Although Paul's strategy was first to reach the Jewish community in diaspora, after the Antioch experience (Acts 13) he also directed his efforts toward the Gentiles. Here again, while focusing on receptive Gentiles, he concentrated on family units.

"A favored technique [in Acts] was to evangelize households" (Hedlund 1985a:226). We come across several examples of the households the apostles evangelized. For example, "[Cornelius] and all his family were devout and God-fearing ... and [he] had called together his relatives and close friends" to hear Peter preach (Acts 10:2, 24). Although

Cornelius was not a Jew, Peter brought him and his whole family to the Lord. It is crucial to note this for it shows how we can influence close relatives and friends for Christ.

Such family solidarity is common in most Eastern societies, and effective evangelism will follow the path of these "bridges of God" (McGavran 1955).

Once a family or household becomes Christian, other relatives and friends encounter them and receive their introduction to the gospel. Paul and his companions repeat this pattern in the city of Philippi, a Roman colony and the leading city of the district of Macedonia, where they baptized Lydia and the members of her household (Acts 16:12-15).

We find the most striking example of family conversion, however, in Acts 16. In response to the jailer's question, Paul and Silas instruct him to "believe in the Lord Jesus, and you will be saved—you and your household." Consequently, the jailer and his whole family were baptized. Here it is important to note that the appeal was made to the jailer's whole family to believe in Jesus, and it was natural and normal for Paul and Silas to do so.

In Acts 18 we find that the family of Priscilla and Aquila were part of the community of believers. Further, we read about the conversion of "Crispus, the synagogue ruler, and his entire household . . ." (Acts 18:8). One of the major reasons the early church became strong and grew quickly despite persecution is because of the conversions of families and households.

The gospel moved across cities and spread from family to family. Paul's strategy clearly shows that he not only accepted the existing social system but also used it effectively for the spread of the gospel. McGregor rightly points out that use of the social structure aided the rapid spread of the gospel and the expansion of the early church through the household system. "When a total family is reached for Christ it can become a tremendous force for Christ in winning other

153

households. This is a natural, spontaneous and lifelike process of increase" (1980:37).

When these families united and formed a church, they exerted a tremendous influence on their relatives and friends. These households became centers for further evangelism. "The house church phenomenon of the New Testament (Rom. 16:5-15; Col. 4:15; Phil. 2) was an accompaniment of the family evangelism pattern" (Hedlund 1985a:227). It is, therefore, evident that "the life and ministry of the early church were deeply rooted in the home of the Christian believer" (McGregor 1980:35). The gospel penetrated in and through family networks, making evangelism effective and churches stronger.

Families were the starting point for evangelization in Acts. This approach was effective in winning large segments of different societies for Christ. Paul could boast of preaching the gospel to the whole of Asia, although he only went to some strategic cities and preached the gospel there. But Paul's secret was that he preached to family units—and these families, probably through their networks, spread the gospel to their own kin and clans.

MISSION ACTION

The New Testament pattern of household evangelism has tremendous implications for evangelism in our modern cities today. As we apply New Testament principles in evangelizing families in Indian cities, Christians in India will have to confront several issues. George Peters' comment is worth noting: "Household evangelism and household salvation are the most basic biblical and cultural approaches and expectations and need revival in our days" (1970:147). To be more effective in urban evangelism, we need to examine our approaches in light of the New Testament.

Sensitivity toward social structure

Many Indians blame the Christian church for fostering social disintegration, and say that Hinduism finds its strength in its well-integrated family system. It is true that through the caste system, Hinduism has successfully kept its grip on every aspect of Hindu life. So it may not be wrong to say that Hinduism contributes to family cohesion, or at least helps to maintain it.

The history of the church in India clearly shows that whenever individuals and their families were encouraged to become Christians, great people movements took place. "It is easily proved from history that the great advances of the Christian faith have generally occurred along the lines of natural kinship relationships" (Greenway 1988:4).

Such movements to Christ can bring segments of people into the church without isolating them from their people. Family-focused evangelism and church planting may produce strong churches in India.

The context in which the church ministers in urban India is ripe for employing the biblical approach of household evangelism. Since Indian cities show a pattern of settlement according to caste and kinship group, churches could target each segment of the city, keeping the family as the focus.

Most people in urban areas tend to crave a sense of belonging. This means that people do not break their family ties even after they move to the city. Even urban dwellers in India consider family loyalty a virtue. Presenting the gospel in a way that would strengthen one's family loyalties needs serious consideration. Understanding group patterns of decision-making, close-knit family units, interpersonal relationships, and networking is essential for urban evangelism in India.

Focusing on decision-makers

Although India's urban families are leaning toward fragmentation, the head of the household—normally an elderly man—exerts tremendous authority. The elders deal with most of the household affairs. Often, they are the decision makers. The elders usually make a decision, however, only after discussion with other family members. Decisions such as becoming a Christian affect the whole family, the kinship group, and the community. Therefore, urban churches must take care to focus on and influence the family's decision-makers.

The question of how to present the gospel to the whole family, particularly to the decision-makers, is a crucial one. The Bible indicates that the head of the household is the key to bringing the household to Christ. We must show great sensitivity to a family's decision-making process. This especially influences the way we understand conversion in the context of urban India.

Conversion and social shame

Indians often interpret conversion as a negative social act, particularly when an individual becomes a Christian. Hinduism is the dominant religion in India. It is not only a religion; it is also a system that influences every aspect of society.

When individuals decide to leave their traditional religion, they are considered traitors. The church must take care to allow the gospel to penetrate through families and kinship webs: ". . . The decision making process in strong group-oriented societies influences the way people come to Christ" (Hiebert 1987b:6).

If the church encourages individuals to become Christian, further penetration of the gospel may stop there. Family members may expel that person and close the door to the gospel.

156

As stated in the story at the beginning of this chapter, Indians consider this an act of rebellion and a blow to family solidarity. But if sufficient time is given for the families, kinship networks, and close social groups to think about and make decisions for Christ, then a wider penetration of the gospel is possible. This way there is considerably less resistance from Hindu peers, relatives, and community members. This helps to maintain family coherence.

Indians also link conversion with social shame. They often believe that becoming a Christian means leaving one's centuries-old religion, caste, and traditions. This, in itself, is a major cause for bringing shame on the community.

Indians take great care not to do things that would bring shame to their community. When Christians present the gospel to a community, they should do it in a manner that would make people proud of their decision. Having family members join in making a decision to become Christian normally reduces the intensity of social shame. Granted, this is a big challenge, but we must take the issue of shame and conversion in India seriously.

Dealing with caste

Caste is not only a Hindu social structure, it also has subtle and deep religious roots. Although many believe that the caste system in urban India is changing, it still remains a formidable obstacle to the spread of the gospel. It advocates inequality, granting special privileges and rights to the higher castes. It denies the rights of the lower castes, and particularly of women. The concept of *karma* is the foundation for such practices, and it has led to fatalism, intolerable suffering, and social injustice.

Although Christians outwardly oppose the caste system, in reality it exists even in the church. In turn, the evangelism and witness of the church reveal this reality. Christians with a lower caste background find it difficult to reach out to

157

members of higher castes with the gospel. And only rarely does the church reach the lowest strata of society.

Higher castes are seen as more reluctant to respond to the gospel. For them Christianity is a religion of the low castes and the outcasts. Part of the problem, however, is that Indians believe Christianity is a foreign religion with an individualistic focus. In many cases conversions among members of the high castes occurred on an individual basis, generating much antagonism toward Christianity. The stigma of Christianity as a religion of the low castes still prevails in India. By becoming Christians, members of the higher castes are afraid that they may have to lose their status and privileges for the sake of the gospel.

In recent decades, however, some elements of the caste system have gone through several changes. Caste no longer carries the same importance in the lives of city dwellers as it does in the lives of rural people. The church needs to study the implications of such changes and use its knowledge effectively for the wider and deeper penetration of the gospel in India's cities. The whole issue of the caste system and the implications for urban evangelism also warrants careful study.

Equipping Christian families

Since we must evangelize urban families, then we must equip Christian families for the task. Sharing the gospel with urban dwellers requires personal communication. George David observes that ". . . where there is actual church growth and church planting today, it is taking place largely through the form of interpersonal communication" (1990:103). He further suggests that mission to urban Hindus requires cultivation of face-to-face family friendships with members of the community. This means that the challenge is to develop family friendship evangelism for reaching urban families in India. To a large extent, the church in India has not taken seriously the ministry of equipping Christian families for evangelistic purposes. This remains a crucial challenge before the urban church today.

Urban dwellers crave a sense of belonging and family solidarity. Urban stresses can lead to isolation and alienation. The church can equip Christian families to become centers of hospitality, love, and concern where alienated people can find a sense of belonging. The church should train Christian families to share the gospel in a natural and sensitive way that would reestablish and strengthen family and social solidarity. The gospel brings transformation. It transforms relationships. It reinforces the view that God is creator of all humankind, and there are no high or low castes for all are created in his image. Presenting this redeeming aspect of the gospel can have a liberating effect in the cities of India.

The context in which the church ministers in urban India is ripe for employing the biblical approach of household evangelism. That Indian cities tend to follow a pattern of settlement according to caste, tribe, and kinship groups shows that the church could target each segment of the city and focus on a particular people group. Pastors, evangelists, and missionaries alone could never complete the task of reaching hundreds of segments of migrant peoples. The key here is equipping Christian families with specific training in urban witness and evangelism. This is the need of the hour.

RETELLING THE STORY

After completing my B.D. at Union Biblical Seminary in 1977, I was appointed to minister in the city of Nagpur. This city of over a million people had only about sixty churches then, and my task was to plant a church there. Most of the Christian churches and activities were centered in the civil lines and cantonment, the *Chavni* area of the city. After doing some research, I decided to focus on the western fringe of the

159

city. I rented an apartment in Gandhi Nagar in the western part of the city.

One afternoon, a young man named Himmat came to our neighborhood, inquiring about me. Someone pointed out my apartment to him. I welcomed Himmat and offered him a cup of tea. He told me that he was from the village of Darapur in the Amaravati district and had had some exposure to the gospel there. He had moved to Nagpur and was involved in gambling, drinking, and gang fights. The police had arrested him several times and he was exposed to more crimes while in prison. The last time he was released, he had returned to his village. While he was there, he met a Christian couple who directed him to us. Himmat wanted to leave his criminal way of life, but did not know how.

I found out later that part of his determination to find me was because of my roots in the Amaravati district. My denomination, the Christian and Missionary Alliance, has been working in the Amaravati district for several decades. Both I and my colleague, Sudhir Ingle, originally came from this district. This was one of the reasons Himmat attempted to see us and establish his links with us.

We took a keen interest in Himmat's life, and he began visting us regularly. We soon found out that he was married and was living with his wife, children, and stepmother in a Telankhadi slum. We witnessed to Himmat, who was clearly receptive to our message. We began to visit him in his rented hut.

Because of Himmat, Shashikala (his wife) and her mother became interested in the gospel. We also found out that Himmat was planning to move to the Pandhrabodi slum. This slum was not very far from Gandhi Nagar, and many new migrant families from different villages were settling there. Himmat also wanted to move there because he knew that several people from his own caste were living in that slum.

160

Himmat's move to Pandhrabodi slum gave us easy access to his family and friends. They heartily welcomed us. Himmat began to invite his relatives, friends, and neighbors to join us during our visits to his house. After a time, Himmat, his wife, and his stepmother decided to receive baptism.

Eventually, Himmat's two brothers, Rajaram and Prakash, also joined him in settling down in the same slum. Rajaram, a younger brother, was married to Ratnamala, whose mother Sakhwar Sawle lived in the Takli slum in northern Nagpur. She was a widow with two sons, Manohar and Ashok, and a daughter. Himmat's and Rajaram's family also influenced Sakhwar Sawle and her family, and after a few months they too were baptized.

Soon Prakash, Himmat's youngest brother, decided to marry. He wanted to marry Himmat's sister-in-law, Vatsala. Through the influence of Himmat and his wife, both Prakash and Vatsala also became Christians and were baptized in our church.

I must note a few things at this point. Himmat was a rural migrant to the city. Someone from his village connected him with us. He made a deliberate attempt to find us, primarily because we were from his district and his caste background. He became amazingly open to the gospel during those initial weeks of his arrival in the city. He felt at home with us and with the faith we shared with him, because he knew us and trusted our similar rural roots.

Himmat influences his family for Christ

Himmat became ready for baptism and continued to exert influence on his family. As the eldest male in his family, he was able to influence other members of his extended family for Christ. Over several months, fourteen people from the Thorat, Ingle, and Sawle families became Christians.

Looking at the family ties, we noticed that initially Himmat and his family received the gospel. Even after becoming a Christian, Himmat continued to live with his own relatives and caste people. This gave him and us an opportunity to witness to relatives and lead them to Christ.

Notice also that only the Thorat and Ingle families were living in the Pandhrabodi slum. The Sawle family was living in the Takli slum, yet because of family ties they also came under the influence of the gospel through their Thorat relatives. They retained their strong family ties even after moving to the city. This provided a natural networking structure for the spread of the gospel. As a result, many families came to know Christ, became part of the church, and the church was strengthened.

The churches in the cities of today's world need to be wiser and more intentional about allowing the gospel of God's love to flow freely and naturally through the deep channels of family and kinship.

PART THREE

Being Present
in the City

8

Nairobi and Naomi: Immigration into the city

Stanley Mutuku Mutunga

THE STORY

MOLI HAD just completed high school. At eighteen he joined other Kenyan youths in the streets of Nairobi, looking for a job. For three months his friends and relatives gave him food and shelter. Since most of them were low-income working class people, however, they could help only so much. They firmly challenged him to be "serious" in looking for a job.

For some time, Moli worked as a youth clerk for an aspiring political candidate. The incumbent, however, had defeated the candidate, and Moli never heard from him again. Moli did not know any power broker in the city who could help him find reliable employment. It was becoming very clear to Moli that life in Nairobi did not live up to his

Stanley Mutuku Mutunga is a native of Kenya. He has done pastoral work and Bible college teaching with the Africa Inland Church of Kenya and is currently working on his second Ph. D. Please see the contributing authors section.

expectations. He soon discovered that his friends from the rural area had changed after coming to the city and that economic terms now defined their friendship. To exist, they all had to pool their resources together.

Like many youths in Kenya who complete high school and college, Moli came to Nairobi expecting to get a white-collar job. When reality did not meet his expectations, Moli found it difficult to accept menial jobs just for survival. At one point, he even considered going back to his rural home to pursue another career, such as farming. But he recalled that a major reason for his coming to Nairobi was the scarcity of farmland in his home district.

Before coming to Nairobi, Moli had been a Sunday school teacher at his local Revival Movement Church (RMC). Before he left, his pastor had given him a letter of recommendation that he could present to an RMC church in the city. One Sunday Moli decided to look up a church of his denomination in Nairobi, hoping that he could get not only spiritual nourishment but financial help as well.

The first Sunday Moli attended the church the pastor was extremely busy and could not meet with him. On his third visit he met the pastor and explained to him his predicament. The pastor assured him of his prayerful support but explained that the church could not provide financial help. Moli learned that the church's policy about financial help was this—since they could not help everyone, they should not help anyone.

Moli left feeling discouraged that even his church would not help him. The political system had failed him. The socioeconomic system would not allow persons of his educational background and social status to get jobs easily unless they were "put through" by some power broker. Now the church had thwarted his final hope when it failed to meet his felt needs. What was he to do?

READING THE CONTEXT

Moli's experience is not an isolated case. Many people can cite similar situations in other African cities, and in most cities of the developing world. Several "pull" and "push" factors are increasing the rate of rural-urban migration, especially in tropical Africa. Reports show that at least 500 persons are added to Nairobi's population every day. Of these, over 90 percent are under thirty years old and looking for jobs.[1]

Why are so many Kenyans migrating to Nairobi today? What historical factors (both internal and external) have led to Nairobi's growth? Specifically, how did the events in Europe and North America in the late nineteenth and early twentieth centuries directly influence the growth of this city?

Many people know of the issue of rural-urban migration in Africa. For decades the government of Kenya has been acutely aware of the need to control the rural-urban movement.

The founding president of Kenya, the late Jomo Kenyatta, constantly urged the unemployed to go back to their rural areas to engage in farming. In almost every national address, he would emphasize his motto: *Turudi Mashambani* (a Kiswahili phrase that means "Let us go back to the farms"). Despite this call, rural-urban migration has continued unabated.

In a recent publication, the Kenyan government conceded that "the conventional centralization of management and decision making at the headquarters in Nairobi has proved inefficient" (Development Plan 1989:34). It then proposed that "decentralization of the planning process as reflected in the 'District Focus for Rural Development Strategy' be drafted" (1989:34).

The government hopes that this decentralization of management and decision-making will create more satellite cities that can eventually attract some would-be Nairobians.

167

This new direction is still only an idea and it remains to be seen what effect it will have on the rate of rural-urban migration to Nairobi.

Six key factors have led to the population influx into Nairobi: historical, economic, social, physiographic, population growth, and educational.

Historical causes

Writing on the growth of the cities of developing countries, Benjamin Tonna observed:

> A decisive factor in the origin and development of almost all Third World metropolises was the historical fact of colonization on the part of European peoples. Cities such as Madras and Calcutta, Hong Kong and Singapore were born as support bases for imperialistic interests; they exercised commercial, administrative, and military functions. These cities, and many others, in Latin America and Africa as well, sprang from the concerns of the European population residing in them and the interests of the overseas metropolitan center— not from the needs of the local populations (1985:11).

Although Nairobi was flourishing as a commercial center for the local communities before the coming of the Europeans,[2] the latter were responsible for transforming the city into an administrative center. This transformation was definitely not an African agenda. Shortly after the arrival of the Europeans, the Africans became mostly spectators and guests in their own city, rather than partners. G. Hamdan, writing barely a year after Kenya's political independence (1963), explains how colonialism transformed Nairobi.

> Since its founding in 1899 Nairobi has grown from a small railway encampment to become the capital and primary city of an important political state in Africa south of Sahara. During seven decades of colonial rule,

Nairobi, as other political capitals of Africa, came to bear the most evident fingerprint of Europe on African life (1964:239).

The arrival of the Europeans in Nairobi changed everything. Not only were the Europeans the new rulers of the city, there was also a new attraction to the city, with the focus gradually changing from simple barter trade to more organized economic structures.

To succeed in their economic pursuit, the Europeans saw the need to build a railway line stretching from the coastal city of Mombasa (Kenya) to Uganda in the west. With urbanization, this move brought more people. Fatima Alikhan writes,

> . . . The railway brought in Indian workers in large numbers when construction began on it in 1895. It also brought in white settlers to "open up" the highlands so that the railway could be made a "paying concern." This introduction of white settlers led to the establishment of rapid growth of a network of settlements ribboned along the railway (1987:85-86).

Before the construction of the railway and the coming of the White settlers, the small urban centers were located along Kenya's east coast. Only Mombasa was of some significance. Furthermore, these coastal cities sprang up to facilitate trade between the coastal Africans and the Arabs.

With the arrival of colonial rule, however, "the center of government was shifted from Mombasa the commercial center on the coast to Nairobi, to the railway town in the midst of white farmland in 1907" (Alikhan 1987:92). This shift signaled the emergence of the so-called "White Highlands" as Kenya's economic core, heralding the increased importance of the interior over the coast, and establishing the colonial power's firm political control over the mainland.

169

Circumstances now compelled Africans who had lived in the rural areas for centuries to migrate to the urban centers mushrooming across the colony. Alikhan explains the predicament in which the Africans found themselves:

> By means of various measures including the imposition of the Hut Tax and Poll Tax designed to create a need for cash among Africans, an African labour force class was created to cater for the White needs [in the city] (1987:87; cf. Little 1974:9 and Mitchell 1969:196-200).

Coupled with the above pressure was the need to fill various menial posts in the colonial bureaucracy with Africans. As a result, many Africans were pulled from their rural homes to Nairobi. The traditional trade with the coastal merchants at Mombasa received less and less attention, with the focus now on Nairobi.

Economic factors

Until the European partition of Africa, most of the continent south of the Sahara was predominantly a peasant economy. As the Western economic enterprise with its market economy invaded African life, two major economic factors came into play: the imposition of taxes, and new employment opportunities.

The Europeans needed workers to provide cheap labor for their various economic enterprises. Initially, the idea had little appeal to the nineteenth century Africans, because working for money was a foreign concept. A desperate labor shortage developed, especially in the territories under British control (Little 1974:9). This situation forced the British to impose taxes that the Africans had to pay in cash. This forced the Africans into wage labor, most of which they could find only in towns.

Today people migrate to Nairobi in search of jobs. A substantial body of research on rural-urban migration in various world regions shows that most people move to the city for economic reasons. The rate of urban influx corresponds to the income differentials between rural and urban regions.[3] As to Nairobi, both S. G. Kerkhofs (1981:4) and Alikhan (1987:178) agree that the search for economic alternatives is the key factor leading to increased rural-urban migration. Most of the unemployed are female, and 90 percent of them are less than forty years of age (Mwaniki 1986:viii). Mwaniki writes,

> Women are twice as likely to be unemployed as are men. Rates are highest for the youngest members of the labor force and remain high for all males under 30 and females under 40. . . . Unemployment rates are higher in Nairobi than in other urban centers. Forty per cent of job seekers have been looking for work for less than one year, and over 35 per cent have been searching for over two years (1986:x).

Although rural-urban migration to Nairobi is approximately 500 people per day, job vacancies are decreasing annually. In 1991, for example, the Ministry of Manpower Development and Employment reported that 92 percent of applicants could not find placement.

Social "push-pull" factors

A variety of other push-pull factors draw people to Nairobi, including the availability of money, access to better facilities, and opportunity for visits by relatives.

Money has increasingly become an important commodity, because it is acceptable in all social and economic transactions, including "bride price" and other traditional compensations. Before colonization, Africans used only domestic animals such as goats, cows, and sheep for such transactions. Today, however, social prestige dictates the use of money to finalize these transactions.

171

Nairobi also represents better access to various social needs like housing, medicine, transportation, communication, and electricity. Alikhan explains,

> Nairobi has attracted seventy-five per cent of the National Housing Corporation investment in housing and has one hospital bed for every 152 people. Outside Nairobi the facilities are much worse . . . (1987:101).

In a similar vein, R. Obudho adds that the ". . . provision of public utilities like water supplies, electricity, and rail and road traffic are an index of importance and contribute to the growth of cities like Nairobi" (1983:61-63). People find better income, more entertainment facilities such as movie theaters and sporting events, and more privacy and freedom in Nairobi, amenities that are not as available in rural areas (cf. Hanna and Hanna 1971:42-44). Yet while the above is true of greater Nairobi, the slum dwellers do not have most of these social amenities. Housing is worse in the slums of Nairobi than in most rural areas.

Sometimes new migrants prolong their visits and decide to settle in the city with the hope of upward social mobility and gaining status and power. As it turns out, the reality of city life dashes many of these hopes, and most of the new migrants end up in the slums (Mutunga 1989:31).

Physiographic factors

Kenya's physical geography also influences rural-urban migration. Only a few parts of the country have enough rainfall and good soil to sustain a large population. Faced with inadequate natural resources, many migrate to urban centers—especially Nairobi—to look for jobs.

Although many people would prefer to work on the farms instead of live in Nairobi slums, the physiographic factors force them into these unsanitary places. Almost all of the northeastern province of Kenya, for example, is semidesert and the inhabitants are now leaving nomadic life for formal schooling, producing an even larger influx into Nairobi.

Population factors

Over the years Kenya's runaway population has been reported as growing at 4.1 percent per annum[4]—the highest in the world. A study of the spatial dimensions of Nairobi's dwellers indicates a direct correlation between rural out-migration and the rate of population growth in a particular region. Alikhan writes that the

> High density of population appears as the critical push factor at district level, the largest number of migrants having come from among the most densely peopled districts. These districts have densities ranging from 151 to 220 persons per square kilometer (1987:167).

Alikhan is referring to the districts that are also agricultural zones. Due to overpopulation, available farmland has radically decreased. Robert Caputo observes,

> By tradition a farmer's land is divided among his sons when he dies. Since subdivision can only proceed so far before farming becomes uneconomical, many young men seek land or living elsewhere (1988:918).

The 1979 census put Kenya's urbanization rate at 15 percent. According to the 1989 provisional census report, however, the rate has risen to about 18 percent, with Nairobi holding the highest percentage (*Daily Nation* 1991:2).

Educational factors

Kenyan society is one of the most literate among the developing nations. Johnstone reports that at least 65 percent of Kenyans are literate (1987:265). With the growing scarcity of land, it is common to hear parents reminding

173

their children that the only "land" they can afford to give them today is education. Such a view shows a shift in values from *land* to *education*.

Christian missionaries and colonial rulers first introduced formal schooling to Kenya. When Kenya formally became a British protectorate, the government took over the development of the educational system.

The government was "primarily motivated by the need to provide education for the children of the settlers, but also to some extent, by the need for an educated African working class" (Bigsten 1984:52). The children of the latter were sent to school primarily to better serve the interests of the British bureaucracy and to serve as catechists. Further, the introduction of Western formal education led to a greater expectation of economic gain. As Kenneth Little puts it, "The Africans realized that there were more favorable opportunities of earning a living if one had an education; and to be educated improved a person's social standing" (1974:11).

Kenya's system of education prepares its graduates for clerical jobs, most of which are available in Nairobi and other towns. In recent years, however, the government introduced a new system of education (called "8-4-4") which—at least in theory—is more skill- and job-oriented than previous systems. In this system, a child spends eight years in primary school where most of the basic skills are taught. This is followed by four years in high school and four years in college. The government hopes that at whatever level a student graduates, he or she can at least earn a living. This hope, however, has yet to be fully realized. Meanwhile, school graduates continue to flock into the urban centers in great numbers (Downes 1989:13). Noted educator D. P. Ghai laments,

A large and increasing proportion of [rural-urban migrants] tend to be primary and secondary school leavers whose education has been irrelevant to life and problems in the rural areas and who consequently see little prospects of a productive and satisfying career in farming (1979:1).

From its inception, Kenyans equated formal education with white-collar jobs. Consequently, whenever anyone obtains a high school education they migrate to Nairobi in search of jobs. As Paul Thomson explains:

From childhood the country-dweller hears of the enticements of his nation's great metropolitan areas with their promise of comfort, convenience, and wealth. . . . If he could only wrest himself from the provincialism of family and community and move to the capital. There he would find his pot of gold (1984:47).

In the story with which I began, Moli is typical of the situation in Nairobi. He is a victim of a set of subsystems that can give no economic and social relief. What biblical insights may inform our response to a situation like Moli's?

REREADING THE SCRIPTURES

Moli's experience and the failure of his church to respond to his needs raise several key questions. Why did he expect his friends and relatives, his church, or the politico-economic system to provide for him? Is Moli simply using others to meet his selfish needs?

The traditional village lifestyle forms the basis for Moli's expectations. In this lifestyle, society operates interdependently and relatives and neighbors share what they have with each other. But Moli relies not only on his rich cultural heritage, he also sees the church as a legitimate community of support. Furthermore, with his academic qualifications, Moli feels prepared and qualified for a white-collar job. But Moli

175

does not achieve any of his expectations. There is something wrong with the system of forming new leaders for Kenya. And something is awry when the church also fails to respond.

Moli's plight forces us to read the Bible again and reflect on the presuppositions that are the basis for ministry philosophies of urban pastors in Nairobi and elsewhere. Is there a historical precedent for the response such as the one given to Moli, or was the RMC pastor an isolated case?

Our theologies have been dichotomous, urging the church to concern itself with spiritual things and leave social concerns to someone else. Some Nairobi churches have attempted to focus on people's felt needs. But often, most evangelical churches perceive such attempts as detours or at best secondary to the call to evangelize. While acknowledging the danger that the church could become a purely social agency, we cannot perceive of ministry in a context such as Nairobi's without also recognizing the social and economic plight of those who migrate to the city. This calls for a balance in our theologizing, particularly in urban mission. To do this, however, we must raise crucial biblical questions.

In thinking through this process, I read the book of Ruth again. After her husband and sons die, Naomi returns to her native Judah accompanied by her Moabite daughter-in-law, Ruth.

By going to Judah, Ruth leaves behind her familial, social, economic, and psychological support and risks rejection in starting a new life in a foreign land. By stating to Naomi "[I] will go back with you to your people" (1:10), Ruth demonstrates a strong commitment to Naomi's family ties. Like Moli in Nairobi, Naomi's hope for resettlement in Judah depended on a favorable response from her kinfolk, her people, and her faith community.

Naomi, Ruth, and Boaz

As the narrative progresses, the writer introduces Boaz, Naomi's wealthy relative, who provides the initial family and community for both women. Boaz bases his initial response purely on the "kinship" relations legislated by the larger community of Israel (the people of God), which ensured that even strangers would feel welcome in their midst. The Mosaic law provided for social, economic, psychological, and emotional needs (Lev. 19:9; 23:22; Deut. 24:19). Not that there was a dearth of poor people in Israel. Rather, God designed the law to meet the needs of the poor, because he knew that ". . . there will always be poor people in the land. . . ." (Deut. 15:11).

Naomi describes Boaz favorably, saying, "The Lord bless him! . . . That man is our close relative; he is one of our kinsman-redeemers" (2:20). Boaz's commitment to help the two widows is unquestionable. He goes beyond the call of duty in fulfilling his kinsman-redeemer role (2:14-16; 3:14-18).[5]

The law required that if a woman's husband died, the nearest relative would marry the widow. In Boaz's case, he was legally responsible for Naomi, but not necessarily for Ruth. But when Ruth came to glean from his field, Boaz allowed her to get more than the law required (2:15-23), not because he knew who she was, but because he was a relationship—oriented person. He cared for her, not because of what he could get from her, but because of what he could offer her.

Ruth's marriage proposal shows another important aspect of Boaz's response. In Ruth 3:12, Boaz maintains that he cannot legally marry her. In fact, as Morris maintains, "Boaz's primary relationship was Elimelech. He was therefore connected to Naomi only through Elimelech. It was through Elimelech's relationship that he could be called kinsman-redeemer" (1973:268). But Boaz agrees to Ruth's

177

suggestion after he learns that the next of kin cannot marry her. Even then, Boaz does not talk of marriage but of doing the part of a kinsman. Boaz goes beyond the minimal requirement of the law. God's love drives Boaz to do what is good.

Boaz is also conscious of his familial responsibilities. Although he is not next in line to marry Ruth, he takes the initiative to advise her on what to do. Most important, Boaz does not act on his own. He involves the entire community. In leadership terms, Boaz stands alone as a visionary: a wise, caring, networking, community-organizing, knowledgeable and loving leader.

In what ways can the church in Kenya identify "the Boazes" and develop them as church leaders? Are there lessons the church can learn regarding holistic responsibility to its members? Should the church play the kinsman-redeemer role when the next of kin do not have the means to provide for a needy Naomi or Ruth? Is the church responsible to work with "the Ruths" in a way that does not dehumanize them but gives hope and a new beginning? What could the Kenyan church learn from Boaz's wise treatment of a poor young widow? What kind of contextually appropriate leaders will the church in Nairobi need so it can deal effectively with the complex issues facing people like Moli?

NEW MISSION INSIGHTS

In reassessing the kinds of leaders urban churches need in Kenya, we should begin by reexamining our rich African cultural heritage. In the traditional African context, everyone fits in a given social setting based primarily on kinship relations. The Israelites seem to have operated similarly, as we can see in Boaz's life. Such acts of social responsibility are not foreign to traditional African societies. Kinship roles have always played a major part in meeting each family member's needs. Although Western influence and modernity have had negative effects on this cultural belief system, it is possible to recapture it. The belief that everybody is related to everybody else is still prevalent even in the cities. John Mbiti captures this thought well when he observes that

> The kinship system [in most African societies] is like a vast network stretching laterally (horizontally) in every direction to embrace everybody in any given local group. This means that each individual is a brother or a sister, a father or mother, grandmother, or grandfather, or cousin, or brother-in-law, uncle, or aunt, or something else to everybody. That means that everybody is related to everybody else (1969:104).

Until the introduction of "civilization," no one in any given society went without the basics. One tragedy of modernization is the focus on the nuclear family to the exclusion of the extended family. The dictum "I am because we are" is fast losing its impact, especially in the city. Unfortunately, the church has not assisted in recapturing this fast-fading tradition. To do culturally relevant ministry, the church in Nairobi must revisit some indigenous traditions and critically contextualize them to enhance the kingdom of God.

The church in Nairobi must also draw from our rich Kenyan traditions to see in them a new vision of what contextually appropriate urban church leadership would look like today. Whether Nairobi's church leaders develop in the West, the East, or in Africa, we must contextualize their training according to Kenyan needs.

For my purpose here, I will examine two Kenyan leadership metaphors and three related character traits. If we critically appraise these metaphors and character traits, we could use them for effective leadership development in Kenya's urban churches. The metaphors are those for courage and authority. The character traits are those of age, wisdom and relationships.

179

A metaphor is "a figure of speech in which a term is transferred from the object it ordinarily designates to an object it may designate only by implicit comparison or analogy" (The American Heritage Dictionary). In a general sense, the use of a metaphor "implies a way of thinking and a way of seeing that pervades how we understand our world" (Morgan 1986:12). It follows, therefore, that we use metaphors in an attempt to understand one experience in terms of another. For example, in Kenya someone may say, "Mutua is a lion," meaning Mutua is courageous. Or, someone may say, "Ogola is a rhinoceros," meaning he is fast.

Metaphors produce focused insight of the described aspect. In highlighting certain characteristics, metaphors force others into the background. In drawing attention to Mutua's courage, the "lion" metaphor may miss the fact that Mutua is also an "elephant," meaning he is a slow walker. Morgan summarizes well when he points out that "our ability to achieve a comprehensive reading of the man [or woman] depends on our ability to see how these different aspects of the person may coexist in a contemporary or even a paradoxical way" (1986:12).

In my doctoral research among the people of Nairobi, I discovered two major clusters of metaphors that the people of Nairobi use to describe an effective leader. There are metaphors for courage, and metaphors for authority.

Metaphors for courage

Several Kenyan metaphors have an underlying meaning of courage. For many ethnic groups, these metaphors arose out of a need to survive. The groups needed courageous leaders, so they metaphorically described and addressed them as such. The Akamba,[6] for example, had constant battles with the neighboring Akavi (Maasai) over cattle. The Maasai believed that all the cattle in the world belonged to them, so any cattle found in Ukambaland had somehow strayed there.

Only courageous men could be responsible for protecting or retrieving them.

The Luo refer to their warriors or brave leaders as *Thuon* or sometimes *Ondiek* (Kaduwa 1992). Such persons display bravery in executing their leadership role. A *Thuon* is also a gifted negotiator, having outstanding capabilities for such transactions as marriage, interclan negotiations, and land demarcations.

On the other hand, both the Kikuyu and Meru ethnic groups use the term *Njamba* in describing a courageous leader (Mungai 1992; Baabu 1992). Literally, the term means "a rooster." The focus is the aspect of fearlessness in making major decisions. The Meru, however, see another side to this term. *Nja* means home and for them a *Njamba* is one who protects and defends the home. He is the kind of leader who protects the clan or tribe against invaders.

This concept is gaining momentum in Nairobi's political circles today. There is a widespread cry for political pluralism and democracy, especially since the end of the Cold War and the changes taking place in Eastern Europe. The motto now is, "We need a *Njamba* to lead us in Kenya." What Kenyans are saying is that they need a courageous leader who is willing to break with tradition (a we-will-do-what-we've-always-done attitude), and move Kenya to the new global era of democracy.

The Akamba describe a courageous leader as *Nzamba* or *Iku*. Besides fearlessness, the latter term also refers to a fierce-looking person. Other terms are *Ngumbau* (warrior) and *Munyambu* (lion). When the Akamba describe a leader as *Munyambu*, they refer to someone who is lion-like in his or her manner of leadership. To the Akamba, the lion is fast and the most fearless animal. When they say someone is a *Munyambu*-like leader, they are referring to someone who is fearless and can represent their interests with strong conviction.

181

A courageous leader is also an excellent networker with the necessary charisma to inspire people to join in a common cause. Such leaders tend to attract followers because the latter know that the former's courage will carry them through no matter what the obstacle.

Metaphors for authority

Although Kenyans were traditionally very egalitarian in their world view, the seven decades of British domination left a lasting impact, giving Kenyans a hierarchical understanding of power and authority.

The Kamba, Kikuyu, and Meru ethnic groups refer to a person in a position of authority as *Munene* (Mutinda 1992; Baabu 1992; and Mungai 1992). These ethnic groups belong to the Bantu group and have many linguistic similarities. Unlike other Kenyan metaphors, *Munene* is a metaphor that describes an ascribed position. It means "one in authority," or the "Big One."

This concept implies positional power that enables a person to execute duties as leader. During the colonial era, Kenyans used the term primarily for the infamous "colonial chiefs," and it is still in use today (but is no longer a derogatory term). In contemporary Nairobi, Kenyans commonly use the term for church, civic, and political leadership positions.

Another term commonly used by the Akamba is *Kyongo*, while the Meru use *Kiogo* (Mukangu 1992). We can translate both as "the head." The underlying concept is "the one who has the final word on an important matter." A person can execute this form of leadership either at one's home or in a community setting. Other similar terms by the Akamba are *Mutwe* and *Ngomo*. The former literally means "head," the latter, "chisel." Here the underlying concepts are wisdom, power, and authority. No one can be called *Mutwe* unless he or she occupies a high position. A traditional

Kamba family would call the head of a household (usually a man) *Mutwe*.

When a wife faces a major decision, it is common among the Akamba, for example, to hear her say, *"Kweeteela niwe undu Mutwe unukwasya"* ("Let me first find what the head says about this"). Most traditional Africans expect such a response. Such an expectation, however, does not mean the head is dictatorial in his leadership. Instead, the roles are defined for mutual coexistence, both for the nuclear family and the entire community. Similarly, *Ngomo* is commonly used concerning power and authority. A *Ngomo* is important when it comes to making difficult decisions, because it means the leader is not only wise, but also possesses final authority.

The Luo, on the other hand, refer to the head leader as a *Jatelo* (Auma 1992). *Jatelo* is the leader who leads due to his authority, someone who comes first in any major decision-making. Subordinates hesitate to make major decisions without a *Jatelo* because he is likely to challenge other ideas through his positional power. This does not necessarily suggest arrogance. Instead, his authority is interwoven with great wisdom and he can, therefore, make wise decisions for the benefit of every member in the community. The followers are not skeptical about such a leader because they know he has their best interests in mind in whatever decision he makes.

Three character traits

Apart from the metaphors used for leaders, Kenyans look for other important traits in their leaders. Like metaphors, however, traits are not flawless. They do not describe an ideal leader or type of leadership. They only provide a partial—but necessary—bridge to contextual leadership, depending on the local need. An adequate analysis of leadership involves not only a study of the leader's character, but also that of the group and place of leadership execution. Bass notes that

> A person does not become a leader by virtue of the possession of some combination of traits, but all the pattern of personal characteristics of the leader must bear some relevant relationship to the characteristics, activities, and goals of the followers (1981:66).

While the traits are important, we must view them against the backdrop of the followers. The implication is that leaders who possess certain character traits must match the context that fits their traits. Here I will mention three character traits: relationships, age, and wisdom.

Relationships

Traditionally, the strongest bond of relationship in Africa was through kinship. Today, although modernity has influenced urbanites to form other social networks (such as subcultures, and associations based on interests), kinship ties still exist in cities. Among Africans, "I am because we are" is a common belief. Such ideals provide strong bonds of interdependence among peoples of similar regions residing in cities. "Everybody is related to everyone else" is a truism among various ethnic groups in the community. The relationship may be close or remote, but it is always there.

It is not enough, however, to maintain close relationships only with those of one's homogeneous ethnic group. In Nairobi, for example, the government encourages residents to be nationalistic in their thinking and execution of duties, even if they all come from different ethnic backgrounds. To instill this ideal, the government has encouraged the use of Swahili (although English is also widely spoken).

In terms of leadership development, the ability to relate with urbanites of different ethnic and racial groups has broad consequences for the church. A church's willingness and ability to minister effectively in intertribal and interra-

184

cial settings is the main litmus test for determining a church's effectiveness in the future.

Such endeavors require honesty. They call for leaders who think on a national scale and do not limit themselves to the parochial interests of their ethnic compatriots. While appreciating the sociological realities of kinship and common interests, leaders cannot allow such concerns to stand in the place of national cohesiveness. Only leaders who exemplify love and concern across social, political, and racial barriers can nurture a healthy church with a national outlook in the cities of Kenya.

Age

Traditionally, Kenyans have always associated leadership with age. The saying "Life begins at forty" is certainly true in Africa. Kenyans assume that as people get older, their experiences help them become mature leaders. In many Kenyan traditional societies, people perceive a man who can "rule" his family and who lives an exemplary moral life as a good leader. Because such a man was successful in little things, people could entrust him with more. With the exception of prophetesses, most of Kenya's leaders have been men. Although modernization and Christianity have influenced Kenyans in such areas as monogamy and the role of education in leadership selection and development, followers still view older leaders more favorably.

The Luhya employ the term *Nabong* (Adembe 1991) in describing the ideal leader. Literally, this term describes a person of age, someone who has become wise through time and experience. The Luhya believe that experience can help a person in making difficult decisions. A *Nabongo* must, however, live an exemplary life and show competence and ability by the way he governs his home. Furthermore, such a person must have good public relations. These, the Luhya emphasize, are qualities that come only with age and experience.

185

The Luo describe their leader as a *Jaduong* (Kaduwa 1992; Auma 1992). The Luo use this term for those who qualify as elders of the community, charged with arbitration and the reconciliation of disputes. A *Jaduong* can teach and instruct others because he has achieved that position through age and experience.

The Kikuyu employ the phrase *Ithe wa Andu* (Mungai 1992) to describe a leader who has achieved the position through age. Literally, it means "Father of the people." We can also extend this phrase to *Ithe wa Kirindi/Bururi* (Kamau 1992) to mean "Father of the nation." In contemporary Nairobi, Kenyans use this concept to describe the political president of the country. Kenyans use the term more often of the founding father of their nation, *Mzee* (emphasis on age) Jomo Kenyatta. No one can be called *Ithe wa Andu/Kirindi/Bururi* without achieving this status through age and experience (see also Muturi 1992).

Wisdom

Wisdom is related closely to age among most Kenyan ethnic groups. If Kenyans would emphasize one virtue over others, they would emphasize wisdom. Based on the views of the respondents to my research, most Kenyans would rather follow a young wise leader than an unwise old man.

There is a common saying among the Akamba: *"Mundu ndaekwa anange musyi nundu niwe mukuu"* ("One cannot be allowed to destroy or mislead the whole household just because he or she happens to be the oldest"). In this case, it is wisdom (not necessarily education) that many contemporary Nairobians look for when selecting a leader. This transition does not mean education is unimportant. During the 1992 civil and parliamentary elections in Kenya, voters from certain quarters displayed apathy towards uneducated aspirants. One candidate quipped: "Twenty-nine years after political independence we cannot afford to be led by an illiterate person" (Kaduwa 1992). The speaker was referring to

186

an aspiring parliamentary candidate who only had a high school education.

The Kikuyu describe a wise leader as a *Muthamaki* (Nduati 1992), which means "One who rules because he or she is wise." Such a leader is very charismatic. Whenever this leader faces a problem, he or she carefully listens to both sides before making a final decision.

Another common trait among the Kikuyus is *Muthure ni Ngai* (Mungai 1992). This type of leader is not only full of wisdom, but also one "who is chosen by God." Such an individual is visionary in his or her leadership, and has impeccable moral character, with great personality and eloquence. He or she is a well-rounded leader. Again, this comes with age and experience.

The Luhya use the term *Omwemeli* (Adembe 1991) in describing a wise leader. The emphasis is on "One who comes first due to their wisdom qualities." Again, wisdom has nothing to do with one's educational background. The Luhya also use *Omwemeli* for the leader whose character, age, and cultural familiarity serve as an example to the rest of the community.

The Akamba describe a wise leader as *Mutumia* or *Mundu mui*. This is one of the few terms on leadership that can apply to both single and married individuals. A person qualifies as a *Mutumia* through his or her exemplary conduct in morality, ethics, speech, and general character. On the other hand, when the Akamba describe a leader as a *Kimwana*, this derogatory categorization shows that such a leader is "youngish," not necessarily by age, but by character. It means a person's leadership lacks wisdom and nobody would want to listen to such a leader.

The Meru people employ the term *Mugambi* (Baabu 1992) for a wise leader. As in the Kikuyu *Muthamaki*, *Mugambi* is a leader who is an expert in asking probing questions in times of dispute. It is only after such a leader listens to both sides of a particular case that he or she will make the necessary decision. Among the Meru people today, *Mugambi* is a household name and it simply means "the wise one."

RETELLING THE STORY

In Nairobi, the church's ultimate goal and motivation for ministry must be to engage in tranformational ministry in the city. I use the term transformation to emphasize the fact that spiritual conversion must go hand in hand with socioeconomic, political, and relational change. It is my contention that even as the church meets Moli's felt needs, it should also address his spiritual needs simultaneously. Helping Moli secure shelter and a job are not enough; they are only part of the response. While the church should not use shelter as bait to lure Moli back to itself, a holistic transformational model would seek to address Moli's full humanity.

In Boaz's treatment of Ruth, what lessons can we learn about kinship roles, especially in societies where kinship relations still form the core of support networks? Should the church in Nairobi encourage its members to promote and follow up on natural ethnic associations of support, instead of rejecting them simply because of the involvement of non-believers? Does the Christian call not to conform to this world but to be transformed into God's likeness imply total withdrawal from kinship roles or any other association that believers do not initiate? If Christians should abstain from such, is the church providing alternate Christian networks where new urbanites such as Moli can find hope? Can the church in Nairobi learn lessons concerning its holistic responsibility to its members?

Furthermore, should the church intervene when a kinsman-redeemer does not have the means to provide for the present-day Naomis and Ruths, as was the case with Moli? Is it not the church's responsibility to work with people like

Moli in a way that does not dehumanize them but gives hope for a new beginning?

To suggest that Moli's expectations are unrealistic is to go against his world view. In most African societies, communities live very interdependently. The dictum "I am because we are" is more than a slogan. Nairobi's churches must operate with the knowledge that more people like Moli will continue to knock at their doors in the years to come. It would be unrealistic of me to suggest a simple way to handle the challenge. It does seem, however, that if Nairobi's churches are going to be relevant to their city, they must serve as *bridges* for those who are migrating from rural areas.

MISSION ACTION

It seems to me that a place to start is to define what mission is in the context of a city like Nairobi. I see mission in this context as the church's intentional role to welcome the strangers in its midst and work with them to provide the means for full spirituality and humanity. To realize this goal, I believe the church in Nairobi should engage in a twofold endeavor.

The church should strive to be the light and salt of the city. The church should develop a kinship role even though it has limitations. In African societies, kinship roles have always played a major role in meeting the needs of each member. The dictum "I am because we are" is fast losing its impact in the city. Unfortunately, the church has not been helpful in recapturing some good customs and traditions. Nairobi's churches have a unique opportunity to become a new kinship network for rural migrants to the city.

The church must also challenge the state's politico-economic structure, which perpetuates injustices in all areas of society so that bribery, tribalism, and nepotism are the order of the day. Going back to our Bible story, we notice that Boaz was not only faithful to the dictates of the law, he was also a

189

man of integrity (Ruth 4:1-7). Given the situation of people like Moli, I suggest that the church in Nairobi could take the following specific steps.

Understand the community's tradition

Church leadership must first seek to understand Moli. This means going beyond the casual greeting and seeking to understand his community and culture. Alinsky points out,

> The first stage in the building of a people's organization is the understanding of the life of a community, not only in terms of the individual's experiences, habits, values, and objectives but also from the point of view of the collective habits, experiences, customs, controls and values of the whole group—the community traditions (1969:76).

Such an approach would help the church minister in a culturally appropriate way. Many urban mission agencies in Nairobi have failed because "experts" addressed the needs as they saw them, not from the recipients' point of view. This led to paternalism, thereby crippling the projects when the expert had to leave. To avoid this mistake, the church must study the needs in each neighborhood, and learn what kinds of networks or associations exist that it can use without compromising the gospel to meet some of the needs. The church must seek to fully understand the people's needs so that it can do ministry concretely and relevantly, and with full local involvement.

Get involved in the community

The next natural step is to identify as much as possible with Moli's community. We can assume that as the church attempts to understand its members' cultures and traditions, it will also engage itself in identifying the key poles for organizing.

There are at least two important steps in community organizing. First, the church must seek to network not only with its members, but also with others in the area who may share common goals.

Boaz knew the power of networking. He knew that if he was going to meet Ruth's needs, he had to network with members of "City Hall" (Ruth 4:1-6). But, as Linthicum points out, if networking is built upon biblical foundations, "It will enable the urban church to reorder and prioritize its life and mission so that it will be able to join effectively with the poor and exploited in its city" (1991a:198). Such networking would include building intentional relational bridges between rural and urban churches.

The second step in effective community organization is the proper selection of leadership. A goal of community organization is helping the needy discover their power and using it to its fullest extent. This can only be done through their leaders.

By their leaders we mean those persons the local people define and look up to as leaders. Alinsky says that it is not easy to identify the real leaders and suggests that "It means participating in countless informal situations and being constantly alert to every word or gesture which both identifies and appraises the role of certain individuals within the community" (1969:72). In short, we cannot achieve community organizing and empowerment without forming the necessary networks and engaging the real leaders, the power brokers.

Identify the real needs

It is pointless for Nairobi's church leaders to join the bandwagon of politicians whose talk remains rhetorical and irrelevant to the needs of urbanites. In church-related ministries, the leader cannot go outside the people's experiences. If Moli's real need is shelter, the church should begin its ministry to Moli by addressing that particular need. In this case, the church could help Moli solve his own problem. Moli will not only solve the problem of his homelessness, but the exercise can lead him to build his own community and make him feel empowered.

Seek the community's transformation

I use the term "transformation" here to denote the need for spiritual transformation. It is my contention that even as the church meets Moli's felt needs, it should simultaneously address his spiritual needs. Helping Moli secure shelter is not an end in itself; it is only part of a larger response. What I am advocating is a holistic transformational model that affirms Moli's full humanity.

This suggests the need to overhaul leadership formation for urban pastors. In Moli's case, the pastor and leaders of the church in Nairobi were neither interested in nor prepared for responding to Moli in a holistically transformational and culturally appropriate way.

Leadership formation must reflect an understanding of, and appreciation for, the traditional Kenyan expectations of leaders. These include courage and authority, as well as age, wisdom and communal relationships. Pastoral candidates must be people of impeccable character both in their spiritual vitality and their social responsibility. They need to be creative enough to lead their churches to holistic and transformational ministries in the city.

Moli's story has no end. Instead, it remains as a question in our minds. The next time someone like Moli approaches the church in Nairobi or in any other city, will it turn him or her away? I hope the response will be different. "For I was hungry and you gave me something to eat . . ." (Matt. 25:35).

NOTES

1   See Stanley Downes, et al., in *Summary of the Nairobi Church Survey*.

2   Samuel Kobiah in *The Origins of Squatting and Community Organization in Nairobi* (1984) and Godfrey Muriuki argue that the ethnic groups involved in this trade were Maasai, Agikuyu, Kamba and Andorobo. In an earlier study (1974), Muriuki does not include the Andorobo as part of this lucrative trade. This difference of opinion, however, does not constitute any major discrepancy regarding the historical occurrence of the trade.

3   L. Squire (1981) in *Employment Policy in Developing Countries: A Survey of Issues and Evidence* summarizes data on rates of unemployment by level of education in ten developing countries. In eight cases, the rate is highest, frequently by a large margin, for those who have had a secondary education. Kenya, the only African country represented, shows a regular decline in unemployment as the level of education increases. This may reflect an educational system only beginning to adjust to the enormous influx of rural-urban migration since the 1970s. Unemployment is lower among those with a post-secondary education than among those with only a secondary education in every country.

4   There is no consensus on this figure. According to the United Nations estimates of 1982, the annual growth rate is reported at 4.1 percent. During the same period, however, Kenya's Bureau of Statistics put it at 3.8 percent. Meanwhile, the provisional report on Kenya's census taken in 1989 indicates that growth decreased to 3.4 percent. More recently, in an article carried in the July issue of *The Economist*, growth is recorded at 3.0 percent. This indicates that although population growth in general may not be as high as it was, say, four years ago, it is still an issue that the government cannot push to the periphery in any future strategic planning for the country, particularly as it relates to Nairobi.

5   The "kinsman-redeemer" was responsible for protecting
     the interests of needy members of the extended family,
     such as providing an heir for a brother who had died
     (Deut. 25:5-10), redeeming land that a poor relative had
     sold outside the family (Lev. 25:25-28), redeeming a rela-
     tive who had been sold into slavery (Lev. 25:47-49), and
     avenging the killing of a relative (in Num. 35:19-21,
     "avenger" and "kinsman-redeemer" are translations of the
     same Hebrew word).

6   The name *Akamba* is given to a Kenyan ethnic group that
     lives in the southeastern part of the country. They are also
     called *Kambas*, and the three districts that they reside in
     are called *Ukambani* or *Ukambaland*. A similar observation
     can be made about the *Kikuyu* ethnic group, occasionally
     referred to as *Agikuyu*.

9

Toward redefining urban poverty

Jayakumar Christian

THE STORY

ONCE PEOPLE called them skilled laborers. Now they are unskilled laborers who have to wait for someone to pick them up by the highway, so they can work for daily wages. New factories have taken over the agricultural land, their work place. The poor from Mogalliwakkam are no longer wanted in these factories. Their agricultural tools lie silent in a dark corner of their houses. The people of Mogalliwakkam themselves are now tools in the hands of the urban elite.

The Harijans of Mogalliwakkam[1] live in a semi-urban village on the outskirts of the city of Madras, away from the main road. It is a community of landless agricultural laborers, which is what they have been since time immemorial. "God

Jayakumar Christian was born and raised in India. He has worked at World Vision of India since 1978, where he serves as an associate director, and is involved in such issues as community development. Please see the contributing authors section.

had willed that we should be agricultural coolies and live on the income we get through our hard labor," explained the wife of Arumugam, a laborer of Mogalliwakkam.

It was always their land, although they did not own it.[2] It was their sacred work place. Over the years, however, the changes[3] Mogalliwakkam has undergone have shaken the very foundation of its community life.

The pain of transition

The Madras Metropolitan Development Authority wanted to relieve the congestion in nearby Madras. So they permitted the elite from Madras to buy the agricultural land in Mogalliwakkam for housing. "Now there is not much of an agricultural operation. . . . We do not produce rice paddy anymore; we are forced to buy rice from the market and it is expensive," explained Selvam, a community leader from Mogalliwakkam.[4]

Madras is taking over this small agricultural community. New factories have emerged that use skilled laborers. The factory owners bring the skilled laborers from other states. They no longer consider the landless laborers from Mogalliwakkam, once proficient in agricultural operations, as skilled workers. Mogalliwakkam's residents are not wanted in the new factories constructed on the land that was once their work place. Even when they get jobs in the factories, the factory owners pay these laborers low wages.

These former agricultural laborers now help skilled bricklayers. The city's encroachment is gradually alienating them from the land to which they "belonged." "Thus it is said that the poor flood to the nearest large city, pushed off their land by economic, political and social forces far bigger than themselves, and pulled to the city by its seductive allure" (Linthicum 1991b:9). In Mogalliwakkam, the city's "pushing," not its "pulling," is hurting the people. Mogalliwakkam is going through an extremely painful transition.

Mogalliwakkam is beginning to feel the ripples caused by the growth of the nearby city. The urban trap is sucking it in. Very soon people will know Mogalliwakkam as the "fringe" of a vast urban metropolis.

What will that mean for a quiet rural community like Mogalliwakkam? What is poverty in this context? How can we understand the pain that Arumugam and his family are going through as they become useless to the emerging urban economy? What clues emerge from Mogalliwakkam's experience that will enable us to understand the urban poor in our cities today? Who are the poor in this context?

Mogalliwakkam is a community in poverty. Very soon its citizens will join the millions who go by the name of "the urban poor."[5] We need new categories to describe Mogalliwakkam's pain and struggle as this urban giant, Madras, threatens it. Perhaps by inquiring into the pain of a poor community in transition such as Mogalliwakkam, we may identify some clues to describe why present-day urban communities are so fractured.

Looking at this challenge of urban poverty from the city's point of view, sociologists may call it "urbanization," or "the results of urbanization." They describe the kind of transition experienced by communities such as Mogalliwakkam as a shift in land ownership, changes in the economic base, changes in the employment profile, family profile changes, and so on.

But how does urbanization look from the losers' perspective? How do the victims of urbanization view urbanization? We need new categories to describe this mission context. Let us examine some possibilities.

READING THE CONTEXT

Urban poverty demands careful investigation. Traditional rural values do not help us, and simply adapting traditional rural values does no good. We need a new framework, one that involves a holistic view of urban poverty. By examining the various dimensions of a community that is fast becoming an urban poor community (like Mogalliwakkam), we can probably construct a new framework for defining "urban poverty."

Poverty is relational

Before examining some specific themes from our study of Mogalliwakkam, we must recognize the fundamental nature of all poverty. Poverty is relational. The network of relationships that affect poor communities form the roots of poverty's pain. The poor are powerless when it comes to the many relationships that seek to hold them permanently as captives. The very relationships that God ordained to help humans become like the triune God are instead a source of hurt for the poor and the oppressed.

Being made in God's image assumes that God shaped humans after his triunity image. God made humans to be persons-in-relationships, shaped by, and contributing toward, such relationships. However,

> ... too easily a system created by God to bring humanity into relationship with God, and through that relationship to create a politics of justice and nurturing of the "common wealth," becomes a system of economic exploitation and political oppression that uses the values of the community to control and oppress the people (Linthicum 1991a:17).

Figure 3 on page 199 seeks to bring together the "web of relationships" that hold the poor captive. It portrays the relational nature of the powerlessness of the poor. The poor are powerless about many aspects of their life. Some dimensions involved are the following:

◆ *Community memory*: The community's perception and shared memory of its history, including in its scope the

Figure 3: A profile of powerlessness

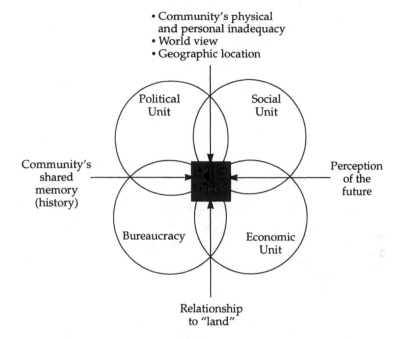

- Community's physical and personal inadequacy
- World view
- Geographic location

Political Unit

Social Unit

Community's shared memory (history)

Perception of the future

Bureaucracy

Economic Unit

Relationship to "land"

sociocultural, economic and political past. Very often, the powerful write or dictate the histories of the poor. This compels the poor to live with a marred version of their history.

◆ The *political, economic, social and bureaucratic units*: These units have both internal (internal to the community) and external dimensions. The individual poor feel powerless about their own community structures, and the community of the poor feels powerless about the external world.

◆ The *world view element*: This plays a more central and dominant role in perpetuating poverty. The world views of both the poor and the nonpoor tend to sanction and perpetuate poverty. In Indian communities,

199

the religious systems (within their world view) play a significant role and sanction some of the oppression that takes place in society. Included in this is the role of the principalities and powers, affecting the self-esteem, habits, and beliefs of the poor and the nonpoor.

◆ The *perception the poor have of their future*: This affects their present very strongly. It reinforces the distorted power relations in the community today. The poor bring a deeper sense of hopelessness from their view of the future.

This framework provides some handles for further probing the relational dimensions of urban poverty. The poor are powerless concerning various entities in society. Further, we see that the relational understanding of poverty enables us to go beyond the traditional spiritual, social, physical, and mental categories. Poverty is relational through and through.

Having set the stage for understanding urban poverty as a relational phenomenon, let us now examine three specific aspects of Mogalliwakkam's transition—a transition from a quiet self-contained rural community to becoming an urban poor community on the fringe of an urban giant.

From belonging to not belonging

In the past, people in Mogalliwakkam defined themselves by their land. Although the land did not belong to them, it was their sacred work place. They looked to the sky to bless the land with rain. They worshiped the gods of their agricultural tools once a year. Now the tools lie silent. The people do not look to the sky for blessing. Their industrial work tools are dead. They themselves are a tool in the giant urban economic mill.

Land for the poor in Mogalliwakkam meant more than an impersonal piece of property. It caused them to look to God for blessing, because they depended on the land for their survival. In many ways this piece of land shaped their identity. For the new owners of the land (the factory owners and the urban elite), however, it was merely a piece of space they could use.

We see an interesting parallel here in Naboth's encounter with Ahab in 1 Kings 21. Briefly reflecting on this encounter, we see again a clash of two different perceptions about land. For Naboth, land meant "the inheritance of my fathers" (21:3). For Ahab, land was a piece of property that he could put to good use—as a vegetable garden. "What is at stake in this confrontation [Naboth's encounter with Ahab] are two views of the land. For Ahab, land was a means of wealth, and as such a tradeable commodity" (Lilburne 1989:14).

For the poor in Mogalliwakkam, their land had a history. Although it did not belong to them, in profound ways they belonged to it. Their identity as skilled persons and the significance of their festivals came from the land's presence. Land was more than a piece of dirt that they could put to better use.

Reflecting on the role of the land in biblical history, Brueggemann comments that "[in the Bible] land is never simply physical dirt but is always physical dirt with social meanings derived from historical experience" (1977:2). For the poor in Mogalliwakkam, land was a reminder of their dependence on God. Biblical faith goes further to affirm that "the earth is the Lord's, and everything in it" (Ps. 24:1). Commenting on Israel's recognition of God's ownership of the land, Christopher Wright points out that "Israel, therefore, could make no 'natural' claim to any land. The only one they possessed they owed solely to God's election of and promise to Abraham . . ." (1983:51). For the poor in Mogalliwakkam, in many ways their work tools served as a reminder that all blessing comes from the gods. Each year they worshiped the gods of the work tools.

Today there is no land to which they can belong. There is no land to remind them to look God-ward. They wait along the highway looking for potential employers to pick them up for their day's work. They are now merely an extension of the urban economy. The poor have themselves become tools in the hands of the urban elite. What then shapes the identity of the urban poor?

The poor no longer belong to the land that once defined their being. Isn't the fracturing of urban society a result of the poor not belonging to the land? Aren't quarrels over "urban turf" really the cry of the poor and their need to belong? What is the alternative to land in the urban area? Can it be the neighborhood or the sociogeographical community that it represents?

Clues to understanding the pain of urban poverty

Considering the implications of this shift "from land to no land," from "belonging to not belonging," we see some key clues to understanding the pain of urban poverty. First, *poverty is a marring of identity*. The poor have no land to belong to that they can use to define their being. The city provides no alternative. The urban poor are in many ways "urban orphans." The key determining factor is their usefulness to the urban agenda. If they are useful to the urban economy (economically productive), then they have value. Consequently, the impersonal economic-political order shapes their identity.

For the poor in Mogalliwakkam, the land was their sacred work place. "The land is holy . . . The Hindu religion is the religion of the land. . . . This view of the land as the holy land may go back to the earliest period of the Aryans in India" (E. Shaw 1986:38). The city offers very few alternatives for the emerging urban poor to turn God-ward. Instead, the "god-complexes" constructed by the urban economic agenda hold the poor captive. *Poverty is the result of the many (the poor) becoming the captives of the god-complexes of the few (the nonpoor)*. Moltmann defines this god-complex as "where people and powers make gods of themselves" (1982:4). Isn't urban poverty, then, about these god-complexes that exploit the poor? Isn't the urban economy a "tower of Babel" humans are building in their effort to become gods? Is urban poverty, then, a result of the lack of God-directedness in the city?

Closely related to the aspect of the land is the "silence of the work tools." They seem to speak of the deeper transition that is happening in Mogalliwakkam. Urban poverty is a result of the poor becoming tools in the hands of the urban elite. Until recently, Mogalliwakkam's agricultural laborers were classified as skilled workers. Today they are suddenly unskilled. The factories that sit on the sacred work place of the poor do not need them anymore. These shifts show that this process of becoming the urban poor is essentially a shift from being a person to becoming a non-person, from being skilled to becoming useless. Thus, *poverty means persons become nonpersons*.

Enlarging the scope of our inquiry here, we see that poverty is essentially an attempt by the nonpoor and the structures to make a person that God created from the dust of the ground (Gen. 2:7) into dust again. Is not urban poverty, then, a struggle of this "personhood" within the poor, crying out that they are not dust? Is it a struggle to remain a person?

To sum up, Mogalliwakkam's shift away from the land is a push toward a painful marring of identity, of becoming captives of other human's god-complexes, and turning into non-persons. These pictures can help us more clearly redefine or reenvision urban poverty.

From community to non-community

Mogalliwakkam, once a self-sufficient community, is on a disturbing journey. Selvam, the Mogalliwakkam community leader I quoted earlier, explained: "You see, we are a community—for good or bad we need each other. How can we continue our rivalry?"

In further explaining the changes in the community, Selvam pointed out how the factory owners perpetuate dependency among the poor. He said, "Employees are encouraged to start a union on some political basis. Gradually the employer buys the loyalty of the union leader and the other employees are forgotten . . . and they [the employees] become completely submissive."

Today, the Mogalliwakkam community is being divided from the outside. The resulting *poverty is a community becoming a "noncommunity."* The poor in this small agricultural community are finding themselves isolated from each other. The politicians and employers buy their loyalties. Is a community's drift toward becoming a noncommunity a reason for "the urban problem"? Is the fracturing of the city really the fragmentation of a people who were meant to be a community?

Becoming a noncommunity has a socioeconomic cost as well. We can see a recent example of this in Dharavi slum in Bombay. Dharavi is Asia's largest slum. With a population of six lakhs (600,000), it forms a rich ethnic mosaic with a daily economic turnover of Rs. 75 lakhs ($250,000).

Recent religious tensions, however, have divided the community. For Dharavi, the cost of becoming a noncommunity was the loss of lives, the destruction of small manufacturing and trading units, and a clear halving of its business activities and daily economic turnover (Rahman 1993). Urban poverty, with all its socioeconomic and political expressions, is the result of the community of the poor becoming fragmented into a noncommunity.

There is another interesting dimension to this understanding of poverty. Not only is the bonding among the poor under strain, but the factory owners in the area are also gradually excluding the poor in Mogalliwakkam. They consider the poor from Mogalliwakkam as unskilled workers. Even their former landlords do not need them anymore, because these landlords sold all the land for housing construction.

Nehemiah's encounter with the nobles provides an interesting parallel. One of the many crises Nehemiah confronted was an internal crisis (Neh. 5:1-13) among the Jews who were involved in rebuilding the wall of Jerusalem. There was an outcry (the word used is *hara*: "burn with anger") against exploitation by the nobles. These nobles were exacting interest in a time of dire need. As a result, the poor had to mortgage their land, go into debt, and subject their sons and daughters to slavery (5:3-5).

This exploitation by the nobles, however, was essentially a result of a long-term drifting away from the rest of the population. Earlier, the nobles were unwilling to work alongside the others (3:5). They violated the Sabbath for economic reasons (13:17). In this context, the exploitation of the poor does not come as a surprise. It is a result of the nobles excluding the poor from their community. *Poverty, then, is the exclusion of the poor by the nonpoor.*

From productivity to powerlessness

The poor in Mogalliwakkam started life at a disadvantage. They were from a lower caste and they were poor. But at least they were agriculturally skilled and productive. They had a special kind of dignity. Now, with the pressure from the growing city nearby, the pain of powerlessness becomes acute. There is a clear shift in the power base. The poor within the Mogalliwakkam community are experiencing the pain of increasing powerlessness.

Mogalliwakkam, which was once self-contained, is waking up to a state of dependence. The city market now

decides the price of rice, which the residents of Mogalliwakkam once produced themselves. The skilled agricultural
laborer is now an unskilled laborer who earns low wages.
The sacred work place is now "out of bounds" for Arumugam and his wife. Powerlessness best describes the experience of the community. *Poverty is powerlessness.*

Powerlessness for the poor is relational. Mogalliwakkam's residents are beginning to realize that they are
fast becoming spectators in the urban game. "We do not
have the financial capability to command respect. If we go in
a car or on a motor bike to see these leaders in their offices,
they will respect us. Instead we must go by bus and then
walk," explains Rajasekar, a Mogalliwakkam community
leader.

Society defines the rules for living in a particular way,
causing the further disempowerment of the poor. The nonpoor and their power structures define the systems in ways
that tend to exclude the poor. In Mogalliwakkam, the house
owners, the Madras Metropolitan Development Authority,
and the factory owners devise the new rules. This leads to
the continuous exclusion of the poor in Mogalliwakkam.
"Once the interpreters of law make the practice of the law
designed to protect the poor, bearable for themselves, the
poor lose the protection of the law" (Sugden 1981:30). It is a
question of meaning, the meaning ascribed by the nonpoor
to the realities that shape and bind the lives of the poor. Further, the deceit that the principalities and powers foster also
causes the poor to believe that God ordained their powerlessness. Increasing hopelessness results. *Powerlessness, then,
is the distortion of truth influencing the realities that surround the
poor.*

While I was in Mogalliwakkam, I frequently heard the
phrase, "What can we do? After all, we are poor." This
almost sounded like a creed that the rest of the world had
made the poor believe in. If poverty is powerlessness, then

the urban poor are captives in a system of distorted truths designed to cause them to believe in their poverty.

The Mogalliwakkam experience provides us with some interesting insights for a further analysis of urban poverty. We now see a new set of categories for understanding urban poverty. These new categories help describe the urban poor and identify some roots of the urban problem. Figure 4 below summarizes the categories that have emerged from the Mogalliwakkam story.

Figure 4: Profile of urban powerlessness in Mogalliwakkam

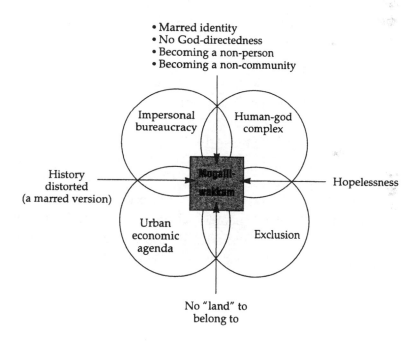

Some clues that emerged from this dialog with Mogal-liwakkam are:

1. Urban poverty is relational; it is the result of hurting and exploitative relationships.

2. Poverty in the cities undermines the poor's identity. In the urban poor's case, there is no alternative to the land that can give them a sense of belonging and help to shape their identity.

3. Poverty is caused when the poor are held captives within the god-complexes of the non-poor.

4. Poverty involves a person, made in the image of God, being reduced to a nonperson.

5. Poverty is the community of the poor being reduced to a noncommunity.

6. Poverty is the poor being intentionally excluded from the "community."

7. Poverty is powerlessness caused by the distortion of the truth, and it is deceit perpetuated by the nonpoor, the structures, and the principalities and powers. Poverty is about meanings ascribed to the realities that influence the lives of the poor.

How should the church respond to a community of poor that is being urbanized, becoming tomorrow's "urban problem"? How should the church respond to the poor who are already urbanized, people whose dreams and shared memories have been shattered in the process? *What will urban mission look like among the powerless poor?*

MISSION ACTION

Jürgen Moltmann rightly points out that theology is ". . . never concerned with the actual existence of God. It is interested solely in the rule of this God in heaven and earth" (1981:191).[7] Johannes Verkuyl continues in this vein by saying that "the kingdom of God has become the hub around which all of mission revolves" (1979:175).

It is very appropriate to probe the many expressions of God's rule to find some clues for a missional response to the urban poor. For God's kingdom does not merely have implications for the poor and the powerless; it is about the poor and the powerless.

> His Kingdom, His power and His glory are already in the midst of this world, in the midst of us. This means liberating judgment on the rich, the violent and the oppressor. This means gracious liberation to the poor, the weak and the downtrodden (Moltmann 1982:8, emphasis added).

There are several foundational themes in the expressions of God's rule that can shape the church's missional response. I will discuss some of these below.

The kingdom is relational

First, the kingdom is relational. Therefore, mission is about rebuilding relationships. A kingdom-based missiology offers a healing alternative to a community whose relationships have become a source of hurt. God's kingdom seeks to build new relationships. This entails most profoundly a new relationship with the One to whom the kingdom belongs. "God's redemptive action among men has the end of bringing them into a new and more intimate relationship with Himself" (Ladd 1974:184).

The God of this kingdom is a king who invites and seeks a response from his people.[8] Searching for a theology of holistic mission, William Dyrness suggests that the kingdom of God seeks an intimacy between God and his people (1983:132). We see, then, that an intimate experience of relationship between the king and his people forms the core of the kingdom. Can the powerless poor that the rest of society excludes have an intimate relationship with the king? For the urban poor, whose various relationships hurt and exploit, the possibility of an intimate relationship with Christ the King is surely a healing alternative.

Further, the kingdom offers "restoration of man's and woman's relationship to each other and even with nature" as the righteousness that we await (2 Pet. 3:13; Verkuyl 1979:168). The kingdom, then, is relational, and the most appropriate and wholesome cure for a fractured society.

Jesus' encounter at Jacob's well with the woman from Sychar is an excellent case in point of the ripples of transformed relationships. In John's narrative we see two distinct descriptions of the woman. First, she was a Samaritan (John 4:7); second, people knew her as a woman with five husbands (John 4:17-18).

Both these identities reveal a person with hurting relationships. The first description had to do with the deep-seated and historical hurting relationship between the Samaritans and the Jews (4:9). The other description meant a state of deprivation that made her believe she had no husband (4:17). She was not lying. That was probably how she understood her primary identity as a woman who had five husbands yet had no husband with whom she could identify.

Jesus' encounter at the well was more than just a time for "personal evangelism." It was a time for healing hurting relationships. In John 4:39, she gives a one sentence testimony: "He told me everything I ever did." It's an expression of gratefulness for the healing and for transformed relationships. When the King and his kingdom enter the reality of the hurting poor, transformed relationships flow out like ripples in a stream.

The kingdom is divine activity

The second foundational theme affirms that the kingdom is divine activity. Let us go back to the narrative of the

210

encounter between Naboth and Ahab. As discussed earlier, the encounter reflected a clear clash of different perceptions of the land. As expected, King Ahab had his way (1 Kings 21:15). Naboth lost his life. King Ahab probably initiated a government-sponsored hybrid vegetable garden on Naboth's land. What is interesting here is how Jezebel and Elijah read the encounter differently. For Jezebel, the encounter between Naboth and Ahab was an issue of prestige, political legitimacy, and a small legal exercise (21:7-15). But for the prophet of God, the encounter was over a piece of dirt with sociohistorical meaning, an issue in which the Lord was interested (21:17-19). Down through history, the single most important theme that dominated the prophets' messages was that God is interested enough to be involved.

The life and ministry of Jesus Christ strongly affirm that the kingdom of God is divine activity. It is not merely a product of human ingenuity. It is the theocentric and dynamic rule of God (Ladd 1974:46). It is a rule for which all other rules will come to a standstill; it is not simply a rule alongside that of other rulers (Henry 1992:41).

Discussing the suggestion that the kingdom of God is essentially an expression of the promise of God, Moltmann points out that the guarantee of the fulfillment lies in the "credibility and the faithfulness of him who gives it" (1967:119). The kingdom empowers the powerless exactly at this point of departure from all other power structures. It is not what the kingdom of God can do for the poor that matters, but what *the kingdom is*. It is not a human kingdom or in any way helplessly dependent on a person.[9] Because it is a theocentric kingdom, it serves as the fulcrum for destroying the god-complexes constructed by men and women.

For the urban poor and the community at Mogalliwakkam, the kingdom of God is more than just a hope. It is the breaking of the vicious cycle of poverty. It is the opening of the prison doors in the god-complexes of the nonpoor and .

211

their structures. Responding to poverty, then, is essentially an encounter between Jezebel's way of ensuring political clout and the kingdom's way of allowing the full realization of God's involvement in history. It is an encounter between the god-complexes constructed by humans and the kingdom of God.

The kingdom rebuilds a community of the free

The third foundational theme affirms that the kingdom seeks to rebuild a community of the free. In the narrative in Nehemiah 5, the nobles who had drifted away from the rest of the community—and in the process excluded the poor—precipitated the crisis among the Jews.

Nehemiah's response as a sensitive and wise leader was to restore community accountability (5:7-8). It required a reversal of roles. Nehemiah called for an assembly of common people to sit in judgment over the nobles. He called on the commoners to judge the powerful. More than just a reordering of relationships, by this action Nehemiah redefined the very nature of accountability—specifically, an accountability in relationships with and within the community.

The scope of the redemptive presence of God's kingdom among the urban poor includes the "redemption of the entire [person]" (Ladd 1974:183). Sugden, explaining the scope of the kingdom's redemptive presence, mentions that

> It [the kingdom of God] found expression in liberated relationships which challenged the distorted personal, social, economic and religious relationships that express rebellion against God. God's Kingdom is His ongoing invasion of liberation (1981:23).

The kingdom seeks to rebuild a community of the free. Metropolitan Geevarghese Mar Osthathios states this emphatically when he mentions that ". . . the Kingdom is the community," with a caution that the community is not the kingdom of God (1982:1). Moltmann argues that a trinitarian hermeneutic enables us to think more naturally of the kingdom in terms of relationships and community (1981:19). It also enables a more communal, instead of individualistic, understanding of freedom.

The kingdom redefines power

The final foundational theme states that the kingdom redefines power. In our analysis of urban poverty we saw that poverty is powerlessness. More specifically, we see that the substance of powerlessness is deeply ingrained in the meanings ascribed to realities. The kingdom does not just reorder the power equation. It is more radical than that. The kingdom redefines the very nature of power itself.

In its response to the urban poor and, specifically, to their powerlessness, God calls the church to "raise the question of meaning" (Moltmann 1967:324). The task of raising the question of meaning is essentially the task of challenging the particular interpretation of the world's rules and regulations. Jesus challenged the criteria for inclusion and exclusion used by the people of his time. "Jesus angered the religious leaders by not only ignoring these barriers but by making His association with 'sinners' a religious issue" (Ladd 1974:175).[10]

We see a battle of meanings in the Lukan narrative of the lawyer's encounter with Jesus (Luke 10:25-37). There are several shifts that Luke records in this brief narrative. First, the lawyer begins his dialog with Jesus by wanting to justify himself. Jesus responds by raising the question of meaning—he presents the case of a Samaritan who got involved as a response to a need, not with the intent of self-justification. Jesus' use of a Samaritan as a model is important. Finally, note how Jesus rephrases the lawyer's question (Luke 10:29, 36). For Jesus, the question of meaning was an integral part of the kingdom's mission.

213

Yet Jesus went further. He challenged the existing leadership by raising the question of meaning. As recorded in the Gospel of Luke, a review of the responses of the leaders in Jesus' time reveals that they were uncomfortable with Jesus. They complained (5:21), questioned (6:2), were furious (6:11), rejected God's purposes (7:30), ridiculed (7:39), were perplexed (9:7), were surprised and insulted (11:45), opposed fiercely (11:53), became indignant (13:14), remained silent (14:4), muttered (15:2), sneered (16:14), were saddened (18:23), sought to rebuke (19:39), tried to kill (19:47), were afraid (22:2), and mocked and beat Jesus (22:63).

On his part, Jesus created dissonance; he raised the question of meaning. Tannehill points out that there were two types of tensions: those initiated by the Pharisees and scribes through their questioning and testing, and those initiated by Jesus through his corrections of their statements and behavior (1969:170).

Jesus was intentional in creating dissonance and conflict. Conflict in Jesus' ministry was not an unintended result. It was an essential part of his mission. Jesus chose the example of a Samaritan for the lawyer, timed his miracle on a Sabbath, dined with sinners, sought after a despised tax collector who had climbed a tree—all these challenged the meanings ascribed by the rulers of the day.

All of this resulted, finally, in the cross. "The crucified God is in fact a stateless and classless God. But that does not mean that he is an unpolitical God. He is the God of the poor, the oppressed and the humiliated" (Moltmann 1974:329). Elliot suggests that a prayer ". . . for the Kingdom is a political statement" (1985:146). Missional response to the powerlessness of the urban poor involves an intentional raising of the question of meaning to redefine the rules of the urban game.

In summary, this inquiry into the redefined presence of the kingdom provides us with some key insights for defining mission and developing a missional response. To begin with, it is absolutely necessary to affirm that when we consider missional response we are not talking only about missional action, as if some effective programming is adequate. For the urban poor whose relationships are hurting, mere programs do not make sense. The poor need an alternative relationship. The kingdom is relational. Therefore, we need to redefine mission response as missional relationships and action, or, more appropriately, as missional being.

How do we demonstrate kingdom-based mission?

Our reading of the kingdom themes specifically suggests that within the relational response, we can demonstrate kingdom—based mission among the urban poor in the following ways:

- ◆ Healing of hurting and exploitative relationships, involving an intimate relationship with the king of the kingdom and a transforming of all other relationships;

- ◆ Allowing the kingdom of God to confront the god-complexes at all levels and to release the captive urban poor;

- ◆ Announcing God's involvement in the issues that concern the urban poor;

- ◆ Rebuilding a community of the free and proclaiming inclusion where there is the hurt of the urban poor's exclusion;

- ◆ Raising the question of meaning to redefine power itself as a response to the powerlessness of the urban poor.

Mission among the urban poor means enabling the poor to pray with conviction, "Thy kingdom come. Thy will be done in earth, as it is in heaven. . . . For thine is the kingdom . . . and the glory . . . (Matt. 6:10, 13, KJV)"

Below are some factors to consider as the local church renews itself to be the kingdom's sign among the urban poor.

1. For the local church, it will mean a time of renewal—a time to clarify its own identity and relationships in light of the issues and relationships with which the urban poor are struggling. For example, what is the church's relationship to the urban economic agenda, or the god-complexes of the rich? What meanings does the church attach to the realities that shape the lives of the poor, in terms of the political powers and other issues?

2. The church must be relational, as opposed to being merely activist. The church needs to provide and demonstrate the richness of the alternative healing relationship available in God's kingdom. The church must intentionally create ripples of transformed relationships among the poor and the nonpoor.

3. The church must become the prophetic voice among the poor, raising the question of meaning. It must be a prophetic voice for the voiceless urban poor, and the yeast that transforms the inadequate relationships and distorted truths among the poor.

4. The church must be a community to which the excluded poor can belong, a community that will shape the poor's identity. The church must also create communities among the poor.

5. The church needs to rediscover the potential of prayer and fasting as a tool for social action, even as it confronts the god-complexes of the urban economy and political systems, and challenges the deceit that the principalities and powers perpetuate to keep the urban poor in their poverty.

The local church among the urban poor must rediscover that it is part of the Father's response to the prayer of the urban poor:

*"Our Father which art in heaven, Hallowed be thy Name. . . .
Thy kingdom come. Thy will be done in earth, as it is in
heaven. . . . For thine is the kingdom, and the power, and the
glory . . ." (Matt. 6:9-10, 13, KJV)*

NOTES

1   Mogalliwakkam is a village located 12.5 miles from the
city of Madras, the fourth largest urban metropolis in
India. As in most of India's rural areas, the lower castes
are tucked away from the main road. The Mogalliwakkam
colony, as it is commonly known, is a community of Harijans. About 12 percent of them are Christians, and the rest
are Hindus. The village has one temple each for Mari-
amman and Venkatesaperumal (Indian deities). There is a
Church of South India within the village, and an Evangelical Church of India outside the community.

Mogalliwakkam has 400 families. Traditionally, this village
was an agriculture-based community. The people were
predominantly landless laborers. The agricultural laborers
earned Rs 15-20 per day (50-60 cents). The higher caste
Mudaliars live in the village next to Mogalliwakkam
colony. Mogalliwakkam has a government school
attended by 600 children. The nearest high school is three
miles away, attended by only 25-30 children, while only 12
children make it to the college located in Madras.

2   The higher caste Mudaliars owned most of the agricultural land in the area. There were some small farmers in
Mogalliwakkam. The houses in Mogalliwakkam, however,
were on land that was legally assigned to them. It was the
Harijans' "home" in many ways. Although they did not
own the agricultural land on which they worked, they
"belonged" to it.

3   With the sale of agricultural land for housing construction
at very high prices, the village's economic base and the
employment profile underwent several changes. The landless do not have a say in the sale of their land, although

their livelihood is at stake. New factories were constructed on the land that once was the workplace of the landless. There is a demand for skilled labor, but the former landless agricultural laborers are categorized as unskilled labor and paid low wages.

4 The interviews and the data on Mogalliwakkam community were gathered during a visit in July 1992.

5 "The most demanding of the urban challenges, unquestionably, is the challenge posed by urban poverty: the challenge of reducing exploitation, relieving misery and creating more humane conditions for working, living and development for those disadvantaged people who have made the city their home already or are in the process of doing so" (Shah 1990:68). Shah is a member of the National Commission on Urbanization in India.

6 This figure describes my present understanding of powerlessness. It is very tentative. My larger study on the "Powerlessness of the rural poor in India" seeks to deal with this question in more detail. Friedmann's model of powerlessness (in *Empowerment: The Politics of Alternate Development*, Cambridge, Massachusetts: Blackwell, 1992), was a useful resource for this purpose.

7 The review of the scholarship related to the study of the kingdom of God has generally included in its scope the contributions of Johannes Weiss in 1892 (*Jesus' Proclamation of the Kingdom of God*, 1971); Albert Schweitzer (*Quest for the Historical Jesus*, 1922), of the "consistent eschatology school"; Rudolph Bultmann, who attempted to bridge the gap between the New Testament and subsequent generations; C. H. Dodd, who presented the "realized eschatology" (*The Parables of the Kingdom*, 1935); Kummel and G. E. Ladd, with their contributions regarding the "already and not yet" explanations of the kingdom of God (Kummel in *Promise and Fulfillment*, 1957, and Ladd in *The Presence of the Future*, 1974); Norman Perrin (*Jesus and the Language of the Kingdom*, 1976) and Amos Wilder (*The Language of the Gospel*, 1964)—Perrin and Wilder's contributions mainly used the perspective of language and symbols in the study of the kingdom of God (Willis 1987:53-54); Hermann Rid-

derbos (*The Coming of the Kingdom*, 1962); Arthur F. Glasser (*Kingdom and Mission*, 1992); and David Bosch (*Transforming Mission*, 1991, pp. 15-180).

8   Sugden, commenting on the two aspects of the relationships in the kingdom, shows that Jesus as the head of the redeemed community summons his people to submit to God's rule and be renewed in their national life. The focus of the renewed group is obedience to Jesus and living out the transformed relationships of the kingdom (1981:27).

9   " . . . it is the Kingdom of God, the Kingdom of Heaven, the Kingdom that Messiah brings down. It is not a program for human rescue shaped by humanity's religious consciousness. It is, rather, one inaugurated and consummated by a King who has nail prints in his hands and who rules his subjects from a higher world" (Henry 1992:49).

10 Ladd, however, commenting on the parable of the tares, points out that the " . . . Kingdom has come into history but in such a way that society is not *disrupted*. The sons of the Kingdom have received God's reign and entered into its blessing" (1974:234, emphasis added). It is not clear how Ladd would reconcile the "non-disruptive" entry of the kingdom with Jesus' angering society's leaders.

10

A common ministry, a communal vocation

Christine Accornero

Few, if any, forces in human affairs are as powerful as shared vision. A shared vision is the first step in allowing people who mistrust each other to begin to work together. It creates a common identity. In fact, an organization's shared sense of purpose, vision, and operating values establish the most basic level of commonality (Peter Senge 1990:206).

THE STORY

SHE WALKED through the door with a mixture of hesitation and enthusiasm. It was the first day of her new job, a new day to start her long-awaited ministry, after so many years of hoping for a place just to be herself. And the Lord had

Christine Accornero was with PUMA (Presbyterians United for Missions Advance) and served as Fuller Theological Seminary's director of human resources. She is now working on her doctoral research. Please see the contributing authors section.

moved so quickly that she could not remember all the circumstances that got her here.

Her past jobs had been with secular companies, and the opportunities for professional advancement had always come with the high price of compromise. She was finally ready to be in a Christian organization, where she could fully use her gifts to further God's kingdom.

She had prayed for so long for that special place where she could be a "people-focused manager" and not just a "project manager." She had refined her skills in team-building through the fire of many trials, difficult circumstances, and situations. These situations had deepened her understanding of people's complexities, and the need to have God's love and grace as the foundation for building effective teams. She was ready to use what the Lord had taught her. Full of hope, she walked through the door and began her new job.

Tales of pain and anger from colleagues

Week after week they came to her door, these people who were now her colleagues in ministry—but they were not what she expected. They came testing the open door with its sign, "All Are Welcome." But they came with bitterness, pain, anger, frustration, and a readiness to defend themselves if necessary.

She had announced at the first staff meeting that she would always leave her door open, that she would put aside projects to listen to the voices of the organization. As the months passed, she was overwhelmed by the numbers that came. She saw deep hurt and pain reflected in their faces, in their eyes. Could they trust her? Would she be just another manager who seemed to care, but in reality had another agenda?

The questions came from hearts filled with too many years of pain. Where did all of this pain come from? Did they bring their personal pain and anger to this Christian place, hoping to find an oasis and healing? It could not be something within the organization that was causing such deep hurt—or could it?

Maybe it was the city—the traffic, the noise, the concrete, the harshness and impersonal nature of a place where too many people lived. After all, she really did not want to move into this urban center and the severe life she knew would be waiting for her. But God had called her to this Christian community, so the problems were not in this place! In this organization, the employees met together for prayer and Bible study—they knew each other's families. Why, then, was there so much pain in her colleagues' eyes?

Through the newly opened lines of communication, they began to tell their stories. At first the stories seemed simple and had issues she dealt with easily. She encouraged her colleagues to communicate more freely with each other and with the other managers.

As the months went on, however, she noticed that the stories kept getting more complicated. The issues were deeper and more painful. The stories spoke of abuse, of deceit, of harassment, of anger. The tears began to flow. The pain surfaced in memos, employees took more sick days, the quality of work decreased, and there was a general decline in the organization's morale.

Where did all of this come from? Wasn't this a Christ-centered organization? Didn't they have a statement of faith, a mission statement, a code of ethics, a policy against harassment? Her tears began to flow too. She became angry. She was angry at God for bringing her to a place that had Christ's name, but not his nature. She was angry at the organization's leaders, who seemed to care more about the mission projects than about the people who had to implement the projects. She was angry because she allowed herself to get angry. Where did that anger come from? She had not brought it with her, had she? She thought back to the joy and excitement that had brought her to this place. Where did that joy go?

As the months passed, she began to see patterns. What she thought were departmental divisions were really people divisions. Managers competed with other managers. They asked the members of their staff—sometimes directly, but mostly through modeling a competitive spirit—to be territorial and protective.

The monthly employee meetings turned into gripe sessions, with fighting and verbal abuse as the rule instead of the exception. Communication channels began closing. People were hurting each other. A general sense of mistrust seemed to be taking the whole organization to the brink of losing sight of its original purpose and mission.

A ministry at the point of inner destruction

She found herself wondering what had happened over the years to bring this vital ministry to a point of inner destruction. The organization's original mission was to reach this sprawling urban center for Christ. People came from around the world to visit and learn from this great ministry that was in the vanguard of evangelism and church planting in the city.

The organization was growing, management was creating more staff positions, their leaders traveled around the world as consultants. They were getting the job done. So why were they disillusioned when they came to her office, with so much pain on their faces? Where was the cancer? Where was the leaven poisoning the internal structures?

This story is a common one told often in organizations around the world. It is a generic story fitting any context or culture, because it describes human weaknesses, misunderstandings, miscommunications, and fears that we can find in the culture of any organization.

Yet too often it also reflects the internal atmosphere found even in communities that claim the name of Christ. Many Christian groups find themselves in situations where internal dynamics are in direct conflict with mission goals. Mission agencies that function in large urban centers have the added task of dealing with very diverse populations, both internally and externally. The community's core identity gets tested on every side.

READING THE CONTEXT

Simply put, the above story is about a person searching for her place of ministry. More broadly, however, it is also the story of a missional institution and its corporate culture. For many years, Christians have talked at length about mission agencies, mission organizations, and mission programs that were designed and structured to take the gospel message around the world. We focused our attention on the projects, the people groups, and the unreached of the world, extending our efforts to reach the world for Christ.

It is my opinion, however, that we have neglected the individual called by God to minister within the context of our mission organizations. If we want to be more effective in reaching our cities with the gospel message, we must take more seriously the evaluation of the corporate cultures of our agencies and organizations.

We must hold ourselves accountable as Christian communities to biblical values, morals, ethics, and to the stewardship of our human resources. We must seek to renew our current structures—even raise new ones—whose core identities are reflected in the faces of their people.

The organizational culture into which God calls a person might be one that reflects the nature of God's kingdom, or might be someone else's little kingdom that cares more for the programs, agendas, and interests of those in positions of power (Tomasko 1993:111). How can a mission organization like the one described in the story above claim to be Christ-centered, and yet be so unlike Christ in how it treats its employees? We need to see that each of our corporations (our mission organizations, our churches) has an internal "being," a personality that is reflected in the lives of those who have come for enabling, equipping, and encouraging in their calling.

The covenantal relationship with God to be stewards of his love and kingdom is one that he nurtured from the beginning of creation (Hall 1990:26). We can trace the threads of this covenant throughout the Scriptures.

From a close examination of the lives of the people in the Old and New Testaments, we can see that God intended for us to bring kingdom values into every aspect of our lives. It also seems that the Lord intended for us to bring those values into the workplace, and apply them to both the individual and the community or organization (DePree 1989:132). Do the goals, values, and structures of our organizations embody this covenantal relationship?

REREADING THE SCRIPTURES

In thinking recently about this city that surrounds me, a reminder came of the variety of Bible accounts that tell us about Jesus walking with the people from the desert to the city, from Nazareth to Capernaum. Jesus lived among us as one who was unadorned, standing with nothing to offer us except God's love. It seems that if we join him in a covenantal relationship, then we must—as individual Christians and Christian communities—be stewards of that same love (Kantonen 1956:3).

God did not choose or call us because of our actions or accomplishments. God chose us because we are his creation, redeemed in love and sent to proclaim that embracing love to the cities and the people, showing them the only true source of life, healing, hope, and forgiveness. In the city's streets, we walk with people who are rejected, broken, wounded, and unpretentious. We only have God's love to offer—nothing more, nothing less (Nouwen 1992a:20). If mission organizations would serve the people of today's cities, they must go as Jesus did—walking on the dirt road with a humble heart, vulnerable, and with an open ear to hear the voices of those they came to serve.

Through the accounts of his temptation in the Gospel of Luke (4:1-13), Jesus shows us how to establish a foundation for ministry in the cities of today's world. He began his ministry in the desert, where God equipped, enabled, and filled him with the Holy Spirit. What began in the wilderness was the development of a core identity as a human being rooted in the power and gentleness of the Holy Spirit (Bosch 1991:100).

I have come to think that maybe Luke offers us an example here, not only for our personal lives, but also for our corporate and organizational lives. All three of the temptations are alienating. All three represent attempts to break Jesus away from his covenantal relationship with God. Jesus shows us a personal response that we can translate into a corporate response. This intentional direction toward a covenantal relationship from within our mission organizations could become a way of countering the forces of the city.

The temptation of appetite

As we walk through our cities today, how can we resist the temptation to turn stones into bread? Many are hungry, homeless, needy. After all, didn't God call us to feed them? Jesus responded that we do "not live on bread alone, but on every word that comes from the mouth of God" (Matt. 4:4). But the city is hungry, Lord! The homeless cry out to us each day as we pass by, Lord. We must provide for them! It seems that looking for "bread alone" was our response throughout the years (Nouwen 1979:85).

The tendency in our organizations is to be almost too focused, too program-oriented, wanting to solve the world's problems, always trying to fill in when the world misses the mark. In urban ministries, this too often reduces us to feeding the hungry or sheltering the homeless. We have set up many mission structures that offer mostly physical answers to practical questions, hoping to heal and transform a hurting world.

In doing so, however, we have taken on the world's standards for efficiency and control, building hierarchical structures as umbrellas for programs and products; measuring success by charting growth; and trying to improve marketing images. How can our success-oriented organizational cultures touch cities filled with lonely and isolated people who lack intimacy; who suffer from broken relationships, boredom, feelings of emptiness and depression; and who have a deep sense of uselessness, and a sense of being used?

It seems that Jesus calls us to a relationship with himself in which we first seek nourishment from the Word. When we are grounded in the Word of God, we can then reach out to feed a hungry child.

Henri Nouwen describes the kind of leader that the church needs for the future as "a leader who dares to claim his or her irrelevance in the contemporary world as a divine vocation that allows him or her to enter into a deep solidarity with the anguish underlying all the glitter of success and to bring the light of Jesus there" (Nouwen 1989:18). This is the kind of leadership that our mission organizations and our cities need. David Bosch describes this type of leadership from another perspective, saying that "it is the community that is the primary bearer of mission." Going further, he quotes Burrows in asserting that

> Mission does not proceed primarily from the pope, nor
> from a missionary order, society, or synod, but from a

community gathered around the Word and the sacraments and sent into the world. Therefore the ordained leadership's role cannot possibly be the all-determining factor; it is only one part of the community's total life (1991:472; Burrows 1981:62).

Those who respond to the programs that we create and implement through our mission organizations are hurting people who need the touch of a Christian community bringing hope wrapped in the power of God's Word, not just food or shelter. The hope comes from a community that reflects Jesus, a community that calls forth the reaction, "See how they love each other!" Our mission organizations and agencies must first be vessels filled with God's love, and have an internal culture that reflects the very essence of God's Word.

It is not enough for us to seek to alleviate the social, political, or economic inequities of our cities. The gospel of which we are witnesses in the city must offer tangible good news, believable reasons for hope, realizable peace, and a corporate experience of joy. We should offer these in the delicate earthen vessels of a common ministry, a communal vocation of Christian people and Christian organizations in the city (Van Engen 1991:139).

The temptation of power

For centuries we have seen Christian leaders and Christian organizations come and go "in God's name," exercising what they claim is their God-given authority to destroy other people. History tells of the Crusades, the Inquisitions, the building of the great cathedrals. We read of the missionaries who went in Christ's name, yet without his nature. In their quests for political, economic, moral, and spiritual influence, Christian leaders and organizations have succumbed to the temptation of power.

If we build and administer great, influential, socially- and economically-powerful mission organizations, are we serving God as the servant-leaders he calls us to be? The temptation for Jesus was to show the world his true identity, to demonstrate his power. Jesus had a very powerful ministry in the eyes of those who witnessed his healings and miracles. He knew he had the power to be at the top, yet he chose to sit with the foolish and the weak. Donald Kraybill, in *The Upside Down Kingdom*, summarizes clearly the point that Jesus made:

> We who manage land and people are not owners. We are stewards accountable to God, the true owner. We dare not use land and people selfishly to build economic pyramids, create social dynasties, or feed greedy egos. Giving the land a vacation in the sabbatical or seventh year fits this understanding. Since the land is the Lord's, it shouldn't be abused. On the seventh year it's given back—restored to God—its original Owner. . . . Natural, human and financial resources are, very simply put, God's. These resources are ours only on loan. As short-term stewards of them, we are accountable to God for their proper use and care (1990:95).

How often do our mission organizations yield to the temptation to be the largest, the best, the most technologically advanced, the most strategically sophisticated? How do we measure church growth? How often do we depend on people with special academic credentials or amazing sales abilities? What is the essence of our marketing strategy, our public image? How often do we expect our pastors to be fantastic preachers, great motivators, and perfect administrators? In our struggle to succeed and "win" the cities for Christ, has the ethos of our mission organizations become one that offers power as an easy substitute for the hard task of love?

If we want our mission organizations to succeed, we must redefine success. Success must become a process toward wholeness, not power. As mission leaders, God did not call us to solve the pain, hurt, and poverty of the cities. God called us to show and to proclaim how he can lead us out of the desert, out of the slavery of poverty and pain, into a new land and a new freedom (Nouwen 1979:23).

We must bring a mission to the cities that articulates a faith in a real God, a real power, a real presence. Through deep theological reflection that shapes the culture of our ministries and organizations, God can show us how to be his people in the midst of the city's noise, pain, and hurt, and how to walk genuinely with the people he loves.

The temptation of the spectacular

It is interesting that the setting for the third temptation is different from the first two. Satan leads Jesus to Jerusalem—a city in need—and tempts him with the desire to stand out as an individual, to be noticed, to be spectacular. In putting aside this desire, Jesus shows us that we have a role in shared, mutual leadership as part of a community, not as isolated spectacular individuals.

Scripture continually calls us back to a corporate lifestyle, to being a community of mutual accountability. The Gospel of Luke shows that Jesus set aside his kingship to sit with his people. Jesus never wanted to stand out in the crowd. He rode into Jerusalem on a donkey; he ate with the poor and homeless; he left before his disciples planted all the churches; he never published his sermon notes; he hung on a cross.

This third temptation brings to mind Scripture's many references to the human body. In 1 Corinthians 12:12-31, Paul offers us a clear picture of the church as one body with many parts that function together.

Thinking of how God created our bodies reminds me of the care he took in putting us together. Our body parts can work as independent units, but they only function cor-

231

rectly in their union with each other around a central core of balance and symmetry. God designed our bodies to eliminate toxins, which occurs only after a careful filtering process so our bodies can use a substance's every possible vital element.

God even placed an internal healing process in our bodies. How interesting, though, that healing comes through rest, and the stronger body parts compensate for the weaker while healing takes place.

Perhaps our mission organizations would function more effectively in the world's confusing and difficult urban centers if we designed them to operate as a body, a corporate community that gives worth to each member. Max DePree, in his book *Leadership Jazz*, describes it well:

> Any organization seeking to progress, to produce, will be required to live up to the potential lying hidden in its diversity. We need to commit ourselves to individual authenticity with openness and expectation, with grace and humor. A good family, a good institution, or a good corporation can be a place of healing. It can be a place where work becomes redemptive, where every person is included on her or his own terms (1992:63).

NEW MISSION INSIGHTS

Perhaps we should reexamine our organizations and see them more in terms of process, growth, and journey than as producers of a product. Jesus seems to view his church in this way as he joins us along the path. He gives us a complete understanding of what his kingdom is and what it will become. He helps us see what many have called "the Already-Not-Yet Kingdom."

I have come to see our mission agencies and organizations in this light, as types of mission structures that I call "the Already-Not-Yet-Organizations." I base this view on certain assumptions:

232

1. We must stop hurting our people. Hurt comes because we do not allow time to carefully define and examine our organizational structures in light of the clearly defined management principles outlined in the Scriptures.

2. A Christian organization should be different—noticeably different—from other corporate structures. A Christian agency's organizational structure must stand and exist for Christian values, principles, truths, and ways of living as declared in its mission statements.

3. The people who work in a Christian organization must be stewards of God's love and accountable to each other.

4. The organization is responsible for being a steward of God's love to its people. It must build into its structure a system of accountability to insure equity, integrity, and the personal worth of each member.

Rereading the section of Christ's temptations in the Gospel of Luke offered me a renewed vision for mission organizations. This vision has enabled me to rework a definition of mission for urban theology, a definition that I developed over many months of reflection. I offer it here as a way of beginning to see how a mission structure can become a flexible, living, growing, and healthy organization in the city, as it attempts to proclaim the coming kingdom of God in Christ Jesus:

> *Mission is intentionally reaching across barriers*
> *from church to nonchurch,*
> *from those who believe in Jesus Christ*
> *to those who do not,*
> *by means of organizational structures,*
> *whether formal or informal,*
> *to proclaim through intentional action, lifestyle,*
> *and goals*

> *the coming of the kingdom of God in Christ Jesus,*
> *through the participation of the people of God,*
> *as stewards of the love and human respect*
> *that is our covenantal obligation.*

MISSION ACTION

So what does all this mean for the mission manager, for the person leading a mission organization in the city into the twenty-first century? From my context and perspective, I feel that the mandate of biblical management and steward-ship means designing new value bases, new processes, new goals, and new definitions of success.

As we examine our mission systems, structures, and organizations, we must consider the people resources that God has entrusted to our care. That means taking care that the details of our organizations (i.e., structure, finances, goals, day-to-day operations, and so on) help us to encour-age, equip, and care for our people. We must become stew-ards of God's love not only to the nations but also to the people who are part of our corporate culture.

Will you and I really lead our people and manage our organizations according to God's agenda or our own? Are we stewards or owners? Do we engineer, strategize, and schedule until our people are weary in welldoing? Or do we nurture and equip them with the kind of human respect that God's order demands? How will we manage and lead our organizations into the twenty-first century?

I would suggest that a framework of God-given stew-ardship might lead us in the right direction. Is it really too much to expect that everyone within our Christian mission organizations—from the board of directors to the part-time employees—embody the same values, the same integrity, and the same desire to show God's love to the hurting cities of this world?

A walk on the periphery

As she walked along the path in the quiet of the morning, the air smelled fresh and clean. She filled her lungs with the newness, hoping to push out the city's dirt and pollution. The six weeks of relaxation, reflection, and contemplation were ending but she was just beginning to feel rested. It had taken four weeks just to forget the city, the noise, the pain.

"Lord, must I return? Can't we just walk here forever?" Her tears had flowed for weeks. She felt like a failure, yet amid the tears she sensed that something was changing. Finally, she was beginning to hear the gentle voice speaking softly in the morning dew.

Months ago the Lord began introducing her to the real meaning of community, and now things were coming into focus. Her own agendas, goals, and desires had clouded the vision she needed to see the community. As her walk continued on this last morning, she could feel the fear of returning to the city subsiding and joy pouring over the wounds. In the quiet, she finally heard what the Lord had to say.

Over the weeks, she realized that she was no different from anyone else in the organization. She came to the Christian community with her own fears and anger, her own ideas and agendas. For years she had thought that she could take her ideas, plans, creativity, and talents to any organization. Hard work and dedication would produce the relationships in the community that she longed for, and where she would find a common vision.

Now she began to understand that what the Lord had in mind was just the opposite. Community is not an organization or group with a common ideology or common mission focus. Community is a group of people, called by God, responding out of their individual aspirations and diversity to come to a place of common ministry and a common vocation—a covenantal community.

The Lord was showing her how he had called her to this place as an individual with special gifts and talents to contribute to the organization's larger vocation. Now he was asking her to return and help the organization rediscover and celebrate its diversity.

The last few weeks of rest had enabled her to see her aspirations and talents as a part of a common task. She realized that she and the other leaders had been working very hard at "managing" the diversity within the organization, instead of embracing it as a variety of manifestations of a common ministry.

The quietness and solitude that she found on the morning path gave her time to see how she too participated in the fast pace and survival atmosphere of the city. She had allowed the emergency-oriented nature of the city to cause her to look for easy and quick solutions, Band-Aid remedies, and temporary ways to care for the immediate. These weeks apart had prepared her to go back as a renewed person, taking joy and hope with her. But what would she tell her colleagues?

The organization had grown so quickly that it seemed impossible for anything to change, but she could not go back to business as usual. She had had a great breakthrough, and she wanted to tell someone.

She wanted to tell her colleagues that what she learned on those long morning walks was that it was not enough to minister to the city's many wounded individuals. It was not enough to offer programs and plant churches, to feed the hungry and shelter the homeless, or to accomplish the organizational goals. All of the external, visible, and measurable products of this organization—her organization—were not enough.

Because, you see, the people producing the products were themselves in pain. The organization had internal bleeding, and the power of common witness and vocation seemed diluted. There was no avenue for expressing real intimacy. The creative witness they needed to offer the angry city was dwindling.

She returned home to the city in peace. She had hoped for so much but all she really had to offer the organization was a renewed awareness of her human weakness. Questions remained. How could they, as a community called by God, awaken hope in their city? How could they develop a communal vocation, a common ministry that would cause the city to say, "Look, they really love each other"?

The first morning back in the office was a dry and dusty one because the demolition crew had started tearing down the building next door. Brick by brick, each beam, piece of iron, and concrete block came down by hand and went out by truck for recycling.

As she sipped her morning coffee and watched the workers, she wondered if an organization must go through the same process before renewal can take place. Is it necessary to dismantle all the internal pieces and rearrange them to find a stronger whole? Whatever an organization needs—partial or complete surgery—the time is right to begin asking the questions.

> In the circus full of lion-tamers and trapeze artists whose dazzling feats claim our attention, the real and true story is told by the clowns. Clowns are not in the center of the events. They appear between the great acts, fumble and fall, and make us smile again after the tensions created by the heroes we came to admire. The clowns don't have it together, they do not succeed in what they try, they are awkward, out of balance, but they are on our side. We respond to them not with admiration but with sympathy, not with amazement but with understanding, not with tension but with a smile. The clowns remind us with a tear and smile that we share the same human weaknesses.

237

The clowns are those peripheral people who by their humble, saintly lives evoke a smile and awaken hope, even in a city terrorized by kidnaping and street violence. In the circus of life we indeed are the clowns. Let us train ourselves well so that those who watch us will smile and recognize that in the midst of our crowded city, we have to keep a place for him who loves his stubborn and hardheaded children with an infinite tenderness and care (Nouwen 1979:58).

PART FOUR

Seeking a theology of mission for the city

11

Constructing a theology of mission for the city

Charles Van Engen

O Jerusalem, Jerusalem, you who kill the prophets and stone those sent to you, how often I have longed to gather your children together, as a hen gathers her chicks under her wings, but you were not willing! Look, your house is left to you desolate. I tell you, you will not see me again until you say, "Blessed is he who comes in the name of the Lord." Luke 13:34-35

WERE THESE WORDS of Jesus a sigh of deep pathos, a cry of excruciating agony, or an exasperated pronouncement of judgment? Matthew (23:37-39) places them after the triumphal entry, closely joined to the seven woes pronounced on the leaders of the Jews,[1] and an integral part of Matthew's

---

Charles Van Engen is associate professor of theology of mission, church growth, and Latin American Studies at Fuller Theological Seminary's School of World Mission. Please see the contributing authors section for more information.

long discourse of eschatological issues concerning the end of the age. In Luke (13:34-35), the nearly identical words of Jesus appear while he is on his way to Jerusalem, before his triumphal entry, and placed alongside Jesus' conflict with Herod, who is plotting to kill Jesus.

Whether viewed through the Matthean paradigm or the Lukan,[2] we could take Jesus' cry, "O Jerusalem, Jerusalem!" as a profound statement by Jesus concerning God's mission in the city.[3] It makes clear God's loving commitment to be involved with, and related to, the city.

God's initiative in sending mission messengers to the city is evident. The Gospels mention Jerusalem's mixed (mostly negative) response to God's love. But the dominant image is one of pained, loving, salvific tenderness: a hen clucking furiously to gather her wayward chicks under her wings.

Although Jerusalem kills the prophets, God does not flee from, or give up on, Jerusalem. Instead, God sends his Son, who comes as King David's descendant, who comes "in the name of the Lord," who comes riding on a donkey on his way to the cross and the empty tomb—events that occur in the midst of, and for the sake of, Jerusalem.

In fact, we may view Jesus' entire ministry from the perspective of his encounter with Jerusalem. These words of Jesus may or may not imply that he knew of the coming destruction of the temple in A.D. 70.

Yet the way both Matthew and Luke structure the text assures us that ultimately, through his death and resurrection, Jesus offers redemption and transformation of the old Jerusalem into the new City of God. This is an eschatological reality that John would later refer to in Revelation 21. True to God's form of response throughout the history of Israel, there is always grace in the midst of judgment; in the end, there is a rewriting of the story of Jerusalem.

As Roger Greenway says,

> The last chapter in the Jerusalem story awaits the future. . . . She is called the Holy City and her Bridegroom is the Lamb. Life in the new Jerusalem is peaceful. There are no tears, nor causes for them. Death and mourning are gone, and so are pain and suffering. Best of all, in this city God in Christ dwells forever with his people in perfect relationship. Grace has triumphed and *shalom* is established (1992:10-11).

When I hear those words of Jesus about Jerusalem, I hear the deep pain of an urban missionary. It also seems to me Jesus offers some profound theological truths that are simultaneously historical, contextual, relational, and missiological. Is it not possible that these words represent for Jesus what today we would call a "theology of mission for the city"?

As was noted at the start, this book is the result of a doctoral seminar that met for forty weeks at Fuller Seminary's School of World Mission to search together for a way to construct a theology of mission for the city. During those months together, we found ourselves returning repeatedly to three basic questions:

1. Why construct a theology of mission for the city?
2. What is a theology of mission for the city?
3. How may we construct a theology of mission for the city?

Because it is a preliminary set of reflections, the authors do not mean for this book to offer the last word on this subject. Instead, we wanted to share with others the methodology and content we discovered through our time together. In this chapter, I want to give a brief summary of the methodology we followed, so that the reader can see how the methodology worked itself out in the particular stories, contexts, reflections, and missiological directions offered by each author in the preceding chapters.

This volume intends to make a contribution to urban missiology, particularly in the arena of method of theology of mission, and considering the unique complexity of urban missiology. In the sixteen months we were together, the seminar group began to shape a methodology that begins on the sidewalks and streets of the city, closely mirroring the way urban missionaries think about mission in the city.

Standing in the city, we began to build a holistic approach that centered on an integrating idea or theme in the midst of the complex multiplicity of urban factors. So the method is very simple, because it begins with a story, but it also takes seriously the complexity of doing theology as related to urban missiology. It is at once practical and theological, relational and reflective, macro-oriented and micro-conscious. In other words, we sought to do for urban mission something akin to what Ray Anderson advocated when he wrote,

> Mission theology is the praxis of Jesus Christ through the presence of the Holy Spirit reaching out to the church through the arms of those whose humanity needs healing and whose hearts need hope. . . . If mission theology is to be integrated with church theology, let there be an authentic orthopraxy, let it dare to submit its concerns and its agenda for the healing and hope of humanity to the One who is the Advocate, the Leitourgos, and the Redeemer of all humanity. . . . If there be an authentic church, let it be found where Christ has his praxis and his pathos—let it pay the price of its orthodoxy in its true ministry and so be empowered by Christ himself (1991:126).

This book is a small step. It seeks to explore how we might create what Ian Bunting, an urban missionary for more than thirty years in northern England's urban areas, called for: "an integrated method of training [urban missionaries]

which can truly be described as global in scope, mission-ori-
ented, and thoroughly contextual." Especially important here
is the search for a correlation of reflection with action, of values with programs, of theology and practice.

Ian Bunting comments,

> While there is general agreement on a method of learn-
> ing theology which involves seeing, judging and act-
> ing, there is no such agreement about the way to
> correlate theology and practice. There is, in fact, a sharp
> disagreement between those who look for more theo-
> retical or systematic correlations (often the trainers in
> universities, colleges, and courses) and those who pur-
> sue more practical theological correlations (normally to
> be found in urban training centers and institutes). The
> issue is as much about where we learn our theology as
> how we go about it. There is not much evidence that
> this divide between the academic and the practical has
> been bridged by more than a few . . . (1992:25).

WHY CONSTRUCT A THEOLOGY OF MISSION
FOR THE CITY?

As the reader can see from the preceding chapters, the
seminar group represented a great deal of diversity on many
fronts. Yet almost from the first day we found a common
conviction that became increasingly significant to us. We
were all looking for ways we might better build on, and
interact with, the literature and programs we knew of that
dealt with urban missiology. Although impressed by the
quantity of literature in the last twenty years written by
those who reflect about issues of urban mission,[4] we
remained restless to find new ways to integrate those
insights with our theology and missiology.

It seems that especially in urban missiology, people
have found it difficult to deal with the whole system of the
city. On the one hand, there are those involved in micro-min-

istry who deal with individuals and their needs in the city—but they are often burning out in the process, in part because they are not dealing with the entire system. Some members of our seminar fell into that category.

On the other hand, there are those who spend much energy doing macro-studies in sociology, anthropology, economics, ethnicity, politics, and religion in the city—but they seldom seem to get down to the level of the streets and the people of the city. Their recommendations for concrete action seem weak, and their activism mostly dulled by the vastness of their scope of investigation. The staggering complexity of an urban metroplex like Los Angeles makes it nearly impossible for students of the macro-structures to convert their findings into specific, timely, compassionate, personal ministry.

Then, too, we found that many authors were caught up in one agenda or another. Community organization theory and practice seemed to need further reflection and interaction with the church in the city, an emphasis that Robert Linthicum has also called for.[5] On the other hand, as William Pannell points out, too much of mass evangelism has been blind to the city's systemic issues and has seldom sought the more radical, holistic transformation of the cities in which its evangelistic enterprises occur (Pannell 1992:6-22).

John McKnight highlighted this tension. "When I'm around church people," he says,

> I always check whether they are misled by the modern secular vision. Have they substituted the vision of service for the only thing that will make people whole—community? Are they service peddlers or community builders? Peddling services is unchristian—even if you're hellbent on helping people. Peddling services instead of building communities is the one way you can be sure not to help. . . . Service systems teach people that their value lies in their deficiencies. They are

246

built on "inadequacies" called illiteracy, visual deficit, and teenage pregnancy. But communities are built on the *capacities* of drop-out, illiterate, bad-scene, teenage-pregnant, battered women. . . . If the church is about community—not service—it's about capacity not deficiency (1989:38,40).

There is a growing interest in planting and growing house churches in the city,[6] yet too few of those have any missional intention to be God's agents for transforming the city itself.

Although generalizations like these are dangerous, our overall shared impression pulled us in two directions. At one end of the spectrum, we knew of many social service agencies "doing for" people with little regard for the city's systems (much less for gathering people into worshiping congregations).

At the other end, we also were aware of many evangelistic, church-planting efforts that did not deal with the entire scope of evil in the city. We kept seeing activists who seldom stopped to do the broader reflection, and reflective investigators who did not often get around to doing anything to change the reality of the city they were studying.

Meanwhile, the churches in the city (including ones where seminar participants are actively involved) continue to struggle to find how to be viable missional communities of faith in the city. For the church of Jesus Christ, life and ministry in the city involves living in profound tensions.

The church is not a social agency—but is of social significance in the city. The church is not city government—but God called it to announce and live out his kingdom in all its political significance. The church is not a bank—but is an economic force in the city and must seek the city's economic welfare. The church is not a school—but God called it to educate the people of the city concerning the gospel of love, justice, and social transformation. The church is not a fam-

247

ily—but is the family of God, called to be a neighbor to all those whom God loves. The church is not a building—but needs buildings and owns buildings to carry out its ministry. The church is not exclusive, not better, not unique—but God specially called it to be different in the way it serves the city. The church is not an institution—but needs institutional structures to effect changes in the lives of people and society. The church is not a community development organization—but the development of community is essential to the church's nature.

So the more we thought about it, the more convinced we became of our need to search for a theology of mission that would give us new eyes to perceive our city, inform our activism, guide our networking, and energize our hope for the transformation of our city. In the months following the Los Angeles riots, our conviction has grown that such action-reflection (or reflective activism) is essential.

What is a theology of mission for the city?

In *The Concise Dictionary of the Christian Mission*, Gerald Anderson defined theology of mission as, "concerned with the basic presuppositions and underlying principles which determine, from the standpoint of Christian faith, the motives, message, methods, strategy and goals of the Christian world mission" (Neill, Anderson and Goodwin 1971:594).

Theology of mission is a multi- and interdisciplinary enterprise. It is a relatively new discipline, with its first text appearing in 1961 in a collection of essays edited by Gerald Anderson, entitled *The Theology of Christian Mission* (Anderson 1961). That volume clearly represented the tripartite nature of theology of mission.

As shown in Figure 5 on page 249, theology of mission has to do with three arenas, shown graphically by three interlocking circles. We apply biblical and theological presuppositions and values (1) to the enterprise of the church's

Figure 5: The tripartite nature of theology of mission

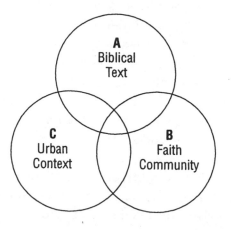

ministry and mission, and (2) set them in the context of specific activities carried out in particular times and places.[7]

First, theology of mission is *theology* (circle A above), because fundamentally it involves reflection about God. It seeks to understand God's mission, God's intentions and purposes, God's use of human instruments in God's mission, and God's working through God's people in God's world.[8] Theology of mission deals with all the traditional theological themes of systematic theology—but it does so in a manner that differs from the normal way systematic theologians operate.

The difference arises from the multidisciplinary missiological orientation of its theologizing. In addition, because of its commitment to remain faithful to God's intentions, perspectives, and purposes, theology of mission shows a fundamental concern for the relation of the Bible to mission. It attempts to allow Scripture to provide not only the foundational motivations for mission, but also to question, shape, guide, and evaluate the missionary enterprise.[9]

Second, theology of mission is theology *of* (circle C in Figure 5 on page 249). In contrast to much systematic theology, here we are dealing with an applied theology. At times it looks like what some would call pastoral or practical theology, due to this applicational nature. This type of theological reflection focuses specifically on a set of particular issues—those concerning the church's mission.

A person would find works dealing with the history of theology of mission[10] that are not especially interested in the theological issues as such, but on their implications for mission activity. These works will often examine the various pronouncements made by church and mission gatherings (Roman Catholic, Orthodox, ecumenical, evangelical, Pentecostal, and charismatic) and ask questions—sometimes polemically—about the results of these for missional action.[11] The documents themselves become part of the discipline of theology of mission.

Third, theology of mission is specially oriented toward and for *mission* (circle B in Figure 5 on page 249). We find the most basic reflection in this arena in the many books, journals, and other publications dealing with the theory of missiology itself.[12] We cannot allow either missiology or theology of mission, however, to restrict itself to reflection only. As Johannes Verkuyl stated,

> Missiology may never become a substitute for action and participation. God calls for participants and volunteers in his mission. In part, missiology's goal is to become a "service station" along the way. If study does not lead to participation, whether at home or abroad, missiology has lost her humble calling. . . . Any good missiology is also a *missiologia viatorum*—"pilgrim missiology" (1978:6,18).

Theology of mission draws its incarnational nature from the ministry of Jesus, and always happens in a specific

250

time and place. Hence circle C involves the missiological use of all the social science disciplines that help us understand the context in which God's mission takes place. This book deals with probably the most complex context missiology has ever faced: the urban metroplex.

To begin to understand the city, first we borrow from sociology, anthropology, economics, urbanology, the study of Christianity and religious pluralism in the city, psychological issues of urbanism, and a host of other cognate disciplines. When we do this type of macro analysis of the city, however, we immediately find ourselves pulled away from the here and now of the gospel's incarnational interaction with the people of the city.

Second, this makes us come to a more particular contextual understanding of the city in terms of a hermeneutic of the reality in which we minister. Third, this in turn calls us to hear the cries, see the faces, understand the stories, and respond to the living needs and hopes of people. This made the seminar group understand that it needed to begin its reflection with stories. But a larger framework of the forces at work in the urban environment encompass the stories. Therefore, an interaction with the stories called us to rethink, to look again, to understand more deeply what went on at the macro level, as that affected the micro structures of the persons we encountered. Circle C involves a strong dialectical tension between seeing people's faces, and seeing those faces in their urbanized contexts.

As we can see in Figure 5 on page 249, the three circles overlap each other. It is not realistic to isolate any of the dynamics mentioned so far, because when urban life and urban ministry happen, they do so in the midst of all three circles at once. This fact slowly made itself felt to us. As our group became more familiar with the interaction of the three circles, we began to see that the complexity of the *content* of the issues of urban missiology forced us to adopt a specifically multi- and interdisciplinary *method* for reflection and action. We discovered that recognizing the necessity of dealing with both the complexity and simplicity of life as it is in the city was our starting point for *how* to construct a theology of mission for the city. We needed to deal with the three arenas together, while simultaneously keeping them separate in our minds.

HOW MAY WE CONSTRUCT A THEOLOGY OF MISSION FOR THE CITY?

In what follows I will give a brief summary of the steps that the seminar group found helpful in constructing a theology of mission for the city. Clearly, this is not the only way to do such reflection. Neither do these steps represent a comprehensive treatment of the method.

In this section I intend only to highlight the broad parameters of what we discovered, allowing the reader to envision the process as it flowed through this book's preceding chapters. Each author intentionally constructed the preceding chapters to follow the process I am about to describe— but the reader should take note that each chapter did so in a slightly different manner. This is because one of our most significant discoveries was that the manner in which the process applies to each given urban context is *itself contextual*. In other words, we must transform not only the content, but also the *method* itself to fit critically and appropriately the particular issues, styles, agendas, and themes arising in each context.

As we can see from Figure 6 on page 253, our method for constructing a theology of mission for the city involved walking through the three multi- and interdisciplinary circles we saw earlier, and adapting and contextualizing their contribution for a particular urban context. So being self-conscious and self-critical in approaching the city was the first step in our process.

Figure 6: Methodological components of a biblical theology of mission for the city

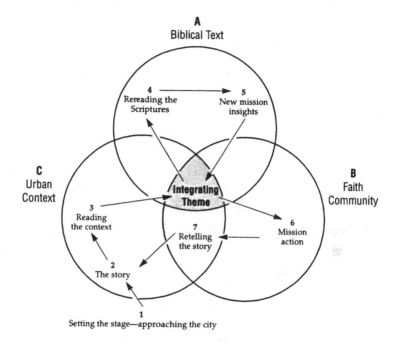

Setting the stage—approaching the city

1. Approaching the city

The earlier discussions in this chapter have already prepared us for the first step in our method. We begin—at the
bottom of Figure 6 above—by setting the stage, asking about
the perceptions, images, and lenses that we use to exegete
the city. Some (primarily in the U.S.) would view the city as
a series of concentric circles: a perspective that led to the language about "inner city" and "suburb." Others (primarily
Europeans) might see the city in terms of "old town" and
"new town." Persons from the Third World see the city as a
central business district with surrounding "barrios," or
"favelas," "districts," "cantonments," or "slums."

As the reader saw in several chapters, we may also
view the city as a network of extended family relationships,

or as a compilation of ethnic subsystems. City planners see streets and buildings, politicians see voters, the police see violence, educators see schools, bankers and economists see businesses, and commuters see traffic. Television sees through a narrow, selected, and restricted lens, looking for sensational stories that will sell.[13]

Still others look at the city through the grid of spiritual warfare, with good and evil forces battling for the allegiance of the city's people and structures. All of us see "but a poor reflection" (1 Cor. 13:12). All of us are insightful in what we see, and blind in what we miss. Yet a full-fledged theology of mission for the city will call for us to look past the limits of our peripheral vision to gain some understanding of the complexity of subsystems (interlocking and independent) that make up the urban metroplex.

The closest visual representation of this reality that the seminar participants could think of was that of a rose. Each petal (subsystem) is different from the others, yet all are interconnected. A petal alone does not make a rose. Yet a rose cannot exist except as the sum of its petals. Also, a rose draws from a whole system of supports involving the rose-bush, just as a city draws from a host of supporting cultural, geographic, national, global, and historical elements that help to sustain the city.

Like a rose, the city also includes intangible elements of beauty and smell that we cannot identify specifically with any given petal—it is the overlapping of the various petals that gives each city its unique image. Like a rose, the city is full of thorns and we must handle it carefully and gingerly. Finally, the city is similar to a rose in its fragility. Cut a rose and it wilts quickly; likewise in the city. As the reader saw in some chapters, life in the city is fragile; death is often too near.[14]

So the first step in our method involved a commitment to view the city systemically, holistically, and critically, while we searched for biblical values and insights to inform our life and ministry in our cities. This in turn forced us to be willing to remain in touch with the complexity of the whole, while also keeping our feet grounded in the specificity of the here and now of persons living in the city. The easiest way to do this was to begin on the sidewalks of our cities by telling a story.

2. The story

The second step of our method involved standing in circle C of Figure 6 (see page 253), and telling not just any anecdote or historical moment, but a specific kind of story. Our method drew somewhat from the anthropological technique known as participant observation, and from the case study approach of sociology and counseling.

Because ours was a specifically *theological* task, however, we found that our stories most fruitfully borrowed from the insights of "narrative theology." "Narrative theology" has been associated with recent hermeneutical developments in the way biblical scholars approach the Bible. Yet the seminar group discovered that the method itself contributed powerfully to seeing the macro issues of the city through the eyes of the micro concerns of persons.[15]

What we meant by this was a method that went beyond the purely historical, sequential retelling of an episode. At the other end of the spectrum, we also felt it necessary to stop short of a totally subjective approach that would ascribe to the event whatever meaning we might feel led to give it.

Instead, we searched for particularly appropriate stories that would serve as specific time and place windows to the larger macro structural issues that we could find highlighted and illustrated by the story. As we saw the stories within the social, cultural, religious, relational, personal, and other urban issues of the original context, we would allow their meanings to illuminate our understanding of missiological praxis in the city.

255

As David Tracy put it, "Human beings need story, symbol, image, myth and fiction to disclose to their imaginations some genuinely new possibilities for existence: possibilities which conceptual analysis, committed as it is to understanding present actualities, cannot adequately provide" (Tracy 1988:207).

Alisdair MacIntyre recognized several diverse uses of narrative that we found echoed time and again in our reflection as a seminar. He argues that (1) intelligible human action is narrative in form; (2) human life has a fundamentally narrative shape; (3) humans are storytelling animals; (4) people place their lives and arguments in narrative histories; (5) communities and (6) traditions receive their continuities through narrative histories; and (7) the construction and reconstruction of more adequate narratives and forms of narrative mark epistemological progress (Hauerwas and Jones 1989:8).[16]

James Gustafson defines narrative in relation to its function, a use that echoed loudly in our own process.

> Narrative functions to sustain the particular moral identity of a religious (or secular) community by rehearsing its history and traditional meanings, as these are portrayed in Scripture and other sources. Narratives shape and sustain the ethos of the community. Through our participation in such a community, the narratives also function to give shape to our moral character, which in turn deeply affects the way we interpret and construe the world and events and thus affects what we determine to be appropriate action as members of the community. Narratives function to sustain and confirm the religious and moral identity of the Christian community, and evoke and sustain the faithfulness of its members to Jesus Christ (Gustafson 1988:19-20).

The story selection was a critical step in our reflective process, because we wanted to focus on narratives that were representative of our ministries, central to our contexts, and rich in hermeneutical meaning for a deeper understanding of the cities in which they happened. We found that when the story was appropriate it naturally led us to broaden our perspectives, to see through it like a window that looked out beyond the event itself and helped us better understand the third step in the process: reading the context.

3. Reading the context

The third step of the process involves listening with new ears, seeing with new eyes, allowing the city to influence the imagination in ways it is not used to—thus yielding a new "hermeneutic" of the city. This use of the word "hermeneutic" does not refer to deriving the meaning from the text of Scripture.[17] Nor does this refer to reading the signs of the times,[18] as was common in the missiology of the World Council of Churches of the 1960s and early 1970s, when there was talk of letting the world set the agenda. Instead, this type of hermeneutic involves rereading the *context* in terms of the symbols, meanings, and perspectives that were there all along but to which we may have been blind.[19]

Juan Luis Segundo's *The Liberation of Theology* (1976) is probably the best methodological treatment of this type of hermeneutic. I would not espouse the way Latin American liberation theologians reduced their hermeneutical method to narrow socioeconomic and political agendas. Yet the process that Segundo describes seems to have much to commend it for reflection on the new reality facing us in today's cities.

> Segundo outlined four decisive steps in the process of the hermeneutical circle.[20] First, we experience reality, which leads us to ideological suspicion. Secondly, there is the application of our ideological suspicion to our understanding of reality in general and to Scripture and theology in particular. Third, we experience a new

way of perceiving reality that leads us to the exegetical suspicion that the prevailing interpretation of the Bible has not taken important pieces of data into account. This calls for rereading the biblical text. Fourth, we develop a new hermeneutic, that is, we find a new way of interpreting Scripture with the new perceptions of our reality at our disposal. This leads us to look again at our reality, which begins the process all over again (Van Engen 1993:31).[21]

The third step leads naturally into the fourth. After looking at the urban context with new suspicions, new agendas and new eyes, we raise our sights and find that we now have new questions to bring to Scripture as well.

4. Rereading the Scriptures

The reader may see from Figure 6 on page 255 that the movement from step 3 to step 4 is by way of an "integrating theme" that forms the central idea interfacing all three circles. Because of the complexity of the inter- and multidisciplinary task, the seminar group found it helpful for each person to focus on a specific integrating idea that would serve as the hub through which to approach a rereading of Scripture. So the reader can quickly review the table of contents and see that each contribution to this book focused on one major concept that best reflected the author's contextual hermeneutic, and most profitably led to looking again at Scripture.

Clearly, we are trying to avoid bringing our own agendas to, and superimposing them on, Scripture. Liberation theologians made this mistake, and have not recovered from it. What we sought is a way to bring a new set of questions to the text, questions that might help us see in the Scriptures what we had missed before.[22] This new approach to Scripture is what David Bosch called "critical hermeneutics."[23]

5. New mission insights

As we reread Scripture, we face new insights, new values, and new priorities that call us to reexamine the motivations, means, agents, and goals of our urban missiology. This, in turn, calls us to rethink each of the traditional themes of theology. Consequently, this will involve us in a contextual rereading of Scripture to discover anew what it means to know God in the city.

The nature of the city and the gods in the city, issues of creation and chaos in the city, revelation, Christology, soteriology, pneumatology, ecclesiology, and eschatology, for example, take on unique hues when colored by the city's realities. Robert McAfee Brown called this type of reflection, "Theology in a New Key" (1978), and "Unexpected News" (1984).

In Latin American theology, this theological process especially focused on issues of Christology and ecclesiology. In the city, it appears that we need to allow our rereading to offer us new insights into the scope and content of our missiology, derived from a profound rethinking of all the traditional themes of theology.[24]

6. Mission action

The move from step 5 to step 6 involves a movement from circle A to circle B (see Figure 6 on page 255). Due to the complex nature of the enterprise, it seems best to allow this step to flow again through the focus of the "integrating theme," which can help hold the various ideas together.

In 1987, the Association of Professors of Mission discussed at length what missiology is, and how it does its reflection. Referring to doing theology of mission, the Association members said that,

> The mission theologian does biblical and systematic theology differently from the biblical scholar or dog-

259

matician in that the mission theologian is in search of the "habitus," the way of perceiving, the intellectual understanding coupled with spiritual insight and wisdom, which leads to seeing the signs of the presence and movement of God in history, and through his church in such a way as to be affected spiritually and motivationally and thus be committed to personal participation in that movement. . . .

Such a search for the "why" of mission forces the mission theologian to seek to articulate the vital integrative center of mission today. . . . Each formulation of the "center" has radical implications for each of the cognate disciplines of the social sciences, the study of religions, and church history in the way they are corrected and shaped theologically. Each formulation supports or calls into question different aspects of all the other disciplines. . . . The center, therefore, serves as both theological content and theological process as a disciplined reflection on God's mission in human contexts. The role of the theologian of mission is therefore to articulate and "guard" the center, while at the same time to spell out integratively the implications of the center for all the other cognate disciplines (Van Engen 1987: 524-525).

Conceptually, our involvement here is with something that the philosophy of science calls "paradigm construction" or "paradigm shift."[25] We know that a paradigm shift is normally understood (especially in the philosophy of science) as a corporate phenomenon that occurs over a long period and involves the reflective community interacting with a particular issue. David Bosch, however, initiated many of us into seeing paradigm formation as a powerful way of helping us reconceptualize our mission concerning specific communities in specific contexts.

In these terms, a paradigm becomes "a conceptual tool used to perceive reality and to order that perception in an understandable, explainable, and somewhat predictable pattern" (Van Engen 1992:53). It is "an entire constellation of beliefs, values and techniques . . . shared by the members of a given community" (Küng and Tracy 1989:441-442). So a paradigm consists of "the total composite set of values, worldview, priorities, and knowledge which makes a person, a group of persons, or a culture look at reality in a certain way. A paradigm is a tool of observation, understanding and explanation" (Van Engen 1992:53).

On the one hand, the mission theologian for the city takes very seriously the biblical text as *text* (circle A), and tries to avoid superimposing particular agendas on the text. It is equally true, however, as Johannes Verkuyl has said, "if study does not lead to participation . . . missiology has lost her humble calling" (Verkuyl 1978:6). So the move from circle A to circle B (see Figure 6 on page 253) is a movement from *text* to *community*. Through the focusing mediation of the integrating theme, we now restate the new insights gained from a rereading of Scripture as contextually appropriate missional orientations of the church in the city.

Experts have offered several different names to describe this process. David Moberg analyzed the "social functions and dysfunctions of the church" as a social institution (1962). On the other hand, Lesslie Newbigin spoke of the congregation as "a hermeneutic of the gospel." This meant that persons and institutions in the surrounding contextual environment read the gospel through the mediation of the local church. "I confess that I have come to feel that the primary reality of which we have to take account in seeking for a Christian impact on public life is the Christian congregation" (Newbigin 1989:227).[26]

David Roozen, William McKinney, and Jackson Carroll developed one of the most creative ways to approach this matter in *Varieties of Religious Presence* (1984). This study examined ten different congregations in Hartford, Connecticut (U.S.A.). The result yielded four "mission orientations": (1) "the congregation as activist," (2) "the congregation as citizen," (3) the congregation as sanctuary," and (4) "the congregation as evangelist" (Roozen, McKinney and Carroll 1984).

These four characterizations do not exhaust the possibilities of describing the missional dimensions, intentions, and relations of the communities of faith—the church—within the city. It might be interesting for the readers, however, to examine their own faith communities and discover how many congregations and missional situations they can encapsulate within one of these four missional orientations.

7. Retelling the story

The final, but at the same time initial, step in the process involves suggestions for contextually appropriate, biblically informed missional action. We called it "retelling the story," because this step brings us back to the here and now of the person on the sidewalks of our cities. It also asks very specifically about the actions within and without the faith community that it must take to respond to the initial situation.

Here we find ourselves in the middle ground between biblically informed missiological theory and contextually appropriate mission action. If our theology of mission does not result in informed action, we are merely "a resounding gong or a clanging cymbal" (1 Cor. 13:1). The intimate connection of reflection with action is essential for urban missiology. Yet if our mission action does not itself transform our reflection, we may have great ideas—but they may be of such heavenly import that they are of no earthly good.

The seminar participants discovered that one of the most helpful ways to interface reflection and action was through the process known as "praxis." Although there have been several different meanings ascribed to this idea,[27] we

262

found that Orlando Costas' formulation was very construc-
tive for us. "Missiology," Costas says,

> is fundamentally a praxeological phenomenon. It is a
> critical reflection that takes place in the praxis of mis-
> sion . . . [It occurs] in the concrete missionary situation,
> as part of the church's missionary obedience to and
> participation in God's mission, and is itself actualized
> in that situation. . . . Its object is always the world . . .
> men and women in their multiple life situations. . . . In
> reference to this witnessing action saturated and led by
> the sovereign, redemptive action of the Holy Spirit . . .
> the concept of missionary praxis is used. Missiology
> arises as part of a witnessing engagement to the gospel
> in the multiple situations of life (1976:8).

In *The Praxis of Pentecost* (1991), Ray Anderson presents
the concept of "praxis" in reflections on Jesus' ministry he
developed through the story of the woman caught in adul-
tery (John 8:1-11). Based on the story, Anderson offers a
hermeneutic of Jesus' ministry as "a paradigm of Christo-
praxis" (1991:48). Following this viewpoint, Anderson then
speaks of Christ's "praxis of liberation," "praxis of sanctification," and "praxis of empowerment" (1991:49-62).

The concept of "praxis" is consistent with what we saw
earlier in circle A regarding narrative theology. It is consistent in the sense that not only the reflection, but also profoundly the *action*, becomes part of the "theology on the
way" of discovering how the church may participate in
God's mission in the city.

The *action* is itself theological, and serves to inform the
reflection, which in turn interprets, evaluates, and projects
new understanding in transformed action. The interweaving
of reflection and action offers a transformation of all aspects
of our missiological engagement with the city. This leads us
back to a faith commitment, a loving engagement, and a

263

hopeful envisioning of ways in which we pray we may retell the story. So we return to where we began, and boldly proclaim the retelling of the story.

> *I saw the Holy City, the new Jerusalem, coming down out of heaven from God, prepared as a bride beautifully dressed for her husband. And I heard a loud voice from the throne saying, "Now the dwelling of God is with [people], and he will live with them. They will be his people, and God himself will be with them and be their God" (Rev. 21:2-3).*

NOTES

1   Please note that the reader can in no way construe these woes as anti-Semitic. On the contrary, they denounce the leaders of the people for misleading the Jewish nation that God cares for so deeply.

2   See David Bosch, 1991, pp. 56-122.

3   In "Biblical Perspectives on the City" (1992), Roger Greenway offered a provocative analysis of Jerusalem as an image of urban missiology, comparing Babylon and Jerusalem. Oddly enough, he omitted reference to this passage. See also John W. Olley, 1990.

4   For example, James H. Cone, 1993; Cain Hope Felder, 1989; Shelby Steele, 1990; Robert Linthicum, 1991a, 1991b; Ray Bakke, 1987 (new edition, 1992); Benjamin Tonna, 1985; Larry Rose and Kirk Hadaway, eds., 1984; David Frenchak and Sharrel Keys, eds., 1979; David Frenchak and Clinton Stockwell, comps., 1984; Viv Grigg, 1984, 1992; Harvie Conn, 1987, Roger Greenway and Timothy Monsma, 1991; Roger Greenway, 1973, 1976, 1978, 1979, 1992; David Claerbaut, 1983; George Gmelch and Walter P. Zenner, 1988; Joel Garreau, 1991; Michael Peter Smith, ed., 1988; Harold J. Recinos, 1989; Elijah Anderson, 1990; William Whyte, 1989; John Gulick, 1989; William Pannell, 1992; Tex Sample, 1984, 1990; Eleanor Scott Meyers, ed., 1992; and other related works like Harvey Cox, 1965, 1984;

Jacques Ellul, 1970; Francis DuBose, 1978; David Sheppard, 1974; Lyle Schaller, 1987; and Edgar Elliston and Timothy Kauffman, 1993.

5   Linthicum says, "Participation in community organization provides the church with the most biblically directed and most effective means for bringing about the transformation of a community—through the assumption of responsibility by the community's residents to solve corporately their own problems" (1991b:109). For some years, Alfred Krass (1978) voiced this concern as well, apparently wanting to keep evangelism, mission, community organization, and urban missiology together in a more integrated fashion. See also Donald Messer, 1992.

6   See e.g., David Sheppard, 1974; Ralph Neighbour Jr., 1990; Del Birkey, 1988; C. Kirk Hadaway, Stuart A. Wright, and Francis M. DuBose, 1987; Lois Barrett, 1986; Bernard J. Lee and Michael A. Cowan, 1986; Robert and Julia Banks, 1989; and John Noble, 1988. It would be interesting to study the base ecclesial community movements in Latin America as possibly a new form of the church in an urban setting—but that is outside the scope of this book. The astounding multiplicity of small Pentecostal storefront churches found in cities all over the world is another well-known phenomenon that receives too little attention from those who study the church's ministry in the city. The megachurches that arose all over the world during the 1980s might have offered themselves as another new model for the church in the city—except few of them have shown any intention of contributing to the holistic transformation of the cities in which they are found.

7   The three arena nature of this method is not original with me. Many others have highlighted something similar, particularly those who deal with contextualization from a missiological perspective. See, for example, Eugene Nida, 1960; Louis Luzbetak, 1963; José Miguez-Bonino, 1975; Shoki Coe, 1976; Harvie Conn, 1978, 1984, 1993a, 1993b; Arthur Glasser, 1979; Charles Kraft, 1979, 1983; Charles Kraft and Tom Wisely, eds., 1979; Bruce Fleming, 1980; John Stott and Robert Coote, 1980a; Paul Hiebert, 1978,

1987a, 1993; Robert Schreiter, 1985; C. René Padilla and Mark Lau Branson, 1986; Alan R. Tippett, 1987; R. Daniel Shaw, 1988; Dean Gilliland, ed., 1989; David Hesselgrave, 1989; Lamin Sanneh, 1989; Charles Van Engen, 1989; William Dyrness, 1990; Stephen Bevans, 1992; and Donald R. Jacobs, 1993.

8   See, for example, Daniel T. Niles, 1962; Georg F. Vicedom, 1965; John V. Taylor, 1972; Johannes Verkuyl, 1978:163-204; and John Stott, 1979.

9   See, e.g., Robert Glover, 1946; G. Ernest Wright, 1952; J. H. Bavinck, 1977; Gerald Anderson, 1961; Harry Boer, 1961; Johannes Blauw, 1962; Roland Allen, 1962; Richard De Ridder, 1975; George Peters, 1972; Orlando Costas, 1974, 1982, 1989; John Stott, 1976; Lesslie Newbigin, 1978; J. Verkuyl, 1978, chapter IV; David Bosch, 1978, 1991, 1993; Dean Gilliland, 1983; Gailyn Van Rheenen, 1983; William A. Dyrness, 1983; Donald Senior and Carroll Stuhlmueller, 1983; Roger Hedlund, 1985b; Marc Spindler, 1988; Ken Gnanakan, 1989; Arthur Glasser, 1992; and Charles Van Engen, 1992, 1993. A combined bibliography drawn from these works would offer an excellent resource for examining the relation of Bible and mission.

10 See, for example, Rodger Bassham, 1979; David Bosch, 1980; James Scherer, 1987, 1993a, 1993b; Arthur Glasser and Donald McGavran, 1983; Arthur Glasser, 1985; Efiong Utuk, 1986; James Stamoolis, 1987; and Charles Van Engen, 1990.

11 See, for example, Donald McGavran, ed., 1972; Arthur P. Johnston, 1974; Harvey Hoekstra, 1979; Roger Hedlund, ed., 1981; Donald McGavran, 1984; and David Hesselgrave, 1988. One of the most helpful recent compilations of such documents is James A. Scherer and Stephen Bevans, 1992.

12 Examples of some readily accessible works would include J. H. Bavinck, 1977; Bengt Sundkler, 1965; Johannes Verkuyl, 1978; C. René Padilla, 1985; James Scherer, 1987; F. J. Verstraelen, 1988; David Bosch, 1980, 1991; James Phillips and Robert Coote, 1993; and Charles Van Engen,

Dean Gilliland and Paul Pierson, 1993. Clearly the most comprehensive work that will be considered foundational for missiology for the next decade is David Bosch, 1991.

13 Concerning the Los Angeles riots of 1992, Los Angelenos generally believe that the media significantly contributed to making the riots worse than they would have been. The irresponsible television coverage almost invited additional looting and rioting.

14 At Lausanne II in Manila in 1989, Fletcher Tink offered a "jungle-profile" view of the city that many found helpful. From its subterranean life, surface life, its small plants, lower canopy, middle canopy, and upper canopy, with its diurnal and nocturnal variations, and filled by its symbiotic systems—many aspects of a primeval jungle can be instructive for viewing modern cities.

15 For a discussion of this hermeneutical approach from several differing perspectives, see, e.g., Gary L. Comstock, 1987; David N. Duke, 1986; Gabriel Fackre, 1983; Michael Goldberg, 1981; Ronald L. Grimes, 1986; David M. Gunn, 1987; David Tracy, 1988; Stanley Hauerwas and L. Gregory Jones, eds., 1989; Paul Lauritzen, 1987; V. Philips Long, 1987; Alasdair MacIntyre, 1980; Kurt Mueller-Vollmer, ed., 1989; Richard Muller, 1991; and Grant Osborne, 1991.

16 Quoted by Les Henson, 1992, p. 19.

17 See, e.g., Luke 4:14-30; Luke 24: 27, 45; Acts 2:14ff; Acts 9:30-31; and Acts 15 as New Testament illustrations of this type of hermeneutic regarding the Old Testament. Paul's writings, Hebrews, and 1 Peter are also excellent places to investigate this.

18 See, for example, Matthew 16:1-12.

19 We may find examples of this in Numbers 13 and Deuteronomy 1 (the differing reports of the spies regarding Canaan); Psalm 137:1 and Daniel 1:19-21 (the differing attitudes to being exiles in Babylon); and John 1:36 and John 4:35 (John's and Jesus' differing perceptions compared with those around them).

20 "The idea of the 'hermeneutical circle' has been around since the early 1800's, . . . often associated with Friedrich Schleiermacher, . . . Wilhelm Dilthey, Edmund Husserl, Martin Heidegger, Rudolf Bultmann, and Georg Gadamer, among others. But Latin American liberation theologians transformed the concept into an intentional, creative, and revolutionary methodology for contextual theology" (Van Engen 1993:30).

21 Besides Juan Luis Segundo, 1976, see also, e.g., Gustavo Gutiérrez, 1973; José Miguez-Bonino, 1975; Guillermo Cook, 1985; Roger Haight, 1985; C. René Padilla, 1985; Leonardo Boff and Clodovis Boff, 1987; and Samuel Escobar, 1987.

22 For a more in-depth discussion of this issue, with supporting bibliographical comments, see Van Engen, 1993, pp. 27-36.

23 See David Bosch, 1991, pp. 20-24.

24 Harvie Conn gave us a summary form of just this sort of thing in 1993a, pp. 102-103.

25 See, e.g., Carl Hempel, 1965, 1966; Stephen Toulmin, 1961, 1972; Ian G. Barbour, 1974, 1990; Thomas Kuhn, 1962, 1977; James H. Fetzer, 1993a:147-178, 1993b; Hans Küng and David Tracy, eds., 1989:3-33; and David Bosch, 1991:349-362.

26 The last chapter of Newbigin's *The Gospel in a Pluralistic Society* contains some fascinating beginning points for a new reflection of what it could mean for the church to be intentional about its missiological orientation to the city. Newbigin highlights the local congregations as (1) a community of praise, (2) a community of truth, (3) deeply involved in the concerns of its neighborhood, (4) prepared for and sustained in the exercise of the priesthood for the world, (5) a community of mutual responsibility, and (6) a community of hope.

27 See, e.g., Robert McAfee Brown, 1978, 50-51; Raul Vidales, 1975, 34-57; Gordon Spykman et al, 1988, xiv, 226-231; Robert Schreiter, 1985, 17, 91-93; Orlando Costas, 1976, 8-9;

Leonardo Boff and Clodovis Boff, 1987, 8-9; Waldron Scott, 1980, xv; Leonardo Boff, 1979:3; Deane Ferm, 1986, 15; C. René Padilla, 1985, 83; Rebecca Chopp, 1986, 36-37, 115-117, 120-121; Gustavo Gutiérrez, 1983, 19-32; Clodovis Boff, 1987, xxi-xxx; and Gustavo Gutiérez, 1984, vii-viii, 50-60.

12

Further toward a theology of mission for the city

Charles Van Engen and Jude Tiersma

SO WHERE do we go from here? As our seminar group realized that our forty weeks of praying, reflecting, reporting, and envisioning together were ending, we asked ourselves: Where do we go from here? Where does this pilgrim theology-on-the-way in the city lead us?

One very strong impression with which we ended our seminar was that our praxis into the future would necessarily lead us to work on two fronts at once: content and method. We hope it is as obvious to the reader as it was to us that we barely scratched the surface regarding the content themes of urban missiology.

In the second part of this chapter, Jude Tiersma will highlight some content issues as a way of stimulating further praxeological reflection and action by Christ's church in the city. But first, Charles Van Engen will review in a summary way the methodological issues that have surfaced.

271

When we think of methods of theologizing in mission for the city, profound contradictions confront us.

Methodological contradictions

Although I would feel more comfortable speaking about sets of continua or dialectical tensions, the city's reality forces itself on us much more as contradictory and opposite forces that pull urban missionaries and ministries apart. Here we have space to highlight only four: the secular versus the sacred; the global versus the local; social systems versus personal relationships; integrative approaches versus specialized ministries.

In each case it appears that the urban mission theologian cannot capitulate to choosing between one pole over and against the other. Mission theology for the city can no longer afford to operate on an "either-or" basis. It must, instead, find a way to begin to reshape its approach and rethink its theology in a "both-and" perspective.

The secular versus the sacred, public versus private

One would think at the outset that mission theologians would have overcome this dichotomy by now and that we would no longer have to think about it. This is not true. The city constantly seems to want to secularize our missional approaches. Politics, economics, technology, real estate matters, city planning, demographics, social structures, languages, ethnicities—all appear to want to be dealt with apart from religious values. Society too often leads us to believe that these arenas are not the church's business. The "public square"[1] wants to remain naked concerning religious affiliation and religious values.

Lesslie Newbigin called attention to this split between the public and the private aspects of life in *Foolishness to the Greeks* (1986) and *Truth to Tell: The Gospel as Public Truth* (1991). What Wade Clark Roof and William McKinney have said is especially true of the city:

The truth is that religion has lost much of its great bind-
ing power on the society. The greater religious individualism of the 1960s and 1970s diminished possibilities
of a common universe of religious meanings and
eroded many of the support structures for religion. . . .
By the 1980s there was little question that the social and
religious order was deeply fragmented. The forces of
habit and custom had diminished, and so had many of
the bonds holding Americans together. Religion mani-
fested itself as "private virtue" and "public rhetoric,"
but this was symptomatic of the loss of shared norms.
As Berger said, "Insofar as religion is common it lacks
'reality,' and insofar as it is 'real' it lacks commonality"
(1987:37-38).[2]

If this is true of European and North American culture,
it even more accurately reflects the reality of the cities in
those continents. Religion is a more public phenomenon in
Africa, Asia, and Latin America. Even so, the secularizing
forces of technology, modernity, science, and urbanism are
just as strong there as they are in Europe and North America, and moving in the direction of increased valueless secu-
larism.

Meanwhile, the churches foster this dichotomy by
moving in one of two directions. Either churches in the city
recreate themselves into modified social agencies responding to the inner city poor's "inadequacies" by "doing for"
them, but seldom empowering them;[3] or they become
fortresses primarily interested in their own survival.

Either way, the churches too often fail to confront the
system of the cities in which they find themselves. They also
too seldom see themselves as agents of God's kingdom for
the city's holistic transformation through the proactive
empowerment of marginalized persons in the city. As we
saw intimated in several case studies in this book, this phenomenon seems true of churches all over the world.

And yet choosing *between* totally valueless secularity or institutional churchism can no longer satisfy us. Instead, one of the challenges before us in constructing an urban theology of mission for the city is to find a third way that speaks to *both* forces. Earlier we mentioned a study that moved in this direction (Roozen, McKinney and Carroll 1984). Robert Wuthnow hinted at another way of holding both poles together when he pointed out that belonging to an ongoing faith community had a positive correlation with acts of charitable behavior. This is in sharp contrast with the tendency in Europe and North America toward a highly privatized faith described by people like Robert Bellah (1985).

> Evidence from my survey shows that in general the more often an individual claims to experience divine love, the more likely that person is to spend time on charitable activities. But this effect is limited to individuals who attend church regularly. Among individuals who attend church infrequently or who do not attend, how much or how little they feel God's love has no effect on the likelihood of their being involved in charitable work. . . . Faith was a strong predictor of charitable behavior among the [active participants in their churches or synagogues] but not among [those who are inactive]. . . . I interpret these results to mean that religious inclinations make very little difference unless a person becomes involved in some kind of organized religious community (Wuthnow 1991a: 13).[4]

We should not think, however, that this is only a European or North American problem. Remember that Protestant missions have exported a strongly individualized perception of faith and ecclesiology, and tended to reproduce this dichotomy in the cities of other continents. Several authors in this book have mentioned that fact.

In other words, what we need is a new theological praxis in the city that seeks to find new ways by which the

274

churches of the city can become a "hermeneutic of the gospel" for the people of the city. In our theology of mission for the city we must discover how to respond *in the city* to Lesslie Newbigin's challenge:

> To be faithful to a message which concerns the king-
> dom of God, his rule over all things and all peoples, the
> Church has to claim the high ground of public truth. . . .
> The primary reality of which we have to take account
> in seeking for a Christian impact on public life is the
> Christian congregation. . . . The only hermeneutic of the
> gospel is a congregation of men and women who
> believe it and live by it . . . they have power to accom-
> plish their purpose only as they are rooted in and led
> back to a believing community (1989: 222, 227).

Global versus local

This chapter hinted at a second false dichotomy. In constructing a theology of mission for the city, we can no longer
divorce global issues from local ones, or macro analysis from
micro encounter.

When a person examines the literature on urban missiology, a predominant impression is of two worlds that seldom speak with each other. On the one hand, much of the
literature on urban ministry heavily focuses on Europe and
North America. On the other hand, missiological literature—born of the mission-sending from Europe and North
America to Asia, Africa, and Latin America—mostly concerns itself with the Two-Thirds World, and only recently
has begun to focus on issues of the cities in those continents.[5]

If one examines denominational structures, it is common to see two worlds that often compete with each other
for attention, resources and funds: "world mission" on the
one hand, and "urban ministries" on the other.[6] One notable
exception we could all learn from is the traditional Pentecostal movement that planted churches mostly in cities—

especially in Latin America—during this century. This movement greatly affected both religion and city life in Latin America, although it was not as holistic as some of us would wish.

It was clear to the seminar group—and we hope will be clear to the readers of this volume—that the time for such dichotomies is over. It is time to get "beyond anti-colonialism to globalism," as Paul Hiebert has said (1991). With theology of mission, we must instead learn to carry out the careful and serious praxeological task of a "critical contextualization" (Hiebert 1987a) of our mission in the city. Hiebert describes this task for us.

> What implications does a global view have for theology? During the colonial era theologians spoke of theology as a universal, objective system of truth. In the anti-colonial reaction they speak of "theologies" as particularist, subjective understandings of truth . . .
>
> How do we resolve the tension between theological absolutes and theological pluralism—between Theology and theologies? The answer lies, in part, in developing a theology of how to do theology. This theology must recognize the fact that different persons and different cultures understand the Scriptures differently. It must also enable them to work toward a common understanding of the truth of the Scriptures.
>
> Theologizing must begin with Scripture because it is God's revelation to us . . . Theologizing must be led by the Holy Spirit, who instructs us in the truth. We need also to recognize that the same Holy Spirit at work in us is also at work in the lives of believers in other contexts. . . . Finally, theology must be done in the community (Kraus: 1979). It is ultimately the task not of individuals but the church. This corporate nature of the hermeneutical task helps guard us against the privatization of faith and from our personal misinterpretations of the Scriptures. Just as others see our sins before we see our

own, so Christians in other cultures see our cultural biases and their impact on our theology more clearly than we see them ourselves (Hiebert 1991:276-277).[7]

Social systems versus personal relationships

As this book's editors, we hope that the reader noticed this issue arising as often as we did. Again, in much missiology and in urban ministry, experts often set these two elements against each other. Social analysts seldom speak of personal, spiritual transformation. Those who deal with personal spirituality almost never broaden their focus to the implications their thinking has on the transformation of the social systems of which they are a part.

As for academic disciplines, this issue sets us in the middle ground between sociology and theology—a very tenuous place to be. Yet our seminar participants increasingly felt that they needed the freedom to do *both-and*, not either-or. Almost every case study in this book touches in some way on this matter. Clearly we can no longer afford to talk about *doing* in urban mission unless we also speak of *being*.

Similarly, issues of authenticity and spirituality ring hollow if they do not translate into transforming action for the city's sake. Orlando Costas—who was deeply concerned about pastoral, evangelistic, and missional issues of the church's ministry in the city—did some of the most creative and helpful reflection along this line. Costas' concept of "integral church growth" may become one of his most significant and lasting contributions to missiology, and has much to commend it for constructing a theology of mission for the city.[8]

The reader may want to stop and reflect on how often this theme appeared in the case studies in this book. The issue is so basic it is inescapable, yet it always seems to take a different hue in each contextual reality.

Integration versus specialization

Finally, regarding methodological considerations, we must face what may be the most difficult dichotomy of all. All over the world, the direction of professional and academic investigation during the last half-century was toward greater specialization. This is no less true in the city. We have seen increasingly narrow arenas carved out by specialists in sociology, economics, health, public welfare, education, politics, law, anthropology, real estate, city planning, and so forth.

But is it not time to begin to ask at what point such atomization of life becomes counterproductive? Life itself in the reality of the city does not happen in specialized compartments. When does such specialization lead to a myopic inability to see the whole and, therefore, a blindness about even one's own small part in proper perspective? Especially when the urban conglomerate of interlocking subsystems confronts us, it appears we need to find ways to develop multi- and interdisciplinary approaches to doing theology for the city.

The implications of this for theological education are profound. Can mission in the city still afford to subdivide theological education and leadership formation into the small categories of traditional theological education? As our seminar group progressed in its reflection, we became more convinced that biblical studies, systematic theology, historical theology, pastoral ministries, preaching, church administration, and missiology must work together simultaneously to give us the necessary tools for confronting the complexity of our cities.

If we work only from an integrative standpoint, however, two unworkable alternatives may confront us. On the one hand, our praxis may become so complex and multivariable that it paralyzes us—no one could understand or respond to it. On the other hand, a purely integrative approach may be so superficial and broad that it does not delve deeply enough into particular issues, causes, and problems.

We have no answers—only more questions. Is there a way that we can learn to theologize about our mission in the city, a way that is *both* integrative, but also draws from the best of each pertinent specialization? I hope that as we network in our urban mission in the world's cities, we will stimulate each other to find a way to do this.

A few things seem clear. First, in theologizing in the city, we can never allow ourselves to lose sight of the persons living in the city. Second, theologizing in the city must be done *primarily* by those living in the city, by the members of base ecclesial fellowships of faith who are part of the city's fabric. Third, this theologizing process presented itself to us as never ending. It involves a continuous pilgrimage of discovery of the meaning of Jesus' mission in the city.

David Bosch concluded his *magnum opus* with an open-ended list of "Elements of an Emerging Ecumenical Missionary Paradigm" (1991:368-510). Similarly, the seminar participants felt that the only appropriate way to end this book was not to do so. We leave this work with many threads loose and dangling. They are open invitations to all our brothers and sisters of the world church who would like to join us in *constructing a theology of mission for the city*.

Content considerations

Our seminar did not initially intend to publish the process we experienced. Therefore, we did not systematically decide what topics to include in a theology for urban missiology. The issues raised reflect the most pressing and unresolved questions in the minds and hearts of the participants. Consequently, several themes recur, and we do not mention—or only briefly touch on—other significant issues. Some of these neglected themes could benefit from the ongoing application of the methodology presented in this book.

One area especially noticeable by its absence is the role of the church in government, economics, and politics. Although the importance of the systemic "big picture" view of the city is an underlying assumption the authors had, most of the stories reflect more of a micro perspective, and do not help the reader bridge to the broader perspective. We also only mention the city's various systems and subsystems: education, health care, housing. How should the church understand and interact with the systems and subsystems of the city?

Although half the seminar participants were women, none of the essays deal directly with the special concerns of women in the city, especially the many women living in poverty. The barriers of race, culture, class, and gender continue to loom large in our cities. As Christians we must continually ask what it looks like to embody the fact that Jesus came to destroy the walls that divide us. How does reconciliation come about?

Related to this is the question of church growth and the homogeneous unit principle in a multiethnic city. How do churches grow in the city? How do we resolve the tension between a people's felt need to worship in their own language, and the need for reconciliation (that they may not feel)? Who decides? Is it possible that a church of the homeless can better develop leadership for themselves than if they worshiped elsewhere?

Central City Community Church is a church among the homeless in downtown Los Angeles. Members are active participants in the life of the church, and involved in leadership. This fellowship is a community where they know they belong as much as anyone else. Would this happen if they attended another church?

I remember clearly one December day when I arrived with a group of Fuller students in the loft above a garment shop on Broadway, where the downtown fellowship was then meeting. The young pastor, Scott, was carrying on a conversation with a homeless woman: bandanna pulled back on her head, dirt in the weathered lines of her face, baggy pants rolled up to her knees. Both were intent on the conversation; neither noticed our presence. The woman held two items: earrings and a bag of lollipops. Handing Scott the earrings, she said, "These are for your wife Beth. And these candies are for the kids in the youth club, so they'll have something when they're done with tutoring." Her eyes beamed as Scott thanked her for the gifts.

My heart filled with warmth and joy on that dreary December day, for I realized that we had witnessed a glimpse of the kingdom, the reign of God, the way God intended things to be. This homeless woman—who on most days was the faceless, nameless recipient of services on skid row—in that moment became Sherry, a person of value in God's eyes, with humble gifts to offer others in her congregation.

Another issue too often overlooked is the environment in the city. Many experts have historically not viewed ecology and the environment as urban issues. A brief visit to Mexico City is convincing proof that this is a pressing matter. While Mexico City's central city is much cleaner than Los Angeles, the surrounding settlements are dumping grounds for contamination and waste. In one *colonia*, a boy rode his bike into a canal into which a nearby factory dumped its waste. According to neighbors, the boy died shortly after due to the toxins in the canal that people can smell for up to two miles away from the site. (The custom of dumping toxins where the poor live is not unique to Mexico City.) Related to issues of physical and social environments is the question of beauty. Do humans need beauty? How can we work to improve the environments of our neighborhoods?

Prayer movements and prayer marches in cities are gaining momentum in many places. Examples include Latin America Mission's Christ for the City program, and the prayer marches started in England with Graham Kendrick. How can these movements help in the networking of cities? How do we relate these movements to the transformation of neighborhoods and cities?

Perhaps the greatest urban challenge facing us is the rapid growth of cities in the Two-Thirds World, most of them in countries with very little access by traditional missionaries. Many of these millions live in impoverished squatter settlements, clinging to the hope that their children will have a better life in the city.

Other concerns abound: a Christian response to AIDS; street kids; the elderly; the effects of violence on families. The list is as diverse and endless as cities seem to be. The important thing is to take our context seriously, give concrete shape to our passion, continue to reread the Scripture, and act on what we know. We need to build this kind of reflection into our city ministries, both for those of us who are missionaries in the city, and for those who were there long before us.

Increasingly, the dialogue in urban missiology must include diversity in gender, ethnicity, and class. While some see "political correctness" as only a passing trend, I mention diversity here because of a deep belief that the discussion is only valid if it includes all of God's people, especially those who inhabit our cities.

A story helps us understand the city's reality

As we theologize in this way, starting with stories rooted in a particular urban context, our theologizing is "on the way," our feet covered with the grime of the city streets, our noses filled with the neighborhood's smells and aromas. While cities can become places of statistics and unnamed people, a story brings us back to a flesh and blood person. We can become hardened to numbers, but hearing a story moves us to compassion.

A gang member killed in a driveby shooting becomes Chato from Guatemala. He had no place to call home, so he attached himself to a group of kids, a gang that called itself the Orphans. We remember him as Chris' new friend, the kid who watched us paint a mural from a second story window—but was too shy to let us take his picture. "He was good," everyone said. "Never did none of the bad stuff. Stayed off the streets at night."

One night he was outside, standing near the corner when four shots rang out. Now he is gone. No one knew his last name, or who his parents were. He was given a city cremation. But in the neighborhood we gathered in the courtyard, remembered him, sang, and prayed together. We grieved for Chato, and because we know Chato we grieve for so many others, children killing children.

After we grieve, we begin to reflect. This is not God's will for our city, for our children. Why did these young people call themselves the Orphans? Where are the families God intended them to belong to? What has happened in a society where our children kill each other, often with little remorse or thought for the consequences? Why are guns so easily available? Why are there no job opportunities for these young people? Why does a shooting in a wealthier part of the city cause so much more stir than a shooting where the urban poor live?

The questions will continue, and we will continue to struggle with them, both in reflection and action. We groan inwardly, longing for the day when God will free creation from its bondage to decay, when the promise of Isaiah 65:17-22 (NRSV) reaches its fulfillment:

> *For I am about to create new heavens and a new earth;*
> *the former things shall not be remembered or come to mind.*
> *But be glad and rejoice forever in what I am creating;*
> *for I am about to create Jerusalem as a joy,*
> *and its people as a delight.*

I will rejoice in Jerusalem, and delight in my people;
no more shall the sound of weeping be heard in it,
or the cry of distress.
No more shall there be in it an infant that lives but a few
*   days,*
or an old person who does not live out a lifetime;
for one who dies at a hundred years will be considered a
*   youth,*
and one who falls short of a hundred will be considered
*   accursed.*
They shall build houses and inhabit them;
they shall plant vineyards and eat their fruit.
They shall not build and another inhabit;
they shall not plant and another eat;
for like the days of a tree shall the days of my people be,
and my chosen shall long enjoy the work of their hands.

NOTES

1   Cf. Richard Neuhaus: 1984.

2   Roof and McKinney are quoting from Peter Berger: 1967:133. Benton Johnson wrote with insight about this issue in, "Is There Hope for Liberal Protestantism?" (1986).

3   Cf. John McKnight: 1989:38, quoted earlier in the chapter on "Constructing a theology of mission for the city."

4   This article highlights the findings in Robert Wuthnow, 1991b. See also Robert Wuthnow, 1988.

5   Examples of the latter would include the Latin America Mission's "Christ for the City" program, Roger Greenway's publications about mission in the cities in Latin America, Ralph Neighbour's work in planting house churches in the cities of the Two-Thirds World, Viv Grigg's writings, along with the works of Harvie Conn, Tim Monsma, and Ray Bakke. Hispanics in the U.S. have been challenged by the thoughts, action, and writing of

folks like Manny Ortiz, Jesse Miranda, Oscar Romo, and others.

6   Again, there are notable exceptions personified in such folks as Roger Greenway, Harvie Conn, Al Krass, Tim Monsma, Ray Bakke, and Viv Grigg—who have been cross-cultural missionaries in the Two-Thirds World, and very active in reflection on urban mission.

7   See also C. Norman Kraus, 1993.

8   See Orlando Costas, 1974, 1975, 1979, and 1989.

Bibliography

Adembe, Florence. Personal interview with Stanley Mutunga. Pasadena, July 6, 1991.

Aghamkar, Atulkumar Y. *Lewa Patils of Jalgaon District: A Study of an Advanced Community in Transition and its Challenge to the Church.* Unpublished M. Th. thesis, South Asia Institute of Advanced Christian Studies, Bangalore, India, 1985.

Alikham, Fatima. *Urbanization in Third World: An African Experience.* Hyderabad: Booklinks Corporation, 1987.

Alinsky, Saul D. *Reveille for Radicals.* New York: Vintage Books, 1969.

Allen, Roland. *Missionary Methods: St. Paul's or Ours?* Grand Rapids: Eerdmans, 1962.

Alton, Frank M. "Mutual Transformation of Rich and Poor." *Urban Advance* 3(3):1-7, 1992.

Anderson, Elijah. *Streetwise—Race, Class and Change in an Urban Community.* Chicago: University of Chicago Press, 1990.

Anderson, Gerald H., editor. *The Theology of Christian Mission.* New York: Abingdon, 1961.

Anderson, Gerald H. and Thomas F. Stransky. *Mission Trends No. 3: Third World Theologies.* Grand Rapids: Eerdmans and New York: Paulist Press, 1976.

Anderson, Ray S. *The Praxis of Pentecost: Revisioning the Church's Life and Mission.* Pasadena: Fuller Thelogical Seminary, 1991. (This was republished as *Ministry on the Fire Line.* Downers Grove: InterVarsity Press, 1993.)

Augsburger, David W. *Pastoral Counseling Across Cultures*. Philadelphia: The Westminster Press, 1986.

Auma, Clarise. Personal interview with Stanley Mutunga. Pasadena, July 16, 1992.

Ayrookuzhiel, Abran, A.M. *The Sacred in Popular Hinduism*. Madras, India: The Christian Literature Society, 1983.

Baabu, Elias. Personal interview with Stanley Mutunga. Ontario, June 8, 1992.

Bakke, Ray. "Strategy for Urban Mission." *TSF Bulletin* 8:20-21, March-April 1984.

_____. *The Urban Christian: Effective Ministry in Today's Urban World*. Downers Grove: InterVarsity Press, 1987. (New edition, 1992.)

Banks, Robert and Julia Banks. *The Church Comes Home: A New Base for Community and Mission*. Claremont: Albatross Books, 1989.

Barbour, Ian. *Myths, Models and Paradigms*. New York: Harper & Row, 1974.

_____. *Religion in an Age of Science*. New York: Harper & Row, 1990.

Barrett, David. "Annual Statistical Table on Global Mission: 1994." *International Bulletin of Missionary Research* 18:24-25, January 1994.

_____. *World-Class Cities and World Evangelization*. Birmingham: New Hope, 1986.

Barrett, Lois. *Building the House Church*. Scottdale: Herald Press, 1986.

Bass, Bernard M. *Stogdill's Handbook of Leadership: A Survey of Theory and Research*. New York: Free Press, 1981.

Bassham, Rodger. *Mission Theology: 1948-1975, Years of Worldwide Creative Tension, Ecumenical, Evangelical and Roman Catholic*. Pasadena: William Carey Library, 1979.

Bates, Karen Grigsby. "Shades of Black." *Los Angeles Times Magazine*:22-24, 45-46, May 23, 1993.

Bavinck, J.H. *An Introduction to the Science of Missions*. Nutley: Presbyterian and Reformed Publications, 1977.

Ba-Yunas, Ilyas. "Muslims in North America: Problems and Prospects." A speech given to the Muslim Student Association of the USA and Canada, 1977.

Bellah, Robert N., Richard Madsen, William M. Sullivan, Ann Swidler, and Steven M. Tipton. *Habits of the Heart: Individualism and Commitment in American Life*. New York: Harper & Row, 1985.

Berger, Peter L. *The Sacred Canopy*. Garden City: Doubleday, 1967.

Berney, James E., editor. *You Can Tell the World*. Downers Grove: Inter-Varsity Press, 1979.

Berry, Carmen Renee. *When Helping You is Hurting Me: Escaping the Messiah Trap*. San Francisco: Harper Books, 1988.

Bevans, Stephen. *Models of Contextual Theology*. Maryknoll: Orbis, 1992.

Bigsten, Arne. *Education and Income Determination in Kenya*. Gothenburg: University of Gothenburg, 1984.

Birch, Bruce C. *Let Justice Roll Down: The Old Testament, Ethics and Christian Life*. Louisville: John Knox Press, 1991.

Birchett, Colleen, editor. *Biblical Strategies for a Community in Crisis: What African Americans Can Do*. Chicago: Urban Ministries Inc., 1992.

Birkey, Del. *The House Church: A Model for Renewing the Church*. Scottdale: Herald, 1988.

Blauw, Johannes. *The Missionary Nature of the Church*. Grand Rapids: Eerdmans, 1962.

Boer, Harry R. *Pentecost and Mission*. Grand Rapids: Eerdmans, 1961.

Boff, Clodovis. *Theology and Praxis: Epistemological Foundations*. Maryknoll: Orbis, 1987.

Boff, Leonardo. *Liberating Grace*. Maryknoll: Orbis, 1979.

Boff, Leonardo and Clodovis Boff. *Introducing Liberation Theology*. Maryknoll: Orbis, 1987.

Bosch, David J. "Reflections on Biblical Models of Mission." In *Toward the 21st Century in Christian Mission*. James M. Phillips and Robert T. Coote, eds., pp. 175-192. Grand Rapids: Eerdmans, 1993.

_____. *Transforming Mission: Paradigm Shifts in Theology of Mission*. Maryknoll: Orbis, 1991.

_____. "The Why and How of a True Biblical Foundation for Mission." In *Zending Op Weg Naar de Toekomst: Essays Aangeboden Aan*

289

Prof. Dr. J. Verkuyl and Jerald Gort, eds., pp. 33-45. Kampen: J. H. Kok, 1978.

_____. *Witness to the World: The Christian Mission in Theological Perspective.* London: Marshall, Morgan & Scott, 1980.

Bougue, Donald and K. C. Zachariah. "Urbanization and Migration in India." In *India's Urban Future.* Roy Turner, ed. Berkeley: University of California Press, 1962.

Branson, Mark L. and René Padilla, editors. *Conflict and Context: Hermeneutics in the Americas.* Grand Rapids: Eerdmans, 1986.

Brewster, E. Thomas, and Elizabeth S. Brewster. *Bonding and the Missionary Task.* Pasadena: Lingua House, 1982.

_____. "Incarnation and Mission Among the Urban Poor." Class notes. Pasadena: School of World Mission, Fuller Theological Seminary. No Date.

Brown, Robert McAfee. *Theology in a New Key: Responding to Liberation Themes.* Philadelphia: Westminster, 1978.

_____. *Unexpected News: Reading the Bible with Third World Eyes.* Philadelphia: Westminster, 1984.

Brueggemann, Walter. *The Land: Place as Gift, Promise, and Challenge in Biblical Faith.* Philadelphia: Fortress Press, 1977.

Brush, J. E. "Morphology of Indian Cities." In *India's Urban Future.* Roy Turner, editor. Berkeley: University of California Press, 1962.

Bunting, Ian. "Training for Urban Mission in the United Kingdom." *Urban Mission* X(2):16-27, 1992.

Burrows, William R. *New Ministries: the Global Context.* Maryknoll: Orbis, 1981.

Caputo, Robert. "Kenya: A Population Exploding." *National Geographic.* 174:(6):918-921, 1988.

Carpenter, Joel A. and Wilbert R. Shenk, editors. *Earthen Vessels: American Evangelicals and Foreign Missions, 1880-1980.* Grand Rapids: Eerdmans, 1990.

Chopp, Rebecca. *The Praxis of Suffering: An Interpretation of Liberation and Political Theologies.* Maryknoll: Orbis, 1986.

Christensen, Michael J. *City Streets, City People.* Nashville: Abingdon, 1988.

Claerbout, David. *Urban Ministry*. Grand Rapids: Zondervan, 1983.

Clayton, Janet. "Cornel West: Seeking to Expand America's 'Public' Conversation." Interview in the *Los Angeles Times*: M3, May 9, 1993.

Coe, Shoki. "Contextualizing Theology." In *Mission Trends No. 3: Third World Theologies*. Gerald H. Anderson and Thomas F. Stransky, eds., pp. 19-24. Grand Rapids: Eerdmans, and New York: Paulist, 1976.

Comstock, Gary L. "Two Types of Narrative Theology,." *Journal of the American Academy of Religion* LX(4):687-720, 1987.

Cone, James H. *Martin & Malcolm & America: A Dream or a Nightmare*. Maryknoll: Orbis, 1993.

_____. *Speaking the Truth: Ecumenism, Liberation and Black Theology*. Grand Rapids: Eerdmans, 1986.

Conn, Harvie. *The American City and the Evangelical Church*. Grand Rapids: Baker (forthcoming), 1994.

_____. *A Clarified Vision for Urban Mission: Dispelling the Urban Stereotypes*. Grand Rapids: Zondervan, 1987.

_____. "Contextualization: A New Dimension for Cross-Cultural Hermeneutic." *Evangelical Missions Quarterly* XIV(1):39-46, 1978.

_____. "A Contextual Theology of Mission for the City." In *The Good News of the Kingdom: Mission Theology for the Third Millennium*. Charles Van Engen, Dean Gilliland and Paul Pierson, eds., pp. 96-104. Maryknoll: Orbis, 1993b.

_____. *Eternal Word and Changing Worlds: Theology, Anthropology, and Mission in Trialogue*. Grand Rapids: Zondervan, 1984. (Reprinted by Presbyterian and Reformed Publications, 1992.)

_____. "Unreached Peoples and the City." *Urban Mission* 8:3-5, May 1991.

_____. "Urban Mission." In *Toward the 21st Century in Christian Mission*. James Phillips and Robert T. Coote, editors, pp. 318-337. Grand Rapids: Eerdmans, 1993a.

Conn, Harvie, ed. *Practical Theology and the Ministry of the Church, 1952-1984: Essays in Honor of Edmund Clowney*. Phillipsburgh: Presbyterian and Reformed, 1990.

291

Cook, Guillermo. *The Expectation of the Poor: Latin American Basic Ecclesial Communities in Protestant Perspective*. Maryknoll: Orbis. (This was orignially a doctoral dissertation done at the School of World Mission, Fuller Theological Seminary), 1985.

Costas, Orlando E. *Christ Outside the Gate: Mission Beyond Christendom*. Maryknoll: Orbis, 1982.

_____. *The Church and its Mission: A Shattering Critique from the Third World*. Wheaton: Tyndale, 1974.

_____. *The Integrity of Mission: The Inner Life and Outreach of the Church*. New York: Harper & Row, 1979.

_____. *Liberating News: A Theology of Contextual Evangelization*. Grand Rapids: Eerdmans, 1989.

_____. *El Protestantismo en America Latina Hoy: Ensayos del Camino (1972-1974)*. San Jose, Costa Rica: INDEF, 1975.

_____. *Theology of the Crossroads in Contemporary Latin America: Missiology in Mainline Protestantism, 1969-1974*. Amsterdam: Rodopi, 1976.

Cox, Harvey. *Religion in the Secular City*. New York: Simon & Schuster, 1984.

_____. *The Secular City*. New York: Macmillan, 1965.

Cragg, Kenneth. "Prepositions and Salvation." *International Bulletin of Missionary Research* 17(1):2-3, 1993.

D'Abreo, Desmond A. *Turning the Tide of Injustice*. Bangalore, India: Grandslam Computers Pvt. Ltd., 1991.

Daily Nation. 21(2), April 1991. Nairobi, Kenya.

David, George. "Principles for Indigenous Mission." *India Church Growth Quarterly* 12(3):101-103, 1990.

DePree, Max. *The Art of Leadership*. New York: Doubleday Dell Publishing Group, Inc., 1989.

_____. *Leadership Jazz*. New York: Doubleday Dell Publishing Group, Inc., 1992.

De Ridder, Richard. *Discipling the Nations*. Grand Rapids: Baker, 1975.

Development Plan 1989-1993. Nairobi: Government Printers, 1989.

Deweese, Charles. *Baptist Church Covenant*. Nashville: Broadman, 1990.

Dintaman, Stephan F. *Mennonite Brethren Herald*:6-7, March 5, 1993.

Dodd, C. H. *The Parables of the Kingdom*. London: Nisbet, 1935.

Downes, Stanley, et al. *Summary of the Nairobi Church Survey*. Nairobi: Daystar University College, 1989.

DuBose, Francis. *How Churches Grow in an Urban World*. Nashville: Broadman, 1978.

Duke, David N. "Theology and Biography: Simple Suggestions for a Promising Field." *Perspectives in Religious Studies* XIII(2):137-150, 1986.

Dunn, James D. G. *Romans*. Dallas: Word Books, 1988.

Dyrness, Grace. *Urban Anthropology*. Unpublished syllabus and reader. Pasadena: Fuller Theological Seminary, 1992.

Dyrness, William A. *Learning About Theology from the Third World*. Grand Rapids: Zondervan, 1990.

_____. *Let the Earth Rejoice: A Biblical Theology of Holistic Mission*. Pasadena: Fuller Seminary Press, 1983.

Easum, William M. *How to the Reach Baby Boomers*. Nashville: Abingdon Press, 1991.

The Economist. "More Choice, Fewer Babies," 324:39-40, July 1992.

Elliot, Charles. *Comfortable Compassion?: Poverty, Power and the Church*. Mahwah: Paulist Press, 1987.

_____. *Praying the Kingdom: Towards a Political Spirituality*. Mahwah: Paulist Press, 1985.

Ellison, Craig, editor. *The Urban Mission*. Grand Rapids: Eerdmans, 1974.

Elliston, Edgar J. and J. Timothy Kauffman. *Developing Leaders for Urban Ministries*. New York: Peter Lang, 1993.

Ellul, Jacques. *The Meaning of the City*. Grand Rapids: Eerdmans, 1970.

Escobar, Samuel. "From Lausanne 1974 to Manila 1989: The Pilgrimage of Urban Mission." *Urban Mission* 7:21-29, March 1990.

_____. *La Fe Evangélica y las Teologías de la Liberación*. El Paso: Casa Bautista de Publicaciones, 1987.

Fackre, Gabriel. "Narrative Theology: An Overview." *Interpretation* XXXVII(4):340-352, 1983.

Felder, Cain Hope. *Troubling Biblical Waters: Race, Class and Family.* Maryknoll: Orbis, 1989.

Ferm, Deane William. *Third World Theologies: An Introductory Survey.* Maryknoll: Orbis, 1986.

Fetzer, James H. *Foundations of the Philosophy of Science: Recent Developments.* New York: Paragon House, 1993b.

_____. *Philosophy of Science.* New York: Paragon House, 1993a.

Fleming, Bruce. *Contextualization of Theology.* Pasadena: William Carey Library, 1980.

Fowler, James W. *Becoming Adult: Becoming Christian.* Nashville: Abingdon Press, 1984.

_____. *To See the Kingdom: The Theological Vision of H. Richard Niebuhr.* Nashville: Abingdon Press, 1974.

Freire, Paulo. *Pedagogy of the Oppressed.* New York: Herder and Herder, 1970.

Frenchak, David J. and Sharrel Keys, editors. *Metro-Ministry: Ways and Means for the Urban Church.* Elgin: David C. Cook, 1979.

Frenchak, David J. and Clinton E. Stockwell, compilers. *Signs of the Kingdom in the Secular City.* Chicago: Covenant Press, 1984.

Friedmann, John. *Empowerment: The Politics of Alternate Development.* Cambridge: Blackwell, 1992.

Garreau, Joel. *Edge City.* New York: Doubleday Books, 1991.

Ghai, D. P. "Employment Performance, Prospects and Policies in Kenya." *Institute of Development Studies.* Nairobi, 1979.

Gibellini, Rosino, editor. *Frontiers in Theology of Latin America.* Maryknoll: Orbis, 1975.

Gilliland, Dean. *Pauline Theology and Mission Practice.* Grand Rapids: Baker, 1983.

Gilliland, Dean, editor. *The Word Among Us: Contextualizing Theology for Mission Today.* Waco: Word, 1989.

Glasser, Arthur F. "The Evolution of Evangelical Mission Theology Since World War II." *International Bulletin of Missionary Research* IX(1):9-13, 1985.

_____. "Help from an Unexpected Quarter: or the Old Testament and Contextualization." *Missiology* VII(4):401-410, 1979.

_____. *Kingdom and Mission: A Biblical Study of the Kingdom of God and the World Mission of His People.* Unpublished syllabus. Pasadena: Fuller Theological Seminary, 1992.

Glasser, Arthur F. and Donald McGavran. *Contemporary Theologies of Mission.* Grand Rapids: Eerdmans, 1983.

Glazer, Nathan and Daniel P. Moynihan. "Beyond the Melting Pot." In *Social Science and Urban Crisis.* Victor B. Ficker and Herbert S. Graves, eds., pp. 99-117. New York: The Macmillan Company, 1971.

Glover, Robert. *The Bible Basis of Mission.* Los Angeles: Bible House of Los Angeles, 1946.

Gmelch, George and Walter P. Zenner. *Urban Life: Readings in Urban Anthropology.* Prospect Heights: Waveland Press, 1988.

Gnanakan, Ken R. *Kingdom Concerns: A Biblical Exploration Towards a Theology of Mission.* Bangalore: Theological Book Trust, 1989.

Goldberg, Michael. *Theology and Narrative: A Critical Introduction.* Philadelphia: Trinity Press, 1981.

Gort, Jerald, editor. *Zending Op Weg Naar de Toekomst: Essays Aangeboden Aan Prof. Dr. J. Verkuyl.* Kampen: J.H. Kok, 1978.

Greenway, Roger S. *An Urban Strategy for Latin America.* Grand Rapids: Baker, 1973b.

_____. *Apostles to the City.* Grand Rapids: Baker, 1978.

_____. "Biblical Perspectives on the City." *The Reformed Ecumenical Council Mission Bulletin* XII(3):3-13, 1992a.

_____. *Calling Our Cities to Christ.* Nutley: Presbyterian and Reformed, 1973a.

_____. "The Perils of Neglecting Rural-Urban Bridges." *Urban Mission.* Vol. 6(1):4, September 1988.

_____. "Urbanization and Missions." In *Crucial Issues in Missions Tomorrow.* Donald McGavran, ed., pp. 227-244. Chicago: Moody, 1972.

Greenway, Roger S., ed. "Confronting Urban Contexts with the Gospel." *Discipling the City.* Grand Rapids: Baker, 1992b.

_____. *Guidelines for Urban Church Planting*. Grand Rapids: Baker, 1976.

_____. *Discipling the City: A Comprehensive Approach to Urban Mission*. Grand Rapids: Baker, 1992. (First edition, 1979.)

Greenway, Roger and Timothy M. Monsma. *Cities: Missions' New Frontier*. Grand Rapids: Baker, 1989.

Grigg, Viv. *Companion to the Poor*. Australia: Albotross Books., 1984. (Reprinted by MARC, Monrovia, 1991.)

_____. *Cry of the Urban Poor*. Monrovia: MARC, 1992.

Grimes, Ronald L. "Of Words the Speaker, of Deeds the Doer." *Journal of Religion* LXVI(1):1-17, 1986.

Gulick, John. *The Humanity of Cities: An Introduction to Urban Societies*. Granby: Bergin & Garvey, 1989.

Gunn, David M. "New Directions in the Study of Biblical Hebrew Narrative." *Journal for the Study of the Old Testament* 39:65-75, October 1987.

Gupta, Giri Raj. *Marriage, Religion and Society: Patterns of Change in an Indian Village*. New York: John Wiley and Sons, 1974.

Gustafson, James M. "Varieties of Moral Discourse: Prophetic, Narrative, Ethical and Policy." In *The Stob Lectures*. Grand Rapids: Calvin College, 1988.

Gutiérrez, Gustavo. *The Power of the Poor in History*. Maryknoll: Orbis, 1983.

_____. *A Theology of Liberation*. Maryknoll: Orbis, 1973. (London: SCM Press, 1974).

_____. *We Drink From Our Own Wells*. Maryknoll: Orbis, 1984.

Hadaway, C. Kirk, Stuart A. Wright, and Francis M. DuBose. *Home Cell Groups and House Churches*. Nashville: Broadman, 1987.

Haight, Roger E. *An Alternative Vision: An Interpretation of Liberation Theology*. New York: Paulist, 1985.

Hall, Douglas John. *The Steward: A Biblical Symbol Come of Age*. Grand Rapids: Eerdmans, 1990.

Hamdan, G. "Capitals of New Africa." *Economic Geography*: 239-259, March 1964.

Hanna, William J. and Judith L. Hanna. *Urban Dynamics in Black Africa:*

An Interdisciplinary Approach. Chicago: Aldine-Atherton, 1971.

Hanson, Paul D. *The People Called: The Growth of Community in the Bible.* New York: Harper & Row, 1986.

Hauerwas, Stanley and L. Gregory Jones, editors. *Why Narrative?* Grand Rapids: Eerdmans, 1989.

Hedlund, Roger E. *Evangelization and Church Growth: Issues from the Asian Context.* Madras: C.G.R.C. McGavran Institute, 1992.

_____. *The Mission of the Church in the World: A Biblical Theology.* Grand Rapids: Baker, 1985b.

_____. *Mission to Man in the Bible.* Madras: Evangelical Literature Service, 1985a.

Hedlund, Roger E., ed. *Roots of the Great Debate in Mission.* Madras: Evangelical Literature Service, 1981.

Heim, S. Mark. *Is Christ the Only Way? The Christian Faith in a Pluralistic World.* Valley Forge: Judson Press, 1985.

Hempel, Carl G. *Aspects of Scientific Explanation.* New York: The Free Press, 1965.

_____. *Philosophy of Natural Science.* Englewood Cliffs: Prentice-Hall, 1966.

Henry, Carl. "Reflections on the Kingdom of God." *Journal of Evangelical Theological Society* 35(1):39-49, 1992.

Henson, Les. *The Momina Theme of Life: Developed Biblically, Theologically and Contextually.* Unpublished master's thesis. Pasadena: Fuller Theological Seminary, 1992.

Hesselgrave, David J. *Contextualization.* Grand Rapids: Baker, 1989.

_____. *Today's Choices for Tomorrow's Mission: An Evangelical Perspective on Trends and Issues in Missions.* Grand Rapids: Zondervan, 1988.

Hian, Chua Wee. "Evangelization of Whole Families." In *Perspectives on the World Christian Movement: A Reader.* Ralph Winter and Steve Hawthorn, editors. Pasadena: William Carey Library, 1981.

Hiebert, Paul G. *Anthropological Insights for Missionaries.* Grand Rapids: Baker, 1985.

297

_____. "Beyond Anti-Colonialism to Globalism." *Missiology* XIX(3):263-282, 1991.

_____. "Conversion, Culture and Cognitive Categories." *Gospel in Context* I(4):24-29, 1978.

_____. "Critical Contextualization." *International Bulletin of Missionary Research* XI(3):104-111, 1987a.

_____. "Evangelism, Church, and Kingdom." In *The Good News of the Kingdom: Mission Theology for the Third Millennium.* Charles Van Engen, Dean S. Gilliland and Paul Pierson, eds., pp. 153-161. Maryknoll: Orbis, 1993.

_____. "Form and Meaning in Contexualization of the Gospel." In *The Word Among Us: Contextualizing Theology for Mission Today.* Dean Gilliland, ed., pp. 101-120. Waco: Word, 1989.

_____. "Window Shopping the Gospel." *Urban Mission* 4:6, May 5, 1987b.

Hoekstra, Harvey. *The World Council of Churches and the Demise of Evangelism.* Wheaton: Tyndale, 1979.

Hoyer, Stephen, and Patrice McDaniel. "From Jericho to Jerusalem: The Good Samaritan From a Different Direction." *Journal of Psychology and Theology* 18(4):326-333, 1990.

Jacobs, Donald R. "Contextualization in Mission." In *Toward the 21st Century in Christian Mission.* James M. Phillips and Robert T. Coote, eds., pp. 235-244. Grand Rapids: Eerdmans, 1993.

Jelks, Randal M. "Waters of Babylon: To Be an African American Presbyterian." *Perspectives: A Journal of Reformed Thought*, May 1992.

Johnson, Benton. "Is There Hope for Liberal Protestantism?" In *Mainstream Protestantism in the Twentieth Century: Its Problems and Prospects.* Dorothy C. Bass, Benton Johnson, Wade Clark Roof, eds., pp. 13-26. Louisville: Committee on Theological Education, Presbyterian Church (USA), 1986.

Johnston, Arthur P. *World Evangelism and the Word of God.* Minneapolis: Bethany Fellowship, 1974.

Johnstone, Patrick. *Operation World: A Day-to-Day Guide to Praying for the World.* England: WEC Publications, 1987.

Kaduwa, John. Personal interview with Stanley Mutunga. Nairobi, December 22, 1992.

Kagotho, James. Personal interview with Stanley Mutunga. Nairobi, December 20, 1992.

Kamau, John. Personal interview with Stanley Mutunga. Nairobi, December 16, 1992.

Kantonen, Taito Almar. *A Theology for Christian Stewardship*. Philadelphia: Muhlenberg Press, 1956.

Karp, David, Gregory Stone, and William Yoels. *Being Urban: A Sociology of City Life*. 2nd ed. New York: Praeger, 1991.

Keifert, Patrick. *Welcoming the Stranger: A Public Theology of Worship and Evangelism*. Minneapolis: Fortress, 1992.

Kerkhofs, S. G. "African Cities and the Church." *Pro Mundi Vita*, October 1981.

Kobiah, Samuel. *The Origins of Squatting and Community Organizations in Nairobi*. Ann Arbor: Michigan State University, 1984.

Koenig, John. *New Testament Hospitality: Partnership with Strangers as Promise and Mission*. Philadelphia: Fortress, 1985.

Kraft, Charles H. *Christianity in Culture: A Study in Dynamic Biblical Theologizing in Cross-Cultural Perspective*. Maryknoll: Orbis, 1979.

_____. *Communication Theory for Christian Witness*. Nashville: Abingdon, 1983. (Reprinted by Orbis, 1993.)

Kraft, Charles H. and Tom Wisely, eds. *Readings in Dynamic Indigeneity*. Pasadena: William Carey Library, 1979.

Krass, Alfred C. *Five Lanterns at Sundown: Evangelism in a Chastened Mood*. Grand Rapids: Eerdmans, 1978.

Kraus, C. Norman. *The Authentic Witness*. Grand Rapids: Eerdmans, 1979.

_____. *The Community of the Spirit*. Scottdale: Herald Press.

Kraybill, Donald B. *The Upside Down Kingdom*. Scottdale: Herald Press, 1990.

Kuhn, Thomas S. *The Essential Tension: Selected Studies in Scientific Tradition and Change*. Chicago: University of Chicago Press, 1977.

_____. *The Structure of Scientific Revolutions*. Chicago: University of Chicago Press, 1962.

Kümmel, Werner Georg. *Promise and Fulfillment*. London: SCM Press, 1957.

Küng, Hans and David Tracy, eds. *Paradigm Change in Theology: A Symposium for the Future*. New York: Crossroad, 1989.

Ladd, G. E. *The Presence of the Future*. Grand Rapids: Eerdmans, 1974.

Lauritzen, Paul. "Is 'Narrative' Really a Panacea? The Use of 'Narrative' in the Work of Metz and Hauerwas." *Journal of Religion* LXI(3):322-339, 1987.

Lee, Bernard J. and Michael A. Cowan. *Dangerous Memories: House Churches and Our American Story*. Kansas City, MO: Sheed & Ward, 1986.

Lewis, C.S. *Screwtape Letters*. London: G. Bles, 1963.

Lilburne, Geoffrey R. *A Sense of Place: A Christian Theology of the Land*. Nashville: Abingdon, 1989.

Linden, Eugene. "Megacities." *Time*:28-38, January 11, 1993.

Linthicum, Robert C. "Authentic Strategies for Urban Ministry." In *Discipling the City: A Comprehensive Approach to Urban Mission*. 2nd ed. Roger S. Greenway, ed. Grand Rapids: Baker, 1992.

_____. *City of God, City of Satan: A Biblical Theology of the Urban Church*. Grand Rapids: Zondervan, 1991a.

_____. *Empowering the Poor: Community Organizing Among the City's "Rag, Tag and Bobtail."* Monrovia: MARC, 1991b.

_____. "The Urban Christian: In, to or with the City." *Theology, News and Notes*, October 1991c.

Little, Kenneth. *Urbanization as a Social Process: An Essay on Movement and Change in Contemporary Africa*. London: Routledge and Kegan Paul, 1974.

Long, V. Philips. "Toward a Better Theory and Understanding of Old Testament Narrative." *Presbyterion* XIII(2):102-109, 1987.

Lupton, Robert D. "On Doing Good." *FCS Ministries Newsletter*. Atlanta: November, 1992.

_____. *Theirs is the Kingdom: Celebrating the Gospel in Urban America*. San Francisco: Harper Collins, 1989.

Lusser Rico, Gabriele. *Pain and Possibility: Writing Your Way Through Personal Crisis*. Los Angeles: Jeremy P. Tarcher Inc., 1991.

Luzbetak, Louis. *The Church and Cultures*. Pasadena: William Carey Library, 1963. (Reprinted 1970, 1975 by William Carey Library, reprinted by Orbis, 1988.)

MacIntyre, Alasdair. "The Virtues, the Unity of a Human Life and the Concept of a Tradition." *After Virtue*. Notre Dame: University of Notre Dame Press, 1980.

MacKay, John. *The Other Spanish Christ*. New York: MacMillan, 1993.

Malamat, Abraham. "Love Your Neighbor As Yourself: What It Really Means." *Biblical Archaeology Review* 16(4):50-51, 1990.

Mansmaz, Timothy. "Homogeneous Networks." *Urban Mission* Vol. 5, No. 3, January 1980.

May, Roy H., Jr. *The Poor of the Land: A Christian Case for Land Reform*. Maryknoll: Orbis, 1991.

Mbiti, John. *African Religions and Philosophy*. New York: Praeder, 1969.

McAlpine, Thomas. *Facing the Powers: What are the Options?* Monrovia: MARC, 1991.

McGavran, Donald A. *Bridges of God: A Study in the Strategy of Mission*. New York: Friendship, 1955.

_____. *Eye of the Storm: The Great Debate in Mission*. Waco: Word, 1972. (Updated and reprinted as: *The Conciliar-Evangelical Debate: The Crucial Documents, 1964-1976*. Pasadena: William Carey Library, 1977.)

_____. *Momentous Decisions in Missions Today*. Grand Rapids: Baker, 1984.

_____. *Understanding Church Growth*. Grand Rapids: Eerdmans, 1970.

McGavran, Donald A., ed. *Crucial Issues in Missions Tomorrow*. Chicago: Moody, 1972.

McGregor, D. "The Dynamics of House Ministry." *Global Church Growth Bulletin*. XVII(3):35,37, 1980.

McKnight, John. "Why 'Servanthood' is Bad." *The Other Side*:38-40, January-February 1989.

Melton, J. Gordon. *The Encyclopedia of American Religion*. Detroit: Gale Research, 1985.

Messer, Donald E. *A Conspiracy of Goodness: Contemporary Images of Christian Mission*. Nashville: Abingdon, 1992.

301

Meyers, Eleanor Scott, ed. *Envisioning the New City: A Reader on Urban Ministry*. Louisville: John Knox, 1992.

Miguez-Bonino, José. *Doing Theology in a Revolutionary Situation*. Philadelphia: Fortress, 1975.

Minear, Paul. *Images of the Church in the New Testament*. Philadelphia: Westminster, 1960.

Miranda, Jesse. *La Iglesia Evangélica Hispana en Los Estados Unidos Norteamericanos: Un Analysis Socia-religioso*. D.Min. dissertation, Fuller Theological Seminary, 1979.

Mitchell, Clyde. *Social Networks in Urban Situations: Analysis of Personal Relationships in Central African Towns*. Manchester: University of Manchester Press, 1969.

Moberg, David O. *The Church as a Social Institution: The Sociology of American Religion*. 2nd ed. Grand Rapids: Baker, 1984. (First edition, 1962.)

Moberly, R.W.L. "Story in the Old Testament." *Themelios* XI(3):77-82, 1986.

Moltmann, Jürgen. *The Crucified God*. New York: Harper & Row, 1974.

_____. *Theology of Hope: On the Ground and Implications of a Christian Eschatology*. New York: Harper & Row, 1967.

_____. "Thine Is the Kingdom, the Power and the Glory." *The Reformed Word* 37(3 and 4):3-10, 1982.

_____. *The Trinity and the Kingdom: The Doctrine of God*. San Francisco: Harper & Row, 1981.

Monsma, Timothy. *African Urban Missiology: A Synthesis of Nigerian Case Studies and Biblical Principles*. Ph.D. dissertation, Fuller Theological Seminary, 1977.

_____. "Homogeneous Networks." *Urban Mission* 5(3):14, 1980.

_____. *An Urban Strategy for Africa*. Pasadena: William Carey Library, 1979.

Morgan, Gareth. *Images of Organization*. London: Sage Publications, 1986.

Morris, Leon. *Ruth: An Introduction and Commentary*. Downers Grove: Intervarsity Press, 1973.

Moulder, W. J. *The International Standard Bible Encyclopedia*. Vol. 3, p. 964. Grand Rapids: Eerdmans, 1986.

Mouw, Richard. "Inter-Religious Dialogue: Implications for Ministry in the Contemporary World." *Insights, a Journal of the Faculty of Austin Seminary*, 1991.

Mueller-Vollmer, Kurt, ed. *The Hermeneutics Reader: Texts of the German Tradition from the Enlightenment to the Present*. New York: Continuum, 1989.

Mukangu, Peter. Personal interview with Stanley Mutunga. Pasadena, June 2, 1992.

Muller, Richard A. *The Study of Theology: From Biblical Interpretation to Contemporary Formulation*. Grand Rapids: Zondervan, 1991.

Mungai, Margaret. Personal interview with Stanley Mutunga. Claremont, May 2, 1992.

Muriuki, Godfrey. *A History of the Kikuyu, 1500-1900*. Oxford: Oxford University Press, 1974.

Mutinda, Paul. Personal interview with Stanley Mutunga. Long Beach, June 7, 1992.

Mutunga, Joseph. Personal interview with Stanley Mutunga. Pasadena, January 7, 1993.

Mutunga, Stanley. *Contextual Leadership Development for the Church: An Investigation into Rural-Urban Migration to Nairobi*. Ph.D. dissertation, Fuller Theological Seminary, 1993.

_____. *The Nature of Ghettoes in Nairobi and their Challenges to the Christian Church*. M.A. Project, School of World Mission, Fuller Theological Seminary, 1989.

Muturi. Personal interview with Stanley Mutunga. Nairobi, December 5, 1992.

Mwaniki, J. A. *Urban Labour Force Survey, 1986*. Nairobi: Central Bureau of Statistics, 1986.

Naisbitt, John. *Megatrends: Ten New Directions Transforming Our Lives*. New York: Warner, 1984.

Nduati, Godfrey. Personal interview with Stanley Mutunga. Nairobi, December 20, 1992.

Neighbour, Ralph W., Jr. *Where Do We Go From Here? A Guidebook for Cell Group Churches*. Houston: Touch Publications, 1990.

Neill, Stephen, Gerald H. Anderson, and John Goodwin, editors. *A Concise Dictionary of the World Mission*. London: Lutterworth, 1971.

Neuhaus, Richard. *The Naked Public Square: Religion and Democracy in America*. Grand Rapids: Eerdmans, 1984.

Newbigin, Lesslie. *Foolishness to the Greeks: The Gospel and Western Culture*. Grand Rapids: Eerdmans, 1986.

_____. *The Gospel in a Pluralist Society*. Grand Rapids: Eerdmans, 1989.

_____. *The Household of God: Lectures on the Nature of the Church*. New York: Friendship, 1954.

_____. *Journey into Joy*. Madras: Diocesan Press, 1972.

_____. *The Open Secret*. Grand Rapids: Eerdmans, 1978.

_____. *Truth to Tell: The Gospel as Public Truth*. Grand Rapids: Eerdmans, 1991.

Nida, Eugene A. *Message and Mission*. New York: Harper & Row, 1960. (Reprinted by William Carey Library, 1972.)

Niles, Daniel T. *Upon the Earth: The Mission of the God and the Missionary Enterprise of the Churches*. London: Lutterworth, 1962.

Noble, John. *House Churches: Will They Survive?* Eastbourne: Kingsway Publications, 1988.

Nouwen, Henri. *Clowning in Rome*. New York: Doubleday Dell Publishing Group, Inc., 1979.

_____. *In The Name of Jesus*. New York: Doubleday Dell Publishing Group, Inc., 1992a.

_____. *A Living Reminder*. Minneapolis: Seabury Press, 1977.

_____. *The Return of the Prodigal Son: A Meditation on Fathers, Brothers, and Sons*. New York: Doubleday, 1992b.

_____. *Seeds of Hope*. New York: Doubleday Dell Publishing Group, Inc., 1989.

Nouwen, Henri, Donald McNeil, and Douglas Morrison. *Compassion: A Reflection on the Christian Life*. New York: Doubleday, 1982.

Obudho, R. A. "The Changing Nature of Kenya's Urban Demography, Spontaneous Papers." Dakar: VAPS, 1990.

_____. *Urbanization and Development Planning in Kenya*. Nairobi: Kenya Literature Bureau, 1981.

_____. *Urbanization in Kenya*. Boston: University Press of America, 1983.

O'Connor, Elizabeth. *Journey Inward, Journey Outward*. San Francisco: Harper Collins, 1968.

Olley, John W. "God's Agenda for the City: Some Biblical Perspectives." *Urban Mission* VIII(1):14-23, 1990.

Ortiz, Manny. "Being Incarnational Christians in the City." In *Discipling the City*. R. Greenway, ed. Grand Rapids: Baker, 1992.

Osborne, Grant R. *The Hermeneutical Spiral: A Comprehensive Introduction to Biblical Interpretation*. Downers Grove: InterVarsity Press, 1991.

Osthathios, Geevarghess Mar. "The Holy Trinity and the Kingdom of God." *The Indian Journal of Theology* 31(1):1-14, 1982.

Padilla, C. René. "Hermeneutics and Culture—A Theological Perspective." In *Down To Earth: Studies in Christianity and Culture*. John Stott and Robert Coote, eds. Grand Rapids: Eerdmans, 1979.

_____. *Mission Between the Times: Essays on the Kingdom of God*. Grand Rapids: Eerdmans, 1985.

Padilla, C. René and Mark Lau Branson, editors. *Conflict and Context: Hermeneutics in the Americas*. Grand Rapids: Eerdmans, 1986.

Palmer, Parker. *The Company of Strangers*. New York: Crossroad, 1981.

Pannell, William. *Evangelism from the Bottom Up: What Is the Meaning of Salvation In a World Gone Urban?* Grand Rapids: Zondervan, 1992.

_____. "Go Ye Therefore, and Be Incarnate." *The Other Side*:48-54, 62, March-April 1992.

Pantaleo, Jack. "The Opened Tomb." *The Other Side*:8-12, March-April 1992.

Pasquariello, Ronald D., W. Donald, and Alan Geyer. *Redeeming the City: Theology, Politics, and Urban Policy*. New York: Pilgrim Press, 1982.

Pearlstone, Zena. *Ethnic Los Angeles*. Beverly Hills: Hillcrest Press, 1990.

Perkins, John. *A Quiet Revolution*. Waco: Word Books, 1976.

_____. "A Seek and Touch Gospel." *Restorer*, Fall 1993.

_____. *With Justice for All*. Ventura: Regal Books, 1982.

Perrin, Norman. *Jesus and the Language of the Kingdom: Symbol and Metaphor in the New Testament Interpretation*. Philadelphia: Fortress Press, 1976.

Peters, George. *A Biblical Theology of Missions*. Chicago: Moody, 1972.

_____. *Saturation Evangelism*. Grand Rapids: Zondervan, 1970.

Peters, Tom. *Liberation Management*. New York: Alfred A. Knopf, 1992.

Phillips, James M. and Robert T. Coote, editors. *Toward the 21st Century in Christian Mission*. Grand Rapids: Eerdmans, 1993.

Presbyterian Church, USA. "Hate Crime in America." *Church and Society*. Louisville: Social Justice and Peacemaking Unit of the General Assembly, 1990.

Punekar, Vijaya B. *Assimilation—A Study of North Indians in Bangalore*. Bombay: Popular Prakashan, 1974.

Rahman, M. "Poor and Polarised." *India Today* 18(5):48-50, 1993.

Recinos, Harold J. *Hear the Cry! A Latino Pastor Challenges the Church*. Louisville: John Knox, 1989.

Rico, Gabriel Lusser. *Pain and Possibility: Writing Your Way Through Personal Crisis*. Los Angeles: Jeremy P. Tarcher, Inc., 1991.

Ridderbos, Hermann. *The Coming of the Kingdom*. Philadelphia: Presbyterian and Reformed, 1962.

Riding, Alan. *Distant Neighbors: A Portrait of the Mexicans*. New York: Alfred A. Knopf, 1984.

Romo, Oscar. *American Mosaic: Church Planting in Ethnic America*. Nashville: Broadman, 1993.

Roof, Wade Clark and William McKinney. *American Mainline Religion: Its Changing Shape and Future*. New Brunswick: Rutgers University Press, 1987.

Roozen, David A., William McKinney and Jackson W. Carroll. *Varieties of Religious Presence: Mission in Public Life*. New York: Pilgrim Press, 1984.

Rose, Larry and Kirk Hadaway, editors. *An Urban World: Churches Face the Future.* Nashville: Broadman, 1984.

Rubin, Lillian B. *Worlds of Pain: Life in the Working-Class Family.* New York: Harper Collins, 1992.

Sample, Tex. *Blue-Collar Ministry: Facing Economic and Social Realities of Working People.* Valley Forge: Judson Press, 1984.

_____. *U. S. Lifestyles and Mainline Churches: A Key to Reaching People in the 90's.* Louisville: Westminster/John Knox Press, 1990.

Sanneh, Lamin. *Translating the Message: The Missionary Impact on Culture.* Maryknoll: Orbis, 1989.

Schaef, Anne Wilson. *Escape from Intimacy.* San Francisco: Harper & Row, 1988.

Schaller, Lyle E. *The Change Agent.* Nashville: Abingdon, 1978.

_____. *It's a Different World: The Challenge for Today's Pastor.* Nashville: Abingdon, 1987.

Scherer, James A. "Church, Kingdom, and *Missio Dei*: Lutheran and Orthodox Correctives to Recent Ecumenical Mission Theology." In *The Good News of the Kindgom: Mission Theology for the Third Millennium.* Charles Van Engen, Dean Gilliland and Paul Pierson, eds., pp. 82-88. Maryknoll: Orbis, 1993a.

_____. *Gospel, Church and Kingdom: Comparative Studies in World Mission Theology.* Minneapolis: Augsburg, 1987.

_____. "Mission Theology." In *Toward the 21st Century in Christian Mission.* James M. Phillips and Robert T. Coote, eds., pp. 193-202. Grand Rapids: Eerdmans, 1993b.

Scherer, James A. and Stephen B. Bevans, editors. *New Directions in Mission and Evangelization 1: Basic Statements 1974-1991.* Maryknoll: Orbis, 1992.

Schreiter, Robert. *Constructing Local Theologies.* Maryknoll: Orbis, 1985.

Schweitzer, Albert. *Quest for the Historical Jesus.* New York: Macmillan, 1922.

Scott, Waldron. *Bring Forth Justice: A Contemporary Perspective on Mission.* Grand Rapids: Eerdmans, 1980.

Segundo, Juan Luis. *The Liberation of Theology.* Maryknoll: Orbis, 1976.

Senge, Peter M. *The Fifth Discipline: The Art and Practice of The Learning Organization*. New York: Doubleday Dell Publishing Group, Inc., 1990.

Senior, Donald and Carroll Stuhlmueller. *The Biblical Foundations for Mission*. Maryknoll: Orbis, 1983.

Shah, Kirtee. "Urban Poverty: A Problem Whose Time Has Come." *Religion and Society* XXXVII(2), 1990.

Shaw, Daniel R. *Transculturation: The Cultural Factor in Translation and Other Communication Tasks*. Pasadena: William Carey Library, 1988.

Shaw, Ellis O. *Rural Hinduism: Some Observation and Experience*. Madras: Christian Literature Society, 1986.

Shenk, David and Ervin Stutzman. *Creating Communities of the Kingdom*. Scottdale: Herald Press, 1988.

Sheppard, David. *Built as a City: God and the Urban World Today*. London: Hodder & Stoughton, 1974.

Shriver, Donald W., Jr. and Karl A. Ostrom. *Is There Hope for the City?* Philadelphia: Westminster, 1977.

Sinha, Raghuvir. *Dynamics of Change in the Modern Hindu Family*. New Delhi: Concept Publishing Company, 1993.

Smith, Michael Peter, ed. *Power, Community, and the City*. New Brunswick: Transaction Books, 1988.

Smith, William. *Smith's Bible Dictionary*. Westwood: Fleming H. Revell, 1967.

Sowell, Thomas. *Ethnic America: A History*. New York: Harper Collins, 1981.

Spindler, Marc R. "Bijbelse fundering en oriëntatie van zending." In *Oecumenische Inleiding in de Missiologie*. F.J. Verstaelen, ed., pp. 132-154. Kampen: J. H. Kok, 1988.

Spykman, Gordon, Guillermo Cook, Michael Dodson, Lance Grahn, Sidney Rooy and John Stam. *Let My People Live: Faith and Struggle in Central America*. Grand Rapids: Eerdmans, 1988.

Squire, L. *Employment Policy in Developing Countries: A Survey of Issues and Evidence*, 1981.

Stamoolis, James. *Eastern Orthodox Mission Theology Today*. Maryknoll: Orbis, 1987.

Stedman, Ray. *Body Life*. Glendale: Regal, 1972.

Steele, Shelby. *The Content of Our Character*. New York: Harper Collins, 1990.

Steffan, Thomas. *Passing the Baton: Church Planting that Empowers*. La Habra: Center for Organization and Development, 1993.

Stott, John R.W. *Christian Mission in the Modern World*. Downers Grove: InterVarsity Press, 1976.

_____. "The Living God is a Missionary God." In *You Can Tell the World*. James E. Berney, ed. Downers Grove: InterVarsity Press, 1979.

Stott, John R.W. and Robert T. Coote, eds. *Down to Earth: Studies in Christianity and Culture*. Grand Rapids: Eerdmans, 1980b.

_____. *Gospel and Culture*. Pasadena: William Carey Library, 1980a.

Sugden, Christopher. *Radical Discipleship*. London: Marshall, Morgan and Scott, 1981.

Sumithra, Sunand and Bruce J. Nicholls. "Critique of Theology in Hindu Cultures." In *The Bible and Theology in Asian Context*. Bon Rin Ro and Ruth Eshenaur, eds. Bangalore: Asia Theological Association and Association of Evangelical Theological Education in India, 1984.

Sundkler, Bengt. *The World of Mission*. Grand Rapids: Eerdmans, 1965.

Tannehill, Robert C. *The Narrative Unity of Luke-Acts: A Literary Interpretation. Vol. 1 of The Gospel According to Luke*. Philadelphia: Fortress Press, 1991.

Taylor, John V. *The Go-Between God: The Holy Spirit and the Christian Mission*. London: SCM, 1972.

Thernstrom, Stephen, editor. *Harvard Encyclopedia of American Ethnic Groups*. Cambridge: Harvard University Press, 1980.

Thomas M. M. and Paul D. Devanandan, eds. *Changing Pattern of Family in India*. Bangalore: Christian Institute for the Study of Religion and Society, 1966.

Thomson, Paul. *The Challenge of the City*. Word Team Learning Resources Center Publications, 1984.

Tink, Fletcher L. *Downtown Los Angeles as Urban Jungle: An Alternative Model to the Homogeneous Unit Principle Understanding of the City*. Unpublished presentation. Manila, Lausanne II, 1989.

Tippett, Alan R. *Introduction to Missiology*. Pasadena: William Carey Library, 1987.

Tomasko, Robert M. *Rethinking the Corporation*. New York: American Management Association, 1993.

Tonna, Benjamin. *A Gospel for the Cities: A Socio-Theology of Urban Ministry*. Maryknoll: Orbis, 1985.

Toulmin, Stephen. *Foresight and Understanding*. New York: Harper, 1961.

_____. *Human Understanding: The Collective Use and Evolution of Concepts*. Princeton: Princeton University Press, 1972.

Tracy, David. *Blessed Rage for Order: The New Pluralism in Theology*. San Francisco: Harper & Row, 1988.

Trivedi, Harshad. *Urbanism: A New Outlook*. Delhi: Atma Ram and Sons, 1976.

Utuk, Efiong. "From Wheaton to Lausanne: The Road to Modification of Contemporary Evangelical Mission Theology." *Missiology* XIV:205-219, April 1986.

Van Engen, Charles. *Biblical Foundations of Mission*. Unpublished syllabus. Pasadena: School of World Mission, Fuller Theological Seminary, 1992.

_____. "A Broadening Vision: Forty Years of Evangelical Theology of Mission, 1946-1986." In *Earthen Vessels: American Evangelicals and Foreign Mission, 1880-1980*. Joel A. Carpenter and Wilbert R. Shenk, eds., pp. 203-232. Grand Rapids: Eerdmans, 1990.

_____. *God's Missionary People: Rethinking the Purpose of the Local Church*. Grand Rapids: Baker, 1991.

_____. "The New Covenant: Knowing God in Context." *The Word Among Us: Contextualizing Theology for Mission Today*. Dean Gilliland, ed., pp. 70-100. Waco: Word, 1989.

_____. "The Relation of Bible and Mission in Mission in Mission Theology." In *The Good News of the Kingdom: Mission Theology for the Third Millennium*. Charles Van Engen, Dean S. Gilliland, and Paul Pierson, eds., pp. 27-36. Maryknoll: Orbis, 1993.

_____. "Responses to James Scherer's Paper from Different Disciplinary Perspectives: Sytematic Theology." *Missiology* XV(4):524-525, 1987.

Van Engen, Charles, Dean S. Gilliland, and Paul Pierson, eds. *The Gospel of the Kingdom: Mission Theology for the Third Millenium*. Maryknoll: Orbis Books, 1993.

_____. *Theologizing in Mission*. Unpublished course syllabus. Pasadena: School of World Mission, Fuller Theological Seminary, 1992.

Vanier, Jean. *Community and Growth*. New York: Paulist Press, 1979.

Van Rheenen, Gailyn. *Biblical Anchored Missions: Perspectives on Church Growth*. Austin: Firm Foundation Publications, 1983.

Verkuyl, Johannes. *Contemporary Missiology: An Introduction*. Grand Rapids: Eerdmans, 1978.

_____. "The Kingdom of God as the Goal of Missio Dei." *International Review of Mission* LXVIII(270):168-175, 1979.

Verstraelen, F. J. *Oecumenische inleiding in de missiologie: Teksten en Konteksten van het wereldchristendom*. Kampen: Kok, 1988.

Vicedom, Georg F. *The Mission of God: An Introduction to a Theology of Mission*. Translated by A.A. Thiele and D. Higendorf from the German original, *Missio Dei* (1957). St. Louis: Concordia, 1965.

Vidales, Raul. "Methodological Issues in Liberation Theology." *Frontiers in Theology of Latin America*. Rosino Gibellini, ed., pp. 34-57. Maryknoll: Orbis, 1975.

Vigil, James. *Barrio Gangs: Street Life and Identity in Southern California*. Austin: University of Texas Press, 1988.

Wagner, C. Peter. *Church Growth and the Whole Gospel: A Biblical Mandate*. San Francisco: Harper and Row, 1981.

_____. *Church Planting for a Greater Harvest*. Ventura: Regal, 1990.

_____. *Frontiers in Missionary Strategy*. Chicago: Moody, 1971.

_____. *Your Church Can be Healthy*. Nashville: Abingdon, 1979.

_____. *Your Spiritual Gifts Can Help Your Church Grow*. Glendale: Regal, 1974.

Walsh, Brian J. and Richard Middleton. *The Transforming Vision: Shaping a Christian Worldview*. Downers Grove: InterVarsity Press, 1984.

Wanyama, Patrick. Personal interview with Stanley Mutunga. Nairobi, December 19, 1992.

Webber, George W. "Signs of the Kingdom—Luke 7:18-23." In *Signs of the Kingdom in the Secular City*. David Frenchak and Clinton Stockwell, eds. Chicago: Covenant Press, 1984.

Weiss, Johannes. *Jesus' Proclamation of the Kingdom of God*. Philadelphia: Fortress Press, 1971.

White, Morton and Lucia White. *The Intellectual Versus the City: From Thomas Jefferson to Frank Lloyd Wright*. New York: Oxford University Press, 1962.

Whitehead, James D. and Evelyn Ealon Whitehead. *Method in Ministry: Theological Reflection and Christian Ministry*. San Francisco: Harper, 1980.

Whyte, William. *Rediscovering the Center City*. New York: Doubleday, 1989.

Wilder, Amos. *The Language of the Gospel: Early Christian Rhetoric*. New York: Harper & Row, 1964.

Willis, Wendall. *The Kingdom of God in 20th Century Interpretation*. Peabody: Hendrickson, 1987.

Winter, Ralph D. "Fifteen Changes for Tomorrow's Mission." In *Mission in the 1990s*. Gerald H. Anderson, James M. Phillips, and Robert T. Coote, eds., pp. 46-50. Grand Rapids: Eerdmans and New Haven: Overseas Ministries Study Center, 1991.

Winter, Ralph D. and Stephen Hawthorne, editors. *Perspectives on the World Christian Movement: A Reader*. Pasadena: William Carey Library, 1981.

Wright, Christopher. *An Eye for an Eye: The Place of Old Testament Ethics Today*. Downers Grove: InterVarsity Press, 1983.

Wright, G. Ernest. *God Who Acts: Biblical Theology as Recital*. Chicago: H. Regnery, 1952.

Wuthnow, Robert. *Acts of Compassion: Caring for Others and Helping Ourselves*. Princeton: Princeton University Press, 1991b.

_____. "Evangelicals, Liberals, and the Perils of Individualism." *Perspectives: A Journal of Reformed Thought* VI(5):10-13, 1991a.

_____. *The Restructuring of American Religion*. Princeton: Princeton University Press, 1988.

Younger, George. *From New Creation to Urban Crisis: A History of Action Training Ministries, 1962-1975*. Chicago: Center for the Scientific Study of Religion, 1987.

Ziegenhals, Walter E. *Urban Churches in Transition*. New York: Pilgrim Press, 1978.